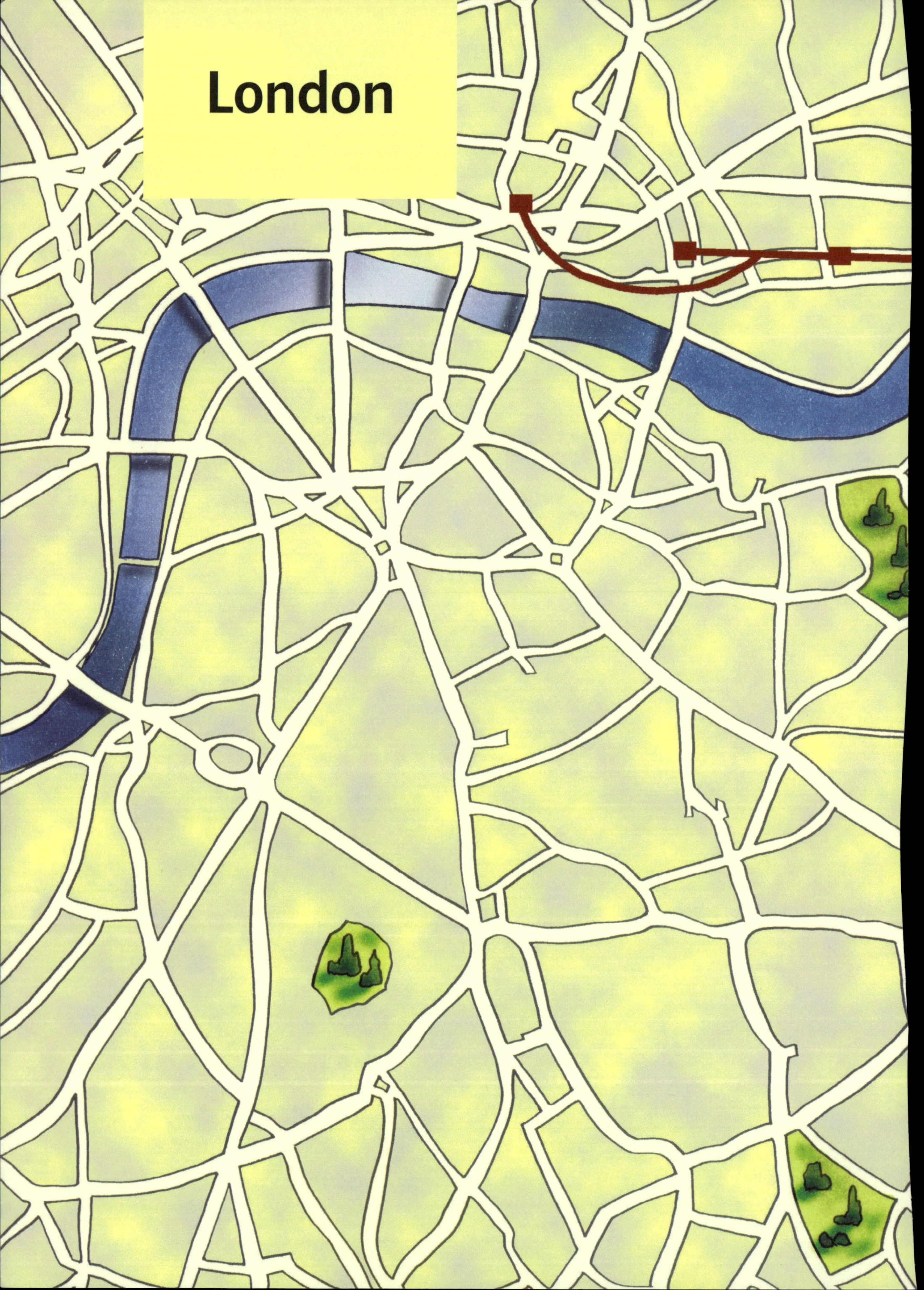
London

DOCKLANDS LIGHT RAILWAY
MILLENNIUM DOME
Terry
ISLE OF DOGS
GREENWICH FOOT TUNNEL
CUTTY SARK
TRAFALGAR ROAD
ROMNEY ROAD
CREEK ROAD
GREENWICH CHURCH STREET
MAZE HILL
GREENWICH
GREENWICH HIGH ROAD
CROOMS HILL
ROYAL OBSERVATORY
GREENWICH PARK
Sam
BLACKHEATH ROAD
GREENWICH MARKET
CHARLTON WAY
SHOOTERS HILL ROAD
Thomas Tallis School
Greenwich
LEWISHAM
Emma
THOMAS TALLIS SCHOOL
Lisa

Orange **Line**

1

von Jennifer Baer-Engel und
Marion Horner

Herausgeber: Frank Haß

Ernst Klett Verlag
Stuttgart Düsseldorf Leipzig

Orange Line 1

für Klasse 5 an Mittelschulen, Regelschulen, Sekundarschulen, Gesamtschulen, verbundenen Haupt- und Realschulen, Orientierungsstufen und sechsjährigen Grundschulen

Im Auftrag des Verlags herausgegeben von:
Frank Haß, Kirchberg

Unter besonderer Mitwirkung von:
Harald Weisshaar, Bisingen

Erarbeitet von:
Jennifer Baer-Engel, Göppingen, und Marion Horner M.A., Cambridge, sowie Pamela Grimes, Stuttgart (Around the year)

Unter besonderer Mitwirkung von:
Sheila McBride, Stuttgart

Beratung:
Manfred Bojes, Lohne; Anette Christiani, Dortmund; Ulf Degen, Braunschweig; Volker Pabst, Stade; Annegret Preker-Franke, Bielefeld

Umschlaggestaltung:
Koma Amok, Stuttgart

Umschlagfoto:
Kerstin Hacker, London

Illustrationen:
David Norman, Meerbusch; Naomi Fearn, Berlin (Link-up-Seiten); Christian Dekelver, Weinstadt (Seite 47)

3-12-990661-4 Sprachtrainer
Bietet abwechslungsreiche Übungsformen zu Vokabular und Grammatik, Leistungs- und Lernzielkontrollen und ein Lexikon mit dem Wortschatz des Lehrwerks.

1. Auflage

1 6 5 4 3 2 1 | 2008 2007 2006 2005 2004

Alle Drucke dieser Auflage können im Unterricht nebeneinander benutzt werden.
Die letzte Zahl bezeichnet das Jahr des Druckes.

Internetadresse: http://www.klett.de

Redaktion: Antje Loydl M.A., Jim Martin M.A., Sheila McBride, Elke Munkelt (Projektleitung), Dr. Gudrun Steinbach, Susann Edele (Assistenz)

Mediengestaltung: Ulrike Wursthorn
Reproduktion: Meyle + Müller, Medien-Management, Pforzheim
Druck: Stürtz, Würzburg
Printed in Germany
ISBN 3-12-547510-4

9 783125 475106

Hallo und herzlich willkommen bei Orange **Line**!

Englischlernen macht Spaß! Damit dir das Englischlernen leicht fällt, möchten wir dir hier dein neues Englischbuch vorstellen. So weißt du wo sich alles befindet.

Es geht los mit **Time for Greenwich** (Zeit für Greenwich). Hier zeigen wir dir den Handlungsort deines neuen Englischbuchs, nämlich Greenwich, einen Stadtteil Londons.

In sieben **Units** (Kapiteln) lernst du die vier Lehrwerkscharaktere kennen und erlebst mit ihnen und ihren Familien deren Alltag mit all seinen Freuden und Problemen.
In der Unit 1 und auf den **Link-up** (Verbindung)-Seiten kannst du all dein Wissen aus der Grundschule noch einmal anwenden.

Check-in: Hier geht es los! Auf zwei Seiten, die dich in die Unit einführen, lernst du neue Wörter und Landeskunde.
Language: Hier geht es um Redemittel und Grammatik.
Chats with Charlie: Eine Radioseite mit DJ Charlie Black. Hier gibt es besonders viel Englisch zu hören.
Story: Geschichten mit den Lehrwerkscharakteren rund um Greenwich!
Wordwise: Alles über Wörter! Hier machst du Wortarbeit und Wortspiele.
Check-out: Alles klar? Am Ende der Unit überprüfst du selber, was du gelernt hast.

In **Extras** findest du eine spannende Fortsetzungsgeschichte, ein kurzes Theaterstück, ein Projekt über Tiere und Texte über Festtage in England.
Nach den Extras folgen **Mediation** und **Grammar** (Grammatikanhang) mit vielen Regeln, Beispielen und Tipps.
Am Ende des Buches findest du den Teil **Vocabulary** (Vokabelliste). Hier kannst du alle neuen Wörter einer Unit mit ihren deutschen Übersetzungen finden.
Das **Dictionary** (Wörterbuch) listet die Vokabeln des ganzen Buches alphabetisch auf. Es ist auch zum Nachschlagen gedacht, wenn du einmal ein Wort vergessen hast.

Alles klar? Dann mache dich bereit für eine Reise nach Greenwich.
Aber bevor es losgeht, *let's sing a song*!

(Music & lyrics: K.-H. Böttcher)

Erläuterungen:

Let's talk	Lasst uns reden
Let's listen	Lasst uns zuhören
For my folder	Für meine Sammelmappe
(CD)	Diese Teile sind auf der Begleit-CD (Langversion) enthalten.
(Symbol)	Diese Übungen sind besonders knifflig.
(Symbol)	Partnerarbeit
(Symbol)	Gruppenarbeit
…………	Diese Übungen sind fakultativ.
▶	Tipp zum Vokabellernen
▶	Tipp zur Grammatik

Inhalt

THOMAS TALLIS EATERY

Unit 7 The school year

Extras

Time for Greenwich

A

Millennium Dome

B

Greenwich Market

C

Thames Barrier

D

24-hour clock

E

Greenwich Park

F

Bus to Greenwich

1 Let's listen: Greenwich sounds

Listen and point.

2 A song: Let's get started!

a) *Listen.*
b) *Sing the chorus:*
Let's get started!
We're on our way.
We're learning English!
Let's go! Hooray!

Unit 1 Thomas Tallis School

Hello! I'm Tom.

1 Let's talk: Hello.

Hello. / Hi!
My name is … .
I'm ten. / … .
I'm a … at … .
I'm from … .
I'm in Year Five.

2 Let's talk: What's your name?

A: What's your name?
B: My name is … .
A: Where are you from?
B: I'm from … .
A: How old are you?
B: I'm … .

3 Let's listen: Phone numbers

a) *Listen and write the numbers.*

b) *Listen and write the phone numbers.*

Lisa: ....
Terry: .... (home)
.... (mobile)

c) *Say your phone or mobile number in English.*

1 one, 2 two, 3 three, 4 four, 5 five, 6 six, 7 seven, 8 eight, 9 nine, 0 oh

My mobile number is 0 7740 915462.

4 For my folder: Let's make a poster.

My name is … .
I'm … .
I'm from … .
I'm in Year Five.
My number is … .

My name is Sven.
I'm ten.
I'm from Leipzig.
I'm in Year Five.
My number is 0341 …

My name is Julia.
I'm eleven.
I'm from Berlin.
I'm in Year Five.
My number is 030 …

Meeting people

You and your sport!

1 Let's listen: Emma, Terry, Lisa, Mrs Carter or Mr Newman?

Example: 1. It's Emma. 2. It's … . *Go on, please.*

2 Thomas Tallis School

a) *Make sentences.*

Example: Thomas Tallis **is** a big school.

b) *Match the* ☐ *and* ☐ *sentences.*

Example: Thomas Tallis is a big school.
It's in Greenwich.

▶ **Thomas Tallis is** a big school.
It's in Greenwich.
→ G2

Thomas Tallis Terry Emma Mrs Carter Mr Newman	+ is +	new in Greenwich. the caretaker. a teacher. a big school. in Year Seven.

It's in Greenwich. • She's from Bristol. • She's nice. • He's OK. • He's twelve.

3 A quiz: What's my name?

Example: A: I'm new at Thomas Tallis.
B: Your name is Emma.
A: No. My favourite sport is football.
B: Your name is Lisa.
A: Yes. That's right!

4 Let's talk: This is Nina

Example: 1. A: This is Nina. **She's** eleven. She's from Stuttgart.
B: Hello, Nina. **I'm** … . I'm ten/eleven/… . I'm from … .
2. C: This is Mehmet. **He's** … . He's … .
A: Hi, Mehmet. *Go on, please.*

▶ I'm
he's
she's
→ G1, G2

1

Nina, 11, Stuttgart

2

Mehmet, 12, Istanbul

3

Nadine, 10, Paris

4
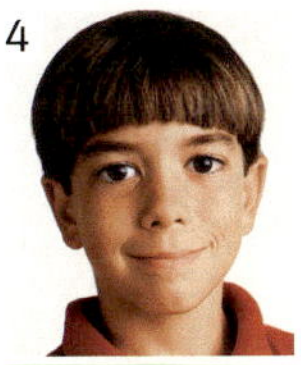
Francisco, 11, Madrid

5

Keiko, 12, Tokyo

6
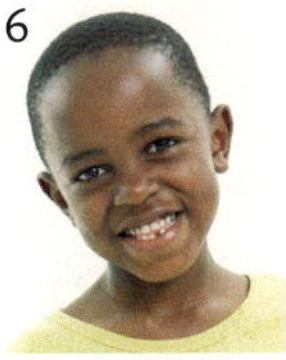
Nelson, 10, Nairobi

5 For my folder: At my new school

Write about your new school.

This is … School. It's my new school.
It's in … .
This is … . She's/He's my teacher.
This is … . She's/He's the caretaker.

The school bag

1 Let's listen: In the bag

a) *Copy the grid into your exercise book. Listen for the words and fill in your grid.*

In the bag	Lisa	Emma	Terry
a pencil case	X		
a pen	X		
a pencil			
a rubber	X		
a ruler			
a book			
an exercise book			
a sandwich			
an apple			
a mobile			

▶ **a book**
an apple

b) *What's in the bag here?*
A pencil, a ruler … . *Go on, please.*

c) *Look at your grid.*
What's the name on the bag in the picture?

Emma Brook | Terry Jackson | Lisa Taylor

2 'A' or 'an'?

1. Here's … exercise book.
2. And here's … pencil case.
3. This is … English book.
4. Mmm, … apple.
5. Here's … shoe.
6. And that's … old ruler.

3 Let's listen: Numbers

a) *Listen and say the numbers.*

b) A: What's 7 and 17?
B: It's 24. What's … and … ?
A: …

c) *Play buzz! Say 'buzz!' for all numbers with seven.*

One, two, three, four, five, six, **buzz!**, eight, nine, ten, eleven, twelve, thirteen, **buzz!**, fifteen, sixteen, **buzz!**, …

13 thirteen
14 fourteen
15 fifteen
16 sixteen
17 seventeen
18 eighteen
19 nineteen
20 twenty
21 twenty-one
22 twenty-two
23 twenty-three
24 twenty-four
30 thirty
40 forty
50 fifty
60 sixty
70 seventy
80 eighty
90 ninety
100 a/one hundred

4 Two pictures

Picture 1: **one pen** …

Picture 2: **four pens** … *Go on, please.*

5 Sounds

Listen and say.

[z]	[s]	[ɪz]
1. bag – bags: The bags are big. pen – pens: My pens are new	2. book – books: My books are in my bag. sport – sports: You and your sports!	3. pencil case – pencil cases: Here are three pencil cases. sandwich – sandwiches: Mmm, two big sandwiches!

6 Let's talk: What's in your bag?

Example: **Two sandwiches, one rubber, …**
Go on, please.

▶ one pen, four pens
one sandwich, two sandwiches
→ G3

7 Let's listen: Alphabet rap

A (clap) B (clap) C D E
Here's a rap for Thomas T.

F (clap) G (clap) H I J
English lessons are OK.

K (clap) L (clap) M N O
Are you new here? Hi, hello.

P (clap) Q (clap) R S T
Say the numbers one, two, three.

U V W *— shout and clap.*

X Y Z (clap) *— do the rap.*

8 Words and numbers

a) *What's your favourite number?*

b) *Read and spell the numbers.*
Go on, please.

forty | four | ninety | …

c) *Make puzzles for your partner.*

A: Here are the letters:
What's the number?
B: It's 'fifteen'.

Asking questions

Sam

Emma: Are we in the right classroom, Lisa?
Lisa: Yes, we are.
Emma: Mrs Carter isn't here. Are you sure?
Lisa: Yes, I am. Look, here's Terry.
Terry: Hi! Where's Sam? Is he here, too?
Lisa: No, he isn't.
Emma: Who's Sam? Is he a friend from your old school?
Lisa: Yes, he is. And he's always late!
Emma: You're lucky, you two. I'm not from Greenwich. My friends aren't at Thomas Tallis.
Lisa: Yes, they are.
Emma: No, they aren't! They're in Bristol.
Lisa: They're here, too – we're your new friends, Emma!
(Brr! Brr!)
Terry: Hey, that's my mobile. – Hi, Sam! What's up? Where –?
Emma: Terry!!! Here's Mrs Carter.
Terry: Bye, Sam. Hello, Mrs Carter. Er – sorry!
Mrs Carter: That's OK. Good morning, boys and girls.

> ▶ Sam is … .
> Sam and Terry are … .
> → G2

1 Right or wrong?

Example: Sam is always late. – That's **right**.
Sam is in the classroom. – That's **wrong**.

1. Lisa and Terry are in the right classroom.
2. Mrs Carter is the caretaker.
3. Emma is from Greenwich.
4. Sam and Terry are old friends.
5. Mr Newman is the teacher.
6. Lisa, Emma and Terry are at Thomas Tallis.

2 People at Thomas Tallis

Fill in: I, you, he, she, it, we, you, they.

Example: **I**'m Lisa. **I**'m from Greenwich.
Go on, please.

1. That's Mrs Carter. …'s my teacher.
2. Here's Terry. …'s from my old school.
3. …'s the right classroom. …'m sure.
4. …'re lucky. Terry and I are friends.
5. Emma and Lisa, …'re in my class.
6. Here are Sam and Terry. …'re my friends.
7. Hello, Mrs Carter. Sorry …'m late.

3 Long forms

Write the long forms.

Example: I'**m** ten. – I **am** ten.

1. You're my new friends.
2. She's eleven.
3. They're new here.
4. You're at Thomas Tallis.
5. He's from Greenwich.
6. I'm in your class.
7. We're friends.
8. It's a big school.

> ▶ you're → you are
> she's → she is
> we're → we are
> they're → they are
> → G2

4 That isn't right.

Look at the pictures and make sentences.

Example: Sam **isn't** here. He is in London.

1. The pupils … here. They … late.
2. I … from Greenwich. I … from Bristol.
3. It … a football. It … a shoe.
4. Mr Newman … a teacher. He … the caretaker.
5. Emma and I … twelve. We … eleven.
6. I … a pupil. I … a mouse.

+	–
I am	I'm not
you are	you aren't
he is	he isn't
she is	she isn't
it is	it isn't
we are	we aren't
they are	they aren't

→ G4

1 
2 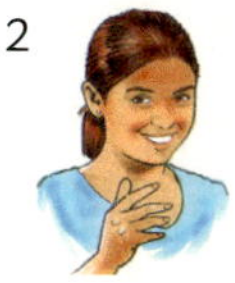
3 
4 
5 

6 

5 Make questions and answers.

Example: Is | Sam | ten? | **No, he isn't.**

Is

Tom · Sam · Terry · Emma · Lisa

from Greenwich? · eleven? · ten? · a mouse? · a boy? · at a new school?

Yes, she is. · Yes, he is. · No, she isn't. · No, he isn't.

Is Emma …?
– **Yes, she is.**
– **No, she isn't.**

→ G5

6 Let's talk: At my school

Example: the girls and boys • OK → **Are** the boys and girls OK? ↗ – Yes, they **are**. ↘ – No, they **aren't**.

1. your friends • from your old school?
2. the classrooms • big?
3. the pupils in your class • ten?
4. your teachers • from London?
5. the caretakers at your school • OK?
6. your school shoes • new?

7 A game

What are the words for your numbers? Make questions and answers.

Example: ⚀ + ⚀

Is Emma eleven? – **Yes, she is.**

Emma …	+	… from Greenwich?
Tom and Mr Newman …		… eleven?
Lisa …		… ten?
Mrs Carter …		… new at Thomas Tallis?
Lisa and Emma …		… German?
the girls and boys in your class …		… English?

Classroom phrases

The classroom

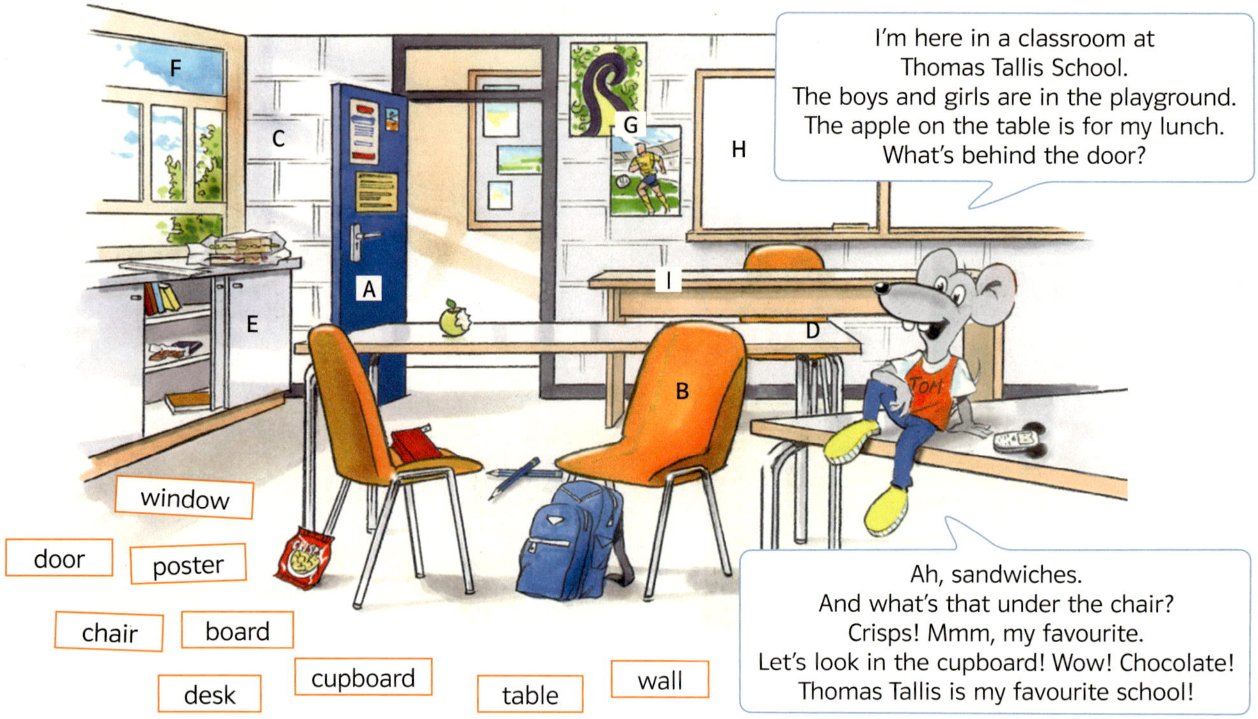

1 Classroom words

a) *Listen and point.*

b) What's the word for A? – The word is **'door'**.
What's the word for B? – …

2 In the picture

Write ten sentences.

Example: The apple is **on** the table.
The books are **in** … . *Go on, please.*

3 A game

Where's the pencil case?

Is it in the bag?

No, it isn't.

Is it on the table?

No, it isn't.

Is it under the chair?

Yes, it is.

4 'Who' or 'what'?

1. …'s TTS? – It's 'Thomas Tallis School'.
2. …'s Mr Newman? – He's the caretaker.
3. …'s Emma? – She's a girl from Bristol.
4. …'s the word 'mobile' in German? – It's '*Handy*'.
5. …'s from Greenwich? – Lisa, Terry and Sam.
6. …'s in the school bag? – A book and two pens.

5 Match the questions and the answers.

1. What's under the chair?
2. What's your favourite sport, Lisa?
3. Where's Greenwich?
4. Who's always late?
5. Where are the books?
6. Where are you from?
7. What's 7 and 7?
8. Where's Thomas Tallis School?

It's a mouse. ✓

I'm from Greenwich.

It's in London.

It's football.

They're on the cupboard.

Sam is always late.

It's 14.

It's in Greenwich.

6 Classroom phrases

Listen and match.

You:
Good morning.
Sorry I'm late.
Can we open the window?
Where are we?
What's '*Auf Wiedersehen*' in English, please?
Can I go to the toilet, please?
What's the homework?
Thank you.
Goodbye.

Your teacher:
That's OK. Sit down, please.
Yes, of course you can.
It's on the board.
Good morning, boys and girls.
We're on page 19, Exercise 6.
You're welcome.
Bye!
No, you can go at lunchtime.
It's 'goodbye'. You can say 'bye', too.

7 Let's talk: In the classroom

What can you say to your teacher?

Example:
Teacher: Good morning.
You: …

1. Good morning.
2. Here's your exercise book.
3. Where's your book?
4. You're late.
5. Let's do a rap.
6. Who's your German teacher?

No problem!

1

A It is lunchtime.
Emma is in the cafeteria with Lisa.

Emma: Look – here's Terry. He's cool.
Lisa: Cool? He's –
Emma: Sssh!
Terry: Listen, you two. Here's a new joke. What's a word with twenty-six letters?
Emma: That's easy! The word is 'alphabet'. Right?
Terry: Uh, yes.
Lisa: That isn't a new joke, Terry. It's a boring old joke. Your jokes are always boring.
Emma: Lisa, that's not very nice. You and Terry are friends.
Terry: No, we aren't. Goodbye, Lisa!

2

B Lisa and Emma are in the playground now.

Lisa: Let's play. Here you are!
Emma: Oh, no! I'm not good at –
Lisa: Oops! The ball is in the tree.
Emma: Oh, Lisa. I'm sorry!

3

C Now Sam and Terry are in the playground, too.

Sam: Hello. What's the problem?
Emma: It's the ball. It's in the tree.
Sam: That's no problem – not for Terry and me.
Terry: Is it your ball, Emma?
Emma: No, it isn't.
Terry: Oh, is it your ball, Lisa?
Lisa: Yes, it is.
Terry: Hm. Your ball – your problem.
Sam: Terry! You and Lisa are friends.
Terry: Friends? No, we aren't. My jokes are boring.
Lisa: I'm sorry, Terry. Your jokes are OK.
Emma: Please, Terry.
Terry: OK, OK.

D Terry is in the tree now.

4

5

1 Terry, you're an idiot!

Talk about the story. This story is … .

very nice | cool | boring | OK

2 What's the right order?

Example: 1. It is lunchtime. 2. …

- Lisa and Emma are in the playground with a ball.
- Mrs Carter is at the window.
- Here is Terry with a new joke.
- It is lunchtime. ✔
- Lisa is not nice to Terry.
- Sam is nice to Terry, Lisa and Emma.
- Emma is not good at football.
- The girls are in the cafeteria.
- The ball is in the tree.

3 Sort the words.

🙂	🙁
Oh, I'm sorry.	You're an idiot!
…	…

Your jokes are boring. • Oh, I'm sorry. • No! • You're cool. • Here you are. • That's wrong. • That's no problem. • Thank you. • Very nice. • You're not cool. • Your ball – your problem. • You're an idiot!

4 Picture five

Write what Mrs Carter says and what Terry says.

5 Act the story.

Make groups and then act the story "No problem!"

1 New words

▶ Neue Wörter behältst du am besten, wenn du sie im Zusammenhang lernst. Dabei kann dir ein *word star* helfen. Übertrage die drei *word stars* auf ein Blatt Papier und lege es in deinen *English folder*. Lass Platz für weitere Wörter, damit du die *word stars* im Laufe des Schuljahres ergänzen kannst.

a)

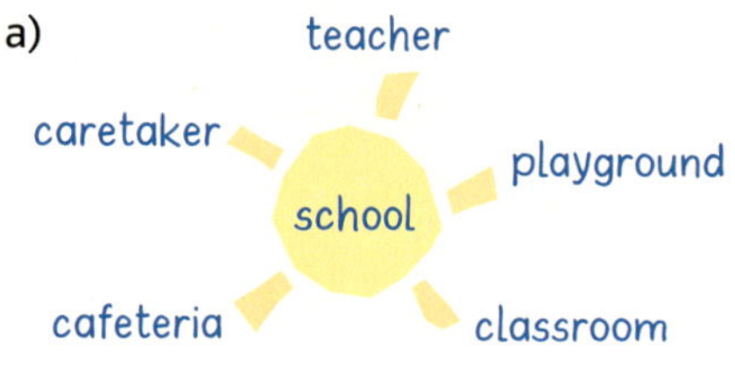

b)

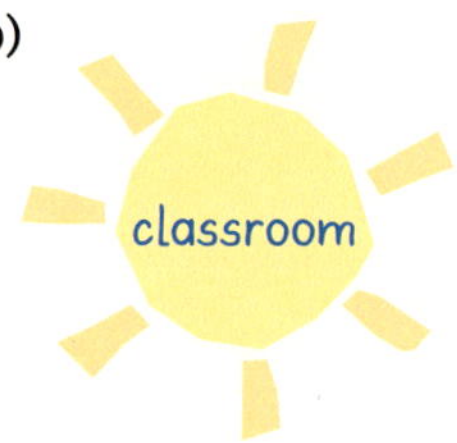

c)

2 Pairs

Find six pairs: old – new

yes	thank you
on	no
girl	bye
old	boy
hi	new
please	under

3 The wrong word

ruler – rubber – mouse – pencil

Example: The wrong word is 'mouse'.

1. girl – chair – boy – teacher
2. cafeteria – playground – caretaker – classroom
3. who – what – hi – where
4. in – on – under – pen
5. homework – apple – chocolate – sandwich

4 Where's Tom?

1. Tom is … .

5 Find the right adjectives.

Example: Tom is a **lucky** mouse.

1. My … sport is football.
2. TTS is a … school.
3. The caretaker is …!
4. Your jokes are …, Terry.
5. Emma is a … girl.
6. How … are you?
7. Lisa isn't … .
8. Sam is always … .
9. Here's Terry. He's … .
10. English is …!

6 Let's listen: Words

Write the letters. What are the words?

1 A new school (Personalpronomen → G1, Die Formen des Verbs *be* → G2)

Look at this letter from Emma to her friend Fiona. Fill in: I, you, he, she, it, we, you, they.

Hi Fiona!
...'s lunchtime here. ...'m in the playground with Terry. Who's Terry? ...'s my new friend and ...'s cool. ...'re in Year Seven now. Terry's friends are Lisa and Sam. ...'re from his old school. ...'re in Year Seven, too. Mrs Carter is nice. ...'s the German teacher. ...'m good at German, but ...'m not good at sport. ... isn't boring here. Greenwich is OK and my new friends are nice. But ...'re my friend, too.

2 School questions and answers (*be* in Fragen/Kurzantworten → G5)

1. **Is** Thomas Tallis a big school? – **Yes, it is.**
2. … Mr Newman a teacher? – No, … .
3. Hi, Terry and Lisa! … you from Greenwich? – Yes, … .
4. Oh, I'm sorry. … I late? – Yes, … .
5. … the girls in the classroom? – No, … .
6. … your school bag new? – No, … .
7. … Mrs Carter a teacher? – Yes, … .
8. Hello, Mrs Carter. … we in the right room? – No, … .

3 Who or where? (Fragen mit Fragewörtern → G6)

Who?	Where?
girl	classroom
…	…

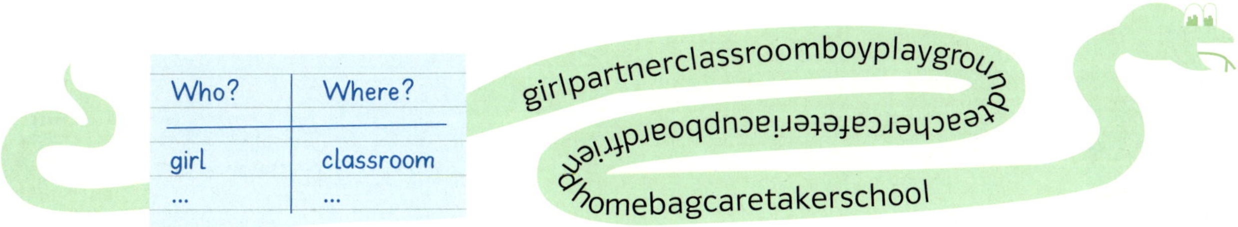

4 A new pupil (Fragen mit Fragewörtern → G6)

Steve:		Lisa:
1. …'s your name?	–	It's Lisa.
2. … are you from?	–	I'm from Greenwich.
3. …'s Mrs Carter?	–	She's a teacher at Thomas Tallis.
4. … are the boys?	–	They're in the playground.
5. …'s your football?	–	It's in my bag.
6. … are 'lucky' and 'cool'?	–	They're adjectives.

Du kannst jetzt

- ✓ dich und andere vorstellen. → *Stelle dich und einen Partner/eine Partnerin vor.*
- ✓ über die Schule reden. → *Stelle deine Schule in fünf Sätzen vor.*
- ✓ zählen. → *Zähle bis 100.*
- ✓ buchstabieren. → *Buchstabiere* 'teacher', 'pencil', 'exercise book'.

Home sweet home

1 Let's listen: Rooms

a) *Listen and write the words on cards, one word per card.*

kitchen
bedroom
dining room
living room
bathroom

b) *Look at the picture and listen. Where is Tom? Show the right card.*

2 Colours

Look at the picture and ask the questions.
A: Is the kitchen yellow?

Close your book. Answer the questions.
B: No, it isn't. It's pink.

1. Is the living room brown?
2. Is the bathroom white?
3. Is the bedroom purple?
4. Is the dining room green?

3 Right colours?

a) *Look at the colours and say the right word.*
b) *Write the words in the right colour.*

Example: Number one is green.

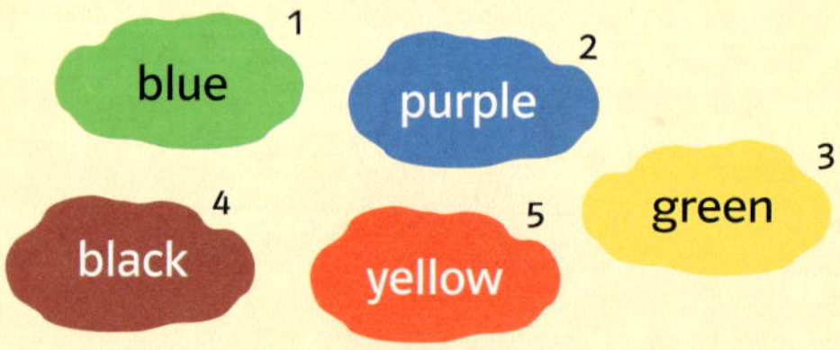

4 Room rhyme

I'm Tom and here's my home sweet home
with table, chairs and bed.
Green and yellow, blue and purple
and my favourite colour, red.
Tiny pictures, tiny sofa
in my funny, tiny house.
Tiny TV and computer –
this is home for Tom, the mouse.

5 Funny furniture

Write and say the words.

1. c • pbo • rd
2. com • • t • r
3. • ha • r
4. ta • • e
5. so • a
6. pi • tu • e

6 Let's talk: Houses

A: What are the rooms in your dream house?
B: Four bedrooms, a … .
A: What furniture is in the rooms?
B: A big bed, a … .
A: What colours are the rooms?
B: The bathroom is yellow. The … .

7 For my folder: My dream house

a) *Now draw your dream house. Write the words for the furniture and the rooms in your picture.*

b) *Show your picture in class. Find new words. Put your picture and the new words in your folder.*

8 Let's listen: Tom Tiny and his family

Example: Who's in picture A?
– That's his brother, Tim. He's three.

1. Who's in picture B?
2. Who's in picture C?
3. Who's in picture D?
4. Who's in picture E?
5. Who's in picture F?

Tina | Tim | Tamara | Tilly | Tony | Thomas

mum | sister | brother | grandad | dad | grandma

9 Write the family words.

1. adragnd
2. itress
3. rrhoebt
4. mraagnd
5. add

10 Link-up quiz

1. Who's in the Tiny family?
2. What are the rooms in the mouse house?
3. What colour are the rooms?
4. What furniture is in the rooms?

Unit 2 At home in Greenwich

The Brooks and the Jacksons

Our computer shop

Emma:

This is my family – my parents, Rob and Farah, and my half-sister, Nasreen. Rob is her stepdad. He's the manager of a computer shop in Holburne Road. Our flat is over the shop. It's very small, so Nasreen and I are in one room. That's a big problem. But the shop is great. I can play computer games with my friends there.

My shed in the garden

Terry:

My parents are Grace and Ted Jackson. Our house is in Hither Farm Road. It's boring at home. I'm an only child. But my cat, Tiger, is funny. Her favourite place is the roof of the shed in the garden. My drums are there. The "Keep out!" sign on the door is only for parents – not for my friends.

1 Emma Brook or Terry Jackson?

Example: Our cat is on the roof of the shed. – That's **Terry Jackson.**

1. Our room is a problem.
2. My drums are there.
3. My dad is the manager.
4. I'm an only child.
5. Our flat is very small.
6. My parents are Rob and Farah.

Emma Brook

Terry Jackson

Our house and garden in Pond Road

2 The Taylor family

Write a text for Lisa.

This is my family. My parents are … .
My sister is …, and Ben is my … .
Barker is our … . Our house is … .

3 Let's listen: Can you come over?

a) *Draw this house.*
b) *Now listen and write the number on it.*
c) *Listen again. What things can you add?*

4 Let's talk: Where's your house?

A: Where's your house?
B: It's in … .
A: What's the number?
B: It's … .
A: What colour is the door?
B: It's … .
A: What colour are the windows?
B: They're … .

5 For my folder: My family

This is my family. My parents are … and … .
I'm an only child. / My brother/sister is … . / My brothers/sisters are … .
Our house/flat is in … .

Families and nationalities

Sam's family

1 Who's who?

Look at Sam's family tree and make sentences.

Example: Tim is **Sam's** uncle.

► Sam**'s** family
Phil**'s** cousin
→ G7

Sarah • James • Tim • Maria • Elena • Phil	+	is	+	Sam's • Tracy's • Phil's • Susan's • David's	+	grandad • grandma • aunt • uncle • cousin • dad • mum • sister • brother

2 For my folder: My family

Make a family tree for your family.

3 Lunch with the Spencer family

Find the names for the letters at the table.

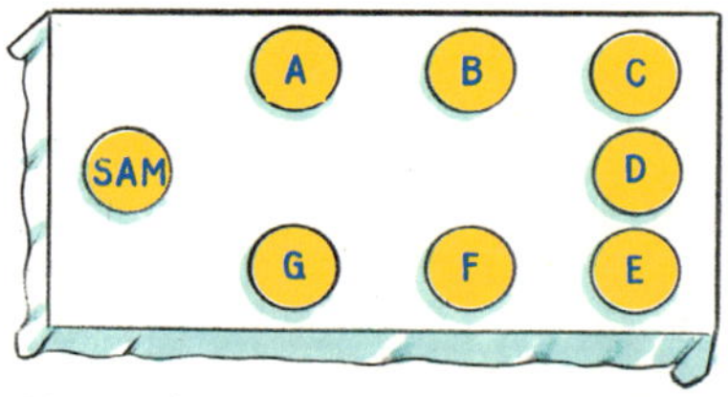

Example: A is … .

1. The girls next to Sam are his cousins.
2. Tracy is on Sam's left.
3. Tracy is next to her Uncle David.
4. Susan is on her dad's left.
5. Phil is next to his dad.
6. David is on his mum's right.
7. Sam's aunt is on his grandma's left.

► … is on the right.
… is on the left.
… is next to …

4 Grandma, are we English?

▶ her parents' name
your cousins' family

→ G7

a) *Copy Sam's family tree.*
b) *Add countries to the tree.*
c) *Where are the people from?*

Example: James Spencer is from England. Sarah Pilch is … .

James Spencer	Sarah Pilch
England	Poland

5 Countries, people and languages

Match a flag with a country and write sentences.

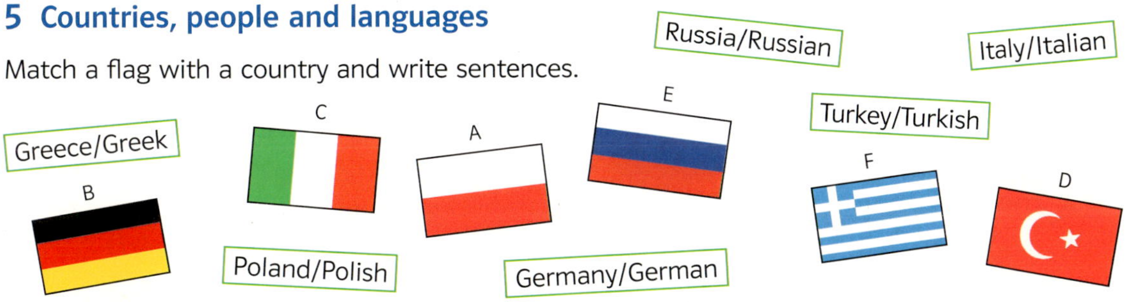

Example: Flag A is from Poland. People from Poland are Polish. The language is Polish.

6 Let's talk: More about my family

A: Where are you from?
B: I'm from … . I'm … .
A: Where's your family from?
B: My family is from … . They're … .
A: And your grandma/grandad?
B: My grandma/grandad is from … . She's/He's … .

Saying what you've got

Emma, you're in big trouble!

Emma has got a big sister, Nasreen. Their bedroom is small, so they have got only one wardrobe. Nasreen hasn't got a lot of time now. Her friends are outside, so she's in a hurry. But her new T-shirt isn't in the wardrobe. Her parents haven't got it, but what about her sister?

Nasreen: Emma? Where are you?
Emma: I'm in the bathroom. What's up?
Nasreen: Where's my new pink T-shirt, Emma? Hurry up! I'm late. Have you got it?
Emma: No, I haven't. Look on the shelf in the wardrobe.
Nasreen: It isn't there. Where is it? You've got two seconds!
Emma: OK, OK! It has er, em – it has got a mark on it.
Nasreen: A mark? Emma, you're in big trouble!
(Later)
Emma: Dad!! Where's Nasreen? She has got my Discman. Just because her T-shirt –
Mr Brook: That's your problem, Emma. I haven't got a Discman and I haven't got a pink T-shirt. Sort it out with your sister.

+	–
I've got	I haven't got
they've got	they haven't got
she has got	she hasn't got

→ G8, G9

1 The Brooks

Read the text and write sentences.

Example: Emma **has got** a big sister.
Nasreen **hasn't got** a big sister.

Emma Nasreen Mr Brook	has got hasn't got	a lot of time. a pink T-shirt. a Discman. a problem. a big sister. friends outside.

2 The girls' room

What have they got? Make sentences.

Example:

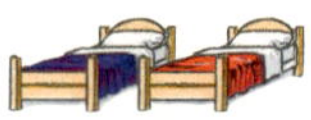

They**'ve got** beds.

They **haven't got** a sofa.

1 

2 

3 

4 

6 

3 Let's talk: Things in your room

A: What have you got in your room?
B: I've got a … and one/two/three … .

4 A quiz: Who is it?

Test your partner.

Example:
A: They've got a house in Pond Road.
Who is it?
B: It's the Taylors.
A: He has got … .
B: It's … . *Go on, please.*

a shed in the garden
only one bedroom
a house in Pond Road
drums
three cousins in Italy
…

5 Nasreen's friend

What are Emma's questions about Nasreen's friend?

Example:
Emma: Has he got a brother?
Nasreen: Yes, **he has.**
Emma: Has he got a dog?
Nasreen: No, **he hasn't.**
Go on, please.

▶ Has he got … ?
– Yes, he has.
– No, he hasn't
→ G10

a brother (yes) • a lot of friends (yes) • a dog (no) • a cat (no) • a mobile (yes) • a computer (yes) • a sister (no) • a TV in his room (no)

6 What have they got?

A: My questions are about the Brooks.
Have they got a computer shop?
B: Yes, they have.
A: Have they got a cat?
B: No, they haven't.
A: Have they got … ?
Go on, please.

▶ Have they got … ?
– Yes, they have.
– No, they haven't
→ G10

the Brooks	?	a computer shop
the Jacksons		a cat/dog
the Taylors		a flat in … Road
the Spencers		a garden
		a shed
		a boy

7 Let's talk: Have you got a red pencil, please?

Describing rooms

1 Look at the pictures.

What's different?

Example: In picture A **there are** two books on the table.
In picture B **there is** one book on the table.

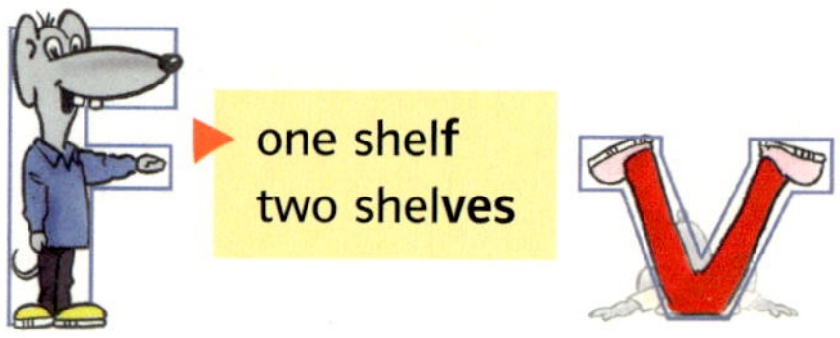

▶ one shelf
two shel**ves**

A

B

2 Let's talk: Questions and answers about the pictures

Your book is closed. Your partner is A.

A: **Is there** a table in picture A?
B: Yes, there is.
A: **Are there** four chairs in picture B?
B: No, there aren't. *Go on, please.*

there is	*es gibt; da ist*
there are	*es gibt; da sind*
Is there ...?	*Gibt es ...? Ist da ...?*
Are there ...?	*Gibt es ...? Sind da ...?*

3 For my folder: My room

Draw a picture of your room, and write about your room.

My room
In my room there is ...

4 Revision: I spy with my little eye ...

A: I spy with my little eye
something beginning with 'C'.
B: Cupboard.
A: No, sorry.
C: Chair.
A: No. That's wrong.
D: Chocolate.
A: Yes. That's right.
Go on, please.

1 Two families

Radio Active has got a new radio show: Chats with Charlie. People can chat about their favourite topics on the show. They can phone Charlie or come to his studio. He is always happy to see new people there.

Before you listen: Who is in the Taylor family? Who is in the Spencer family?

Example: Lisa has got … . dad | sister | brother | …

2 Let's listen: Family and friends

What's the right answer?

1. The topic today is …
   friends. • family. • magazines.
2. Sam has got …
   a brother. • a sister. • a grandma.
3. Lisa's sister is …
   six. • five. • ten.
4. When she's unhappy, Lisa can …
   play with Barker. • sing a song. • play football.

3 Let's listen: Right or wrong?

1. Sam is the DJ.
2. Lisa is in the studio.
3. Lisa can talk about problems with her friends.
4. Sam has got a lot of friends.
5. Lisa has got a problem with Barker.
6. The topic today is 'family'.

4 Sounds

Listen and say.

[tʃ]	[dʒ]
It's Chats with Charlie.	He's the DJ.
She's the teacher.	Here's Mr Jackson.
It's lunchtime.	He's the manager.
What's in the picture?	It's an old joke.

5 A song: I've got a crazy song (Music: K.-H. Böttcher, Lyrics: S. McBride)

1. I've got a crazy[1] song about my brother.
   A really[2] crazy song about my brother.
   I've got a song for free[3] about my family.
   I've got a crazy song about my brother.

2. You've got a crazy song about your sister.
   A really crazy song about your sister.
   You've got a song for free about your family.
   You've got a crazy song about your sister.

3. He's got a crazy song about his grandma.
4. She's got … about her cousin.
5. We've got … about our uncle.
6. They've got … about their grandad.

[1]crazy ['kreɪzi] – *verrückt*, [2]really ['rɪəli] – *wirklich*, [3]for free [fə 'fri:] – *umsonst*

Ghosts in Hither Farm Road?

1 Before you read: Who's who?

What can you say about Terry, Tiger and Emma? They're in this story.

A One Saturday afternoon Terry is in his shed in the garden.

Tiger, the Jacksons' cat, is on the roof of the shed. Terry has got his dad's laptop on one of his drums. He is busy with a new music project. But he has got a problem. The laptop is not very good. It is really slow. He is fed up.

B Who can help? Sam hasn't got a laptop. But what about Emma? He has got Emma's phone number, and he is lucky: she is at home! Emma has got a new laptop and Terry can borrow it.

She has got homework, but she can come over in an hour. Terry is happy now. He can finish his project.

C An hour later, there is a knock on the door of the shed. It is Emma with her new laptop. Terry is really happy to see Emma. Now they can finish his project. And Emma is a great help. They have got a lot of problems, but Emma is really good with computers.

Two hours later, Emma can go home. But she isn't very happy. It is late and it is already dark outside.

D Emma: Terry, it's spooky here. There are strange noises outside.

Terry: Oh, Emma! It's only the wind in the trees. We haven't got ghosts in Hither Farm Road! But I can take you home.

Emma: OK, Terry. That's really nice of –

Suddenly there is a terrible noise outside! Emma is really scared.

Emma: Aargh!!! Terry! What's that?

Terry: I'm not sure. Let's look!

It is dark outside, but they can see two yellow eyes under the window. Meow, meow!

Terry: Tiger! You stupid cat. Your bed is in the kitchen. It isn't on the roof of the shed! Come on, Emma. Let's go!

2 Talk about the story.

This story is … .

very good · really nice · funny · spooky · a bit boring · terrible

3 What's wrong in the sentences?

Example: Terry is in the Jacksons' house.
That's wrong. Terry is in **his shed**.

1. The shed is in Pond Road.
2. Terry has got his dad's drums.
3. Emma is at school.
4. Emma has got an old laptop.
5. There is a knock on the door of Terry's house.
6. They can see two cats under the window.

4 More about Terry, Emma and Tiger

a) *Sort the adjectives.*

strange • busy • new • fed up • slow • not very good • lucky • good with … • happy • nice • scared • stupid • terrible • spooky

Terry	Emma
busy	good with computers
…	…

Tiger	places/things
stupid	not very good
…	…

b) *Use the adjectives and write sentences.*

Example: Terry is busy in the shed.

1 Picture words

A B C D E F

▶ Besorge dir bunten Karton und schneide Kärtchen aus. Schreibe darauf die Wörter, die du lernen willst. Schreibe das Wort als Zeichnung. Befestige die Kärtchen an verschiedenen Plätzen in deinem Zimmer. Immer, wenn du an den Wörtern vorbeikommst, wirst du sie sehen, lesen und damit besser behalten.

Examples:

2 Funny words

What's the right word?

Example: playground

step – top | ~~play~~ – ball | lap – dad | up – board | foot – time | cup – stairs | lunch – ~~ground~~

3 A word puzzle

Find the words.

1. school ➜ teacher
   computer shop ➜ ???
2. bed ➜ bedroom
   sofa ➜ ???
3. grandpa ➜ grandma
   uncle ➜ ???
4. Greece ➜ Greek
   Poland ➜ ???
5. books ➜ shelf
   T-shirts ➜ ???
6. pencil case ➜ pencils
   house ➜ ???

4 Barker's bed

Barker's bed is
in the Taylors' kitchen.
What is there in
Barker's bed?

Example: There is **a mouse**.
There are … .

1 Terry's shed
(Besitzangaben mit -'s → G7, Besitzangaben mit *have got/has got* → G8)

a) *Example:* 1. That's Terry's shed. 2. That's … . *Go on, please.*

b) *What have the people got? Write sentences.* *Example:* Terry has got a shed. *Go on, please.*

2 Two families
(Besitzangaben mit *have got/has got* → G8, *have got/has got:* Verneinung → G9)

	cat	dog	shed	garden	house	flat
The Jacksons	✓	✗	✓	✓	✓	✗
The Taylors	✗	✓	✗	✓	✓	✗

Make sentences.

Example: The Jacksons have got a cat. They haven't got … . *Go on, please.*

3 Funny questions
(*have got/has got:* Fragen und Kurzantworten → G10)

Examples: I • tree • in my bedroom – Have I got a tree in my bedroom?
my • dad • drums • in the car – Has my dad got … ?

1. our cousins • shed • in the playground
2. we • sofa • in the bathroom
3. my grandma • computer • in the garden
4. our school • garden • on the roof
5. I • cupboard • in my school bag
6. Barker • window • in his bed

Du kannst jetzt

✓ über die Familie reden. → *Stelle deine Familie in fünf Sätzen vor.*
✓ über Nationalitäten und Herkunft reden. → *Stelle eine Person vor. Sage, woher sie kommt und welche Sprache/n sie spricht.*
✓ ein Zimmer beschreiben. → *Sage, was es in deinem Zimmer gibt.*

Hobbyland

skate | play computer games | play the drums | break-dance | play football | swim | ride a bike | draw a picture | collect and swap cards | read comics | watch videos | ride a horse

1 What can you do in Hobbyland?

Copy the list of hobbies under the example. Look at the grid and write down where you can do the different things.

Example: 1. ride a bike – A1
2. ride a horse – …

2 Let's listen: Check your list.

Are all your answers right? Correct what's wrong.

3 Let's talk: Hobbies

a) A: Let's say we're in Hobbyland. What can we do together?
B: We can … and we can … .
A: OK. But I can't … .
B: Then I can teach you. / Then we can … .
A: OK. That's a good idea.

Can you … ?
– Yes, I can.
→ G11

b) *Add more hobbies to your list in Exercise 1.*
c) *What hobbies can't your partner do?*

A: Can you … ?
B: Yes I can. / No, I can't. Can you teach me?
A: Yes, I can. / No, I can't.

4 Let's listen: What can't you do today in Hobbyland?

Example: You can't skate today.
Go on, please.

5 Hobbies for Tom and Tina

What can Tom and Tina do?

Example: Tom can ride a bike and … .
Tina can … .

6 Tom's week

a) *What can Tom and his friends do at the Mouse Club?*

Example: On Mondays they can swim or they can draw a picture. On Tuesdays they can … .

b) *Write a plan for Tom's week.*

7 Link-up quiz

1. What can you play?
2. What can you ride?
3. What can you watch?
4. What can you read?

8 What day is it?

1. It's the day after Wednesday.
2. It's two days before Sunday.
3. It's the day after Monday.
4. It's two days after Thursday.
5. It's the day before Monday.

before – *vor*
after – *nach*

9 A song: Seven days in a week (Music: K.-H. Böttcher/Lyrics: K.-H. Böttcher & S. McBride)

At Thomas Tallis after school
There's always lots[1] to do.
From drama club[2] to basketball[3],
It's really up to you[4].
Monday is number one.
Cooking[5] is really fun, yeah[6]!
Tuesday is number two.
Football is the thing for you, yeah!
Wednesday is number three.
Drama club for you and me, yeah!
Thursday is number four.
Gymnastics[7] on the floor[8], yeah!
Friday is number five.
Rap music – and it's live[9], yeah!
Saturday is number six.
Where are the hockey sticks[10]? Yeah!
Sunday is number seven.
Nothing to do[11] is heaven[12], yeah!

[1]lots [lɒts] – *viel*, [2]drama club ['drɑ:mə ˌklʌb] – *Theatergruppe*, [3]basketball ['bɑ:skɪtbɔ:l] – *Basketball*, [4]up to you [ˌʌp tə 'ju:] – *deine Entscheidung*, [5]cooking [kʊkɪŋ] – *Kochen*, [6]yeah [jeə] – *ja!*, [7]gymnastics [dʒɪm'næstɪks] – *Turnen*, [8]floor [flɔ:] – *Boden*, [9]live [laɪv] – *live*, [10]hockey sticks ['hɒki ˌstɪks] – *Hockeyschläger*, [11]nothing to do ['nʌθɪŋ tə ˌdu:] – *nichts zu tun*, [12]heaven ['hevən] – *himmlisch*

Unit 3 Free time

School clubs

Come to the Thomas Tallis
All Sports Club
in the gym on Fridays at 3:30.
Learn to play basketball, badminton and volleyball.

THE COOKING CLUB

- on Mondays
- in room 4C
- at 4:00

THOMAS TALLIS DOG CLUB

Come to the Thomas Tallis dog club in the park on Mondays at 3:30.

Learn about dogs and teach your dog tricks.

▶ 4:00 = four o'clock
3:30 = half past three

Drama Club

Can you sing? Good!
Can you dance? Great!
Can you sing and dance? WOW!

We've got just the right thing for you:

Come to the hall on Wednesdays at 3:00.

The T.T. Football Club

every Tuesday
in the gym
at 4:00

COMPUTER CLUB

Every Tuesday at 3:30 in the computer room.

1 Clubs at Thomas Tallis

What clubs are there at Thomas Tallis? Where are they?

Example: You can go to the **football club.** It's **in the gym**. *Go on, please.*

2 Let's talk: Boring or a good idea?

Talk about clubs with a partner.

A: Let's go to the … club.
B: No, that's … . Let's go to the … club.
A: OK. That's … . When is the … club?
B: It's on … at … . *Go on, please.*

🙂	☹
fun	no fun
easy	terrible
(very) good	a stupid idea
(really) nice	(a bit) boring
a good/great idea	not cool
OK	
cool	

3 Let's listen: What can we do?

a) *Match the clubs with the pupils. Example:* Lisa – dog club, football …

b) *What can the friends do together? Example:* Lisa and Terry – football club

c) *Look at the clubs on page 40 again. When are they? Add the times to the clubs in b) and write sentences.*

Example: Lisa and Terry can go to the football club (in the gym on Tuesdays at 4:00).

football, computer, cooking, dog, all sports, rap, drama

Sam, Emma, Lisa, Terry

4 Let's talk: My clubs

a) *Make a list of clubs at your school or in your town.*

b) *Talk about clubs with your partner.*

A: What are your clubs?
B: My clubs are … and … .
A: When are they?
B: … is on … at …, and … is on … at … .

5 For my folder: My favourite club

Make a poster for your favourite club.

Rules

Clubs at Thomas Tallis

1 Late again?

Sam is on his way to the cooking club. Mr Newman is in the playground.

a) *Read the dialogue.*

b) *Act the dialogue with a partner. Use different times.*

Example: 3:30 – It's **half past three.**

1. 4:30	4. 7:20	7. 4:50
2. 8:15	5. 10:30	8. 9:28
3. 12:45	6. 6:15	9. 11:14

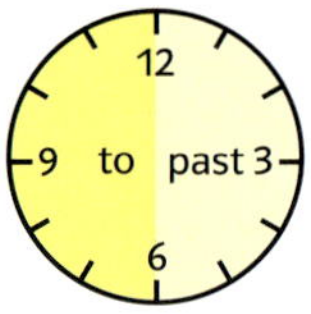

4:15 = quarter past four
4:30 = half past four
4:45 = quarter to five
4:20 = four-twenty

2 At the clubs

Match the pictures of different clubs with the texts.

Example: Picture 1 – **Take** the apples out of the oven at 5:15.

Take .... .
Nimm / Nehmt .... .
→ G12

1

2

3

4

5

6

- Take the apples out of the oven at 5:15. ✔
- OK. It's 4:30. Stop the music, please.
- OK. It's 5:00. Put the balls in the cupboard, please.
- OK. It's 4:30. Walk your dogs to the tree and back, and then you can go home.
- Sorry, it's 4:30. Finish the game now, please.
- It's only 4:50. Sing the song again, please, Emma.

3 Rules for the drama club

Example: **Come** to the drama hall at 2:55. – **Can you come** to the drama hall at 2:55, **please**?

Come to the drama hall at 2:55.
Bring your *Cats* T-shirts.
Leave your bags in my room.
Put your mobiles on my desk.
Learn your lines at home.
Go to the toilet before you come.
Be nice to your partner.
Smile! Drama is fun!

Can you …, please?
…

4 Rules in the T.T. all sports club

It's 3:30 on Friday. Lisa is at the all sports club, but she is fed up. There are a lot of rules.

Don't bring … !
Don't … !
→ G12

a) *Read the rules.*

b) *Make more rules with: be, bring, leave, open, play, put.*

1. Don't … football in the hall!
2. Don't … late!
3. Don't … the gym!
4. Don't … the windows!
5. Don't … dogs!
6. Don't … schoolbags behind the door!

5 Classroom rules

Write rules for your classroom.

6 Funny rules

a) *Look at the poster. What are the rules for the pictures?*

b) *Make a poster with funny rules for your school.*

7 A trick with numbers

Think of[1] a number from one to ten. Multiply the number by[2] two (x2). Add the number eight (+8). Divide the number by[3] two (÷2). Take away[4] the first[5] number (– first number). What's the number?

[1]think of ['θɪŋk ˌəv] – *denk an,* [2]multiply by ['mʌltɪplaɪ ˌbaɪ] – *multipliziere mit,* [3]divide by [dɪ'vaɪd ˌbaɪ] – *teile durch,* [4]take away ['teɪk ə'weɪ] – *subtrahiere,* [5]first [fɜːst] – *erste*

Daily routines

An e-mail to Grandma

Dear Grandma,

Thank you for your e-mail. You ask about my new school. Well, I like Thomas Tallis and I like my teachers. The uniform is OK, but Lisa and I don't like our sports shirts – they're yellow! My school day is very long. We start at 8:40 and most days I don't get home before 4:30. Here's a normal day for me:

Here I am in the computer room :-)

7:45 – I get up and wash – before Nasreen! She's always in the bathroom for hours and she's often late.
8:00 – I dress and go into the kitchen.
8:15 – I eat breakfast with Dad.
8:30 – I leave the house.
1:10 – Lunchtime!!! I eat lunch with my friends, and after lunch we play in the playground.
2:10 – We start afternoon school.
3:20 – We finish school. On Wednesday afternoons we finish at 2:30.
5:00 – I do my homework.
7:00 – We have supper. After supper I help in the kitchen or watch TV.
9:30 – I go to bed.

I sometimes go to a club after school. My friends Terry and Lisa often go to the football club. But I don't like football. I never go there.
There's a sports club, but the kids always play stupid sports – basketball and volleyball! Ugh! Terrible! On Wednesdays Lisa, Terry, Sam and I always go to the drama club. It's *Cats* this year. I love it! And on Fridays Terry and I sometimes go to the rap club. I often go to the computer club with Terry on Tuesdays, too.
Sorry, but it's seven o'clock and my supper is on the table.

Bye, Emma

1 From morning to night

What can Emma say about her day?

Example: I get up and wash at 7:45. I dress and … at … .
Go on, please.

▶ I get up …
I dress …
I eat …
→ G13

2 For my folder: My school day

Write about your school day.

Example: I **get up** and **wash** at 6:30. I … .
Go on, please.

3 School days

Look at a day at your school and a day at Emma's school. What's different?

Example:
1. They **start** at … . We **start** at … .
2. They **eat** lunch at … . We **eat** … .
Go on, please.

4 Let's talk: You and your friends

a) *Talk to a friend about Saturdays.*

I	always often sometimes never	get up late. write e-mails. listen to music. do my homework. watch videos. meet my friends. read comics.

b) *Now say what you and your friend do.*

> always = *immer*
> often = *oft*
> sometimes = *manchmal*
> never = *nie*

5 Emma's clubs

Read about Emma's clubs again and make sentences.

Example: Terry and Lisa • the football club • often • go to
Terry and Lisa often go to the football club.

1. go to • I • the football club • never
2. on Tuesdays • the computer club • go to • often • I
3. the drama club • on Wednesdays • we • go to • always
4. on Fridays • sometimes • go to • Terry and I • the rap club
5. go to • clubs • after school • I • often
6. play • stupid sports • always • they • at the all sports club

> I **always** read comics on Saturdays.
> → G14

6 Pupils don't like homework.

Match and write sentences.

Example: Pupils **don't like** homework. *Go on, please.*

> Pupils **don't like** homework.
> → G15

Pupils Pupils in Greenwich Lisa and her family A lot of young people German pupils Emma and Lisa Mice	don't	eat breakfast. wear uniforms. go home for lunch. live in a flat. like homework. like their sports shirts. like cats.

> one mouse – two mice

7 For my folder: All about my weekends

Write about your weekends.

> At weekends I always go to ... . I don't go to ... . I don't like ..., but I like ... . I sometimes/never/often ... .

Third person singular

Who likes Mondays?

Tiger likes mice. She doesn't like dogs. And she doesn't like Mondays. Terry always comes home early on Mondays and plays his drums in the shed. Tiger often sleeps on the roof of the shed. She doesn't like her bed in the kitchen. She never sleeps there.

Barker likes his bed in the kitchen. He puts his favourite things there. He doesn't like Wednesdays. Lisa always comes home late. But he likes Mondays. Then he always watches *Tom and Jerry* on TV with Jade.

1 Tiger or Barker?

Example: … likes his bed. **Barker** likes his bed.

1. … watches TV.
2. … never sleeps in her bed.
3. … puts his things in his bed.
4. … likes mice.
5. … likes Mondays.
6. … sleeps on the roof of the shed.

▶ He likes … .
She sleeps … .
He watches … .
→ G13

2 Right or wrong?

Example: Barker doesn't like his bed. – That's wrong. **Barker likes** his bed.
Tiger likes mice. – That's right.

1. Tiger doesn't like Mondays.
2. Barker puts his things in the garden.
3. Barker doesn't like Mondays.
4. Terry always skates on Mondays.
5. Tiger likes dogs.
6. Barker likes *Tom and Jerry*.

▶ She likes / doesn't like … .
He watches / doesn't watch … .
→ G15

3 That's wrong.

▶ go – goes
do – does

Example:
Emma likes dogs.
– That's wrong. She **doesn't like** dogs.

1. Terry goes to school at 8:25.
2. Lisa goes to the cooking club.
3. Tom likes cats.
4. Emma gets up after Nasreen.
5. Sam does homework at 5:00.
6. Barker sleeps on the roof.

4 Sam and Terry's Monday

1. Terry **gets up** at 7:00.
He **eats** breakfast at … . He … .
2. Sam **gets up** … . He … . *Go on, please.*

	Terry	Sam
get up	7:00	8:20
eat breakfast	7:30	8:25
go to school	8:00	8:35
do homework	5:00	9:00
watch TV	7:30	7:30

1 Let's listen: A chat with a night nurse

Today Charlie chats with Anna Church, a night nurse.

Match the sentence parts.

1. Anna helps
2. She starts work
3. People sometimes
4. Anna comes home
5. She helps her children
6. She always goes to their school

a. with their homework.
b. at seven in the morning.
c. at half past three.
d. at ten o'clock in the evening.
e. bring chocolate.
f. a lot of people.

2 Let's listen: Anna's day

Listen again. Then match the times with the things that Anna does.

Example: Anna starts work at ten o'clock in the evening. She … . *Go on, please*

Anna starts work. She finishes work.
She goes to bed. She makes breakfast.
She eats lunch. She gets up.

7:00 | 2:30 | in the afternoon | 10:00 ✔ | 8:00 | in the morning | 6:15 | 3:00 | in the evening ✔

3 Sounds

Put the words in three groups.

borrows, comes, dances, does, dresses, finishes, helps, leaves, plays, puts, rides, shouts, sings, skates, sleeps, starts, swims, takes, teaches, washes, watches

[s]	[z]	[ɪz]
sleeps …	borrows …	dances …

4 A poem[1]: Lazy[2] Daisy and Busy Bobby

Lazy Daisy
Sleeps on Monday
Gets up on Tuesday
Washes on Wednesday
Dresses on Thursday
Plays on Friday
Sings on Saturday
Dances on Sunday.
This is what Daisy
Does every week.

Busy Bobby
Washes on Monday
Irons[3] on Tuesday
Shops[4] on Wednesday
Cooks[5] on Thursday
Cleans[6] on Friday
Bakes[7] on Saturday
Dances on Sunday.
This is what Bobby
Does every week.

[1]poem ['pəʊɪm] – *Gedicht,* [2]lazy ['leɪzi] – *faul,* [3]irons [aɪənz] – *bügelt,* [4]shops [ʃɒps] – *kauft ein,* [5]cooks [kʊks] – *kocht,* [6]cleans [kli:nz] – *putzt,* [7]bakes [beɪks] – *backt*

Barker's story

1 Before you read: Answer the questions.

1. Who's Barker?
2. Who's in the Taylor family?

1

A Hello. I'm Barker. My people are the Taylors – Richard and Susan and their children, Lisa, Ben and Jade. The Taylor family lives in my house. I love the Taylors!

2

B Every morning at half past seven I wake up Lisa and wash her face. Lisa is my friend. Then she washes her face again. After that, we make our breakfast.

3

C At twenty past eight the children go to school. I help Susan in the house, or I play in the garden. Sometimes a cat comes into our garden, but I don't like cats. I always bark, and then they run away.

4

D In the afternoons Susan and I go to our café. I often sit behind the window, and I say 'Hello!' when people come in. I'm a very nice dog.

5

E On Saturdays I don't work, and Lisa doesn't go to school. I take Lisa to the park. I often teach Lisa tricks. I sometimes bring Lisa her ball. She often gets lost in the park. Then she calls my name. I always find Lisa again.

F On Sundays I go out of town with my people in our car. There are always a lot of cars. Sometimes there are dogs in the cars, too. We bark. It's great fun!

6

7

G In the evenings my people often watch TV. Then we play a game. I watch TV, too. I sit in front of it, and they throw shoes. I take the shoes into Lisa's bedroom. I like shoes!

8
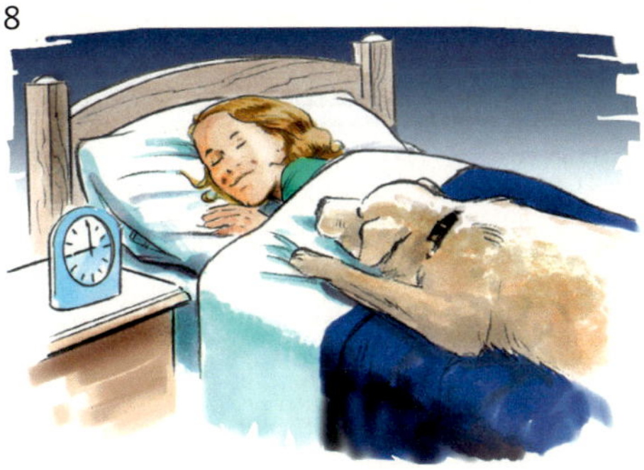

H At nine o'clock I take Lisa to bed. She's nice, so she can always sleep in my bed. I've got a very nice bed in the kitchen, too. But I sometimes sleep on my big bed in the bedroom. After my busy day I'm always dog-tired.

2 Say what you think.

Example: I think this story is really nice/stupid/funny/...
I like/don't like Barker/the pictures/the story/...
Go on, please.

3 Who is it?

Example: Who tells the story? – **Barker.**

1. Who are Barker's people?
2. Who goes to school?
3. Who takes Barker to the park?
4. Who sits behind the window?
5. Who gets lost in the park?
6. Who throws shoes?

4 Let's talk: What can you remember?

a) *Partner A looks at pictures 1 to 4 and then closes his/her book. Partner B asks questions.*

B: Who is in picture 1?
A: Barker and ... .
B: Is there a car in picture 1?
A: ...

b) *Partner B looks at pictures 5 to 8 and then closes his/her book. Partner A now asks questions.*

1 Words in sentences

A B C D E F

▶ Lerne ein neues Wort möglichst in einem ganzen Satz. Das ist für das Gedächtnis leichter. Am besten geht es mit Sätzen, die Bilder in deiner Vorstellung erzeugen, zum Beispiel wie etwas aussieht, wie es sich anhört, wie es sich anfühlt und welche Gefühle es in dir weckt. Du kannst es an diesen Reimen ausprobieren.

a) There's a dog in our rap club,
And breakdance is his thing.
When he dances on the table,
All the children start to sing.

b) Make on Monday, take on Tuesday,
Wash on Wednesday, throw on Thursday,
Find on Friday, sit on Saturday,
See on Sunday.

2 What can you do?

Example: I can wash my face. *Go on, please.*

wake up | eat | help | play | play with | wash

my face | football | computer games | supper | my grandma | my brother | people | breakfast | my dog

3 Fill in the right letters.

Example: fav♥♥rite – favourite

1. choc♥♥♥te
2. r♥♥lly
3. br♥♥kfast
4. T♥♥sday
5. We♥♥♥sday
6. y♥♥ng
7. of♥en
8. e♥♥ning
9. diff♥♥ent
10. cupb♥♥rd

4 Tom's Sunday

Example: Tom gets up at 10:00 in the morning. He … .

does homework
goes to bed
eats supper
gets up
watches TV
makes breakfast

1 Playground rules (Der Imperativ → G 12)

Look at the pictures on the board.
Write the rules.

Example: 1. **Don't bring** mobiles. *Go on, please.*

2 They don't eat chocolate. (Die einfache Gegenwart: Verneinung → G 15)

Look at the pictures and the words. They don't do a lot of things. What can you say?

Example: They **don't** … .

help in the house
eat chocolate
live in a flat
like TV
sleep on the roof
love cats

1

2

3

4

5

6

3 Tiger's Saturday (Die einfache Gegenwart → G 13, Die einfache Gegenwart: Verneinung → G 15)

Example: Tiger ☹ … in her bed. She ☺ … on the roof. sleep
Tiger **doesn't sleep** in her bed. She **sleeps** on the roof.

1. She ☹ … her bed in the house. She ☺ … the shed. There are mice under it. like
2. On Saturday Tiger ☺ … at 6:00 in the morning. Terry ☹ … before 10:00. get up
3. She ☺ … mice. She ☹ … her breakfast. like
4. She ☹ … into the garden. She ☺ … into Terry's bedroom. go
5. She ☹ … on the bed. She ☺ … on his face. sit
6. Terry ☹ …, "Nice cat!" He ☺ …, "You stupid cat!" say

Du kannst jetzt

- ✓ über Clubs und Hobbies reden. → *Was sind deine Hobbies?*
- ✓ Vorschläge machen und darauf reagieren. → *Mache mit deinem Partner eine Aktivität für heute Nachmittag aus.*
- ✓ Verbote ausdrücken. → *Schreibe drei Verbote auf, die es in deiner Schule gibt.*
- ✓ deinen Tagesablauf beschreiben. → *Beschreibe deinen Tag.*
- ✓ die Uhrzeit erfragen und sagen. → *Frage deinen Partner nach der Uhrzeit.*

In town

1 Places in Mousetown

a) *Listen to the words for places on the map. Say the words.*
b) *Now look at the map. What is where?*

Example: The café is in Mouse Road. The park is in … .

2 Let's listen: I'm new in Mousetown.

a) *Look at Tom's map and listen. Where's Tom?*
b) *Listen again. Where are the bus stops? What's the number of the bus?*
c) *Find the way from the department store to number 25 Park Road.*

3 Let's talk: In Mousetown

Look at the map of Mousetown. You are behind the school in Dog Street. How can you get to the computer shop, the museum and the playground? Ask a partner.

A: Excuse me. Can you tell me the way to the computer shop, please?
B: Yes. Go down Dog Street to River Road. Go right into River Road. The computer shop is on your left.
A: Thank you. Goodbye.

on your left	–	*links*
on your right	–	*rechts*
next to	–	*neben*
Go down … .	–	*Geh … entlang.*
Go left.	–	*Biege nach links ab.*
Go right.	–	*Biege nach rechts ab.*

4 A game: Where am I?

A: *Look at the map and then close your eyes.*

B: I'm in Mouse Road, in a place next to the church. Where am I?
A: You're in the … .
B: No, that's wrong.
A: You're in the … .
B: Yes, that's right. *Go on, please.*

5 Link-up quiz: What is it?

1. It's near the supermarket. There are a lot of children there. It's in Old Road.
2. It's near the river. It's in Apple Tree Road. There are old books and pictures in it.
3. It's near the newsagent. It's in Mouse Road. There are a lot of sandwiches there.

6 In Mousetown

You are at the Information Centre. Where can mice go in Mousetown? How can they get there?

Make a poster with six places.

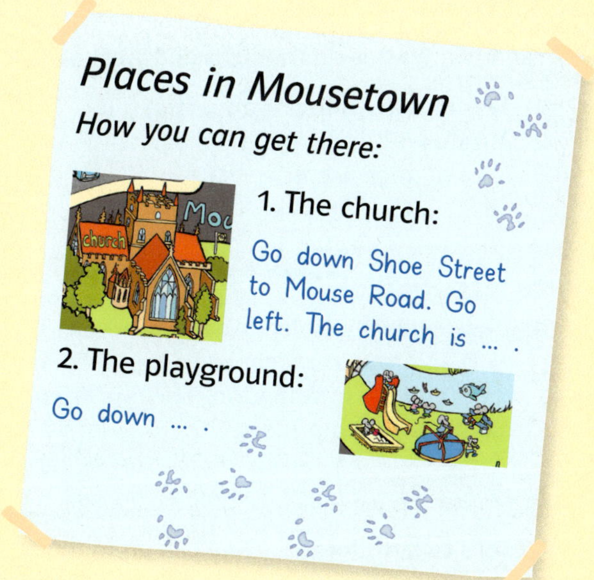

Unit 4 Greenwich Project Week

Out and about in Greenwich

A There is a great playground in Greenwich Park. A lot of young people come here on skateboards or on skates. You can play football here, too.

B The Foot Tunnel goes under the Thames, so you can walk under the river! It starts at Cutty Sark Gardens in Greenwich and goes to the Isle of Dogs.

1 What is it?

Example: East is on the right and West is on the left. – It's the Meridian Line.

1. This famous ship is a museum, too.
2. A train without a driver!
3. A lot of mice use it.
4. Home of the 24-hour clock!
5. Use it and walk under the river!
6. You can skate here.

2 Let's listen: Places for our project

a) It's Greenwich Project Week at Thomas Tallis. The pupils work in groups and choose a topic. Then they go into town and get information. The four friends want to find a topic for their project.

Who wants to do what? Listen and complete the grid.

places	☺	☹
Greenwich Park	Terry	Emma
Cutty Sark	...	...

b) *What's Terry's idea? Complete the text.*

Let's call our topic … . We can go to the … and the … first. Then we can visit the … and … .

C The Royal Observatory is in Greenwich. It is the home of the Meridian Line and GMT (Greenwich Mean Time). When it is 12:00 in Greenwich, it is 1:00 in Germany and 7:00 in New York. The famous 24-hour clock is here, too.

D The name 'Cutty Sark' means short shirt. This famous ship is more than a hundred and fifty years old. It is now a museum. You can see old pictures and maps there.

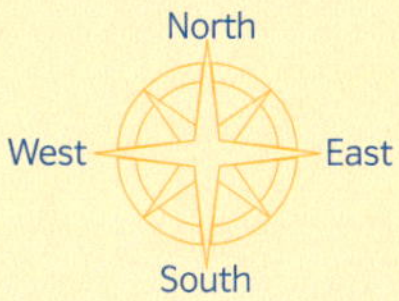

E The DLR (Docklands Light Railway) goes under the river from Greenwich to the Isle of Dogs, too. It is a train without a driver.

3 Let's talk: A visitor in Greenwich

A: Excuse me. I'm a visitor here. Where can I go and what can I do in Greenwich?
B: You can go to … . You can … there.
A: Thank you. That's a good idea.
B: You're welcome.

Cutty Sark Museum:	visit a famous old ship • look at old maps
Greenwich Park:	play football • skate
Royal Observatory:	see the 24-hour clock • see the Meridian Line

4 For my folder: My town

Where can visitors go in your town and what can they do there?

Make a poster with pictures.

Friends and families in Greenwich

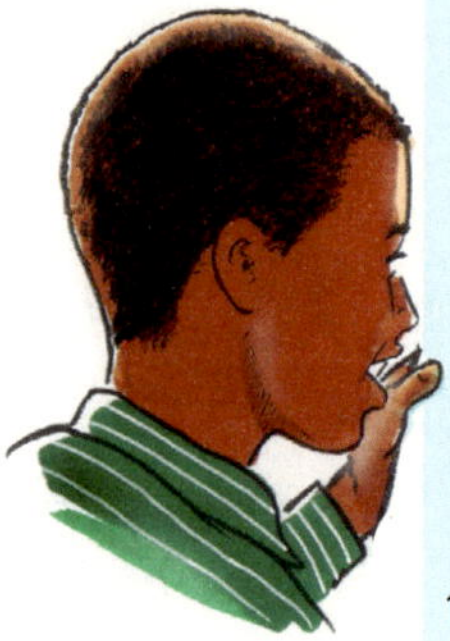

1. Do you live in Greenwich?
2. Do you often go to Greenwich Park?
3. Do you skate there?
4. Do you play football there?
5. Do you ride your bike there?
6. Do you meet friends there?
7. Do you eat lunch in Greenwich Park?
8. Do you listen to music there?
9. Do you read in Greenwich Park?
10. Do you swap cards there?

1 Terry's survey

Terry does a survey for the school project. Look at his questions. What are Emma's answers?

Terry: **Do you** live in Greenwich?
Emma: **Yes, I do.**
Terry: **Do you** often go to Greenwich Park?
Emma: **No, I don't.** *Go on, please.*

> ▶ Do you … ?
> – Yes, I do.
> – No, I don't.
> → G16

2 Let's talk: Our town

a) *Young people in Greenwich meet in the park. Where can you meet in your town? What can you do there?*
Example: We can meet … . We can … there.

b) *Look at Terry's questions again. Write five questions. Ask the group.*
A: Do you … ?
B: … *Go on, please.*

3 Let's talk: Friends and family

Make questions and then ask a partner.

Example: A: **Do** your friends go to town on Saturdays?
B: Yes, they **do**. / No, they **don't**.

> ▶ Do your friends … ?
> – Yes, they do.
> – No, they don't.
> → G16

Do	+	your friends your parents you and your friends/parents	+	go to	+	town the park the shops	+	on … ?

4 How the pupils go to school

One group in Year Seven chooses the topic 'transport'. They make a grid and ask the pupils questions. *Say how the pupils go to school.*

▶ **by** bike
on foot

HOW?	LISA	SAM	EMMA	TERRY	KATE	JOHN	MARY	JENNY
by bike		✔		✔		✔	✔	
on foot			✔		✔			✔
by car	✔			✔	✔			
by bus	✔		✔				✔	
on skates		✔				✔		

Example: Lisa goes **by car** or **by bus.** Sam goes … .

5 Transport

A: **Does Sam** go to school by bus?
B: **Yes, he does.**
A: **Does Lisa** go to school on foot?
B: **No, she doesn't.** *Go on, please.*

▶ Does Sam …? – Yes, he does.
– No, he doesn't.
Does Lisa …? – Yes, she does.
– No, she doesn't.

→ G16

6 A family topic – the Taylors' week

walk Barker | skate in the park | watch TV | play cards | phone Emma

a) *Write sentences about the Taylors' evenings.*

Example: On Mondays Mrs Taylor walks Barker at 7:00. On Tuesdays … . *Go on, please.*

b) *Make dialogues with a partner.*

A: Do Jade and Lisa watch TV on Mondays?
B: No, they don't. They watch TV on … .
Go on, please.

7 Let's talk: Your family

Make questions and answers.

Example: Does your mum get up at … ? – Yes, she does.

Does	+	your mum your dog your grandad …	+	get up meet friends go to the park …	+	on Saturdays? every day? at … o'clock? …

Information questions

Questions about Greenwich

1 What do you know?

1. What does GMT mean?
2. Where do visitors find the 24-hour clock?
3. What do the letters DLR mean?
4. Where does the Foot Tunnel go?
5. What does the name 'Cutty Sark' mean?
6. How do you get from Greenwich to the Isle of Dogs?

▶ What? – *Was?*
Where? – *Wo?*
How? – *Wie?*

Name: Emma Brook

1. Greenwich Meridian Time
2. at the Royal Observatory
3. I don't know
4. under the river
5. old boat
6. by tunnel or by DLR

Name: Sam Spencer

1. Greenwich Meet Time
2. at the Royal Observatory
3. the Docklands Light Railway
4. under the river
5. big shirt
6. by DLR or you can walk

Name: Terry Jackson

1. Greenwich Mean Time
2. at the Royal Observatory
3. the Docklands Light Railway
4. to London
5. short shirt
6. by tunnel or by DLR

2 Read the friends' answers.

Who has got one wrong answer, two wrong answers, three wrong answers? (Look at pages 54 and 55.)

Example: Emma has got … wrong answers. It's/They're number … . Terry has got … . *Go on, please.*

3 How do we get to the Cutty Sark?

Before the pupils go to Greenwich, they ask their teacher a lot of questions.
Put in the right question words.

When …? | What …? | How …? | Where …?

▶ When do we eat … ?
Where do we get … ?
→ G17

Pupil:	Teacher:
1. … do we get to the Cutty Sark?	– You can take the number 386 bus.
2. … does the Royal Observatory open?	– It opens at 10:00.
3. … do we meet you at lunchtime?	– At Mrs Taylor's café.
4. … do we eat lunch?	– At one o'clock.
5. … do we get our sandwiches?	– At Mrs Taylor's café.
6. … do we do in the afternoon?	– You finish your worksheets.

4 On the way to Greenwich

Sort the questions.

Example: get to • the friends • How do • Greenwich
How do the friends get to Greenwich?

1. the friends • What do • in the bus • do
2. the Foot Tunnel • What does • call • Lisa
3. Sam • What does • about the tunnel • know
4. want • What does • Emma • to know
5. the bus • Where do • they • get off
6. get • to school • Lisa • in the morning • How does
7. the pupils • When do • lunch • at the café • eat

5 Let's talk: Where do you skate?

A: Where do you skate?
B: I skate in the park.
A: When do you … ?
Go on, please.

What | Where | When | skate | How | eat lunch | do after school | read | get to school | …

6 A day in town

Look at Terry's answers. What are Sam's questions?

She leaves at nine o'clock.

She meets her sister.

She goes by car.

She goes to the shops.

▶ Where / What / How | does he/she … ?

→ G 17

Using object pronouns

Mr Rose's rules for Project Day

Don't forget your worksheets. Put them in your folders.
Stay in your group. Don't leave it.
One pupil in your group has got a mobile.
Phone Mrs Carter or me with your problems.
But give us your mobile number before you start.
Don't go to Mr Newman and ask him for the answers.
When you've got the answers, write them on your worksheets.
Give them to Mrs Taylor in her café in Park Row.
When she gives you your sandwiches, don't forget to thank her.

I	me
you	you
he	him
she	her
it	it
we	us
you	you
they	them

→ G18

1 Who or what is it?

Read the rules for the project.

Example: Put **them** in your folders. – It's the **worksheets.**

1. Don't leave **it**.
2. You can phone **me**.
3. Give **us** your mobile number.
4. Don't ask **him** for the answers.
5. Write **them** on the worksheets.
6. Don't forget to thank **her**.

2 Can you help me, please?

Match the questions with the pictures.

Example: Picture 1: Can you help me, please?

Can you ask him, please? • Can you find her, please? • ✔ Can you help me, please? • Can I help you? • Can you excuse us, please? • Can we borrow it, please?

1 ✔

2

3

4

5

6

3 A game: Four questions

Ask four questions and try to find the word.

A: The clue[1] word is 'transport'.
B: Is it a place?
A: No, it isn't.
B: Do a lot of people use it?
A: Yes, they do.
B: Does it go under the river?
A: Yes, it does.
B: Is it the Foot Tunnel?
A: No. Sorry! That's question number four.
B: What is it?
A: It's the DLR!

CLUE WORDS
transport
school
town
Greenwich

[1]clue [klu:] – *Hinweis*

1 Let's listen: Sounds in Greenwich

What do you think it is?
Example: 1. It's a bus. 2. … .

clock | football | bus
foot tunnel | skateboard | car
music | café

2 Let's listen: Greenwich for young people

a) *Match the people with the places they like.*
Example: Peter likes … . *Go on, please.*

music shops | Peter | Cutty Sark Gardens | Kate | Mark | the café in Church Street

b) *Listen again. Answer the questions.*

1. What does Peter do in Greenwich?
2. What are Mark's hobbies?
3. What's Kate's problem?

3 Let's talk: In our town

A: What problems are there for young people in your/our town?
B: In my/our town there isn't a … .
A: Are there good/big/ … ?
B: Yes, there are. / No, there aren't.

café	park
playground	sports
…	…

4 Sounds

Write the sentences in your exercise book.
Where do they go up? ↗ *Where do they go down?* ↘

1. Does Sam go to school by bus?
2. Where do we meet at lunchtime?
3. What do the letters 'DLR' mean?
4. Lisa goes by car or by bus.
5. When do they eat lunch at the café?
6. Do Jade and Lisa watch TV on Mondays?

5 A song: Please don't! (Music: K.-H. Böttcher, Lyrics: S. McBride)

I don't want to sit in the house alone[1].
I don't want to talk on my mobile phone.
I don't want to break-dance or to rap.
I only want to play the flute[2] and hear the people clap.

[1]alone [ə'ləʊn] – *allein*, [2]flute [flu:t] – *Flöte*

Cool idea, Sam!

A At nine o'clock on Wednesday morning the groups of pupils in Year Seven leave the school with their worksheets. Terry, Lisa, Emma and Sam take the number 386 bus to King William Walk. Then they walk to the Cutty Sark Museum. It is half past nine. There are no people at the museum. Then Sam reads the sign. Hours: 10:00–17:00, from Monday to Saturday.

Sam: Let's go to the Foot Tunnel first. That's my topic! Then we can come back here.

B They go to Cutty Sark Gardens next to the Foot Tunnel. It is quarter to ten. They see three people and ask them questions. Lisa speaks to a young man.

Lisa: Excuse me. We're from Thomas Tallis School. Have you got time to … ?
Young man: Sorry. I haven't got time. I'm late.

Sam asks a woman.

Sam: Excuse me. Can you help us, please?
Woman: Sorry. No English.

Terry is lucky. An old man has got time.

Terry: Good morning. Excuse me, but have you got time for our questions?
Old man: Of course. I've got a lot of time. What do you want to know?
Terry: Great. Thank you – er! First question: Do you live in Greenwich?
Old man: No, I don't. I live in Poland. I'm a visitor here. I don't know Greenwich.
Terry: Oh, no! Well, thank you.
Emma: Oh, this is terrible. Let's go to the Cutty Sark.

C It is quarter past ten. The children go back to the Cutty Sark Museum. At quarter to eleven they have got only three answers. It is cold and then it starts to rain.

Terry: Let's go to Greenwich Park now and do my survey.
Lisa: Oh, this is so boring. Let's go to mum's café now.
Emma: But what about our worksheets, Lisa?
Sam: I've got an idea. Mr Rose can't tell where we get the answers from. Let's make them up.
Emma: We can't do that.
Sam: Terry, you can ask me. I can ask you. Then I can ask Emma and she can ask Lisa. Mr Rose *can't* find out.
Emma: You two are terrible! And what about your mum, Lisa? She isn't stupid.
Lisa: My mum isn't in the café this morning.

D The children go to Mrs Taylor's café. They find a table and start to do the answers. At half past eleven Mr Rose comes into the café. The friends are busy and they don't see him.

Mr Rose: Hi, you four! Have you got all the answers?
Terry: Oh, Mr Rose! No, we, we –
Lisa: We are –
Emma: – on the way to the Royal Observatory.
Terry: Yes, Lisa just wants to go to the toilet.
Lisa: Oh, yes. I want to go to the toilet.
Mr Rose: Well, hurry up! It's twenty-five to twelve now. Be back here at one o'clock for lunch. Good luck!
Four friends: Thank you, Mr Rose.

1 The right order

Put the sentences in the right order.

- Mr Rose comes into the café.
- It starts to rain.
- The children go to Mrs Taylor's café.
- Lisa speaks to a young man.
- The children walk back to the Cutty Sark.
- Sam reads the sign.
- The pupils leave the school.

2 Timeline

Find all the times in the story and make a timeline.

9:00 The pupils leave the school.
9:30 They are at the … .
9:45 …
Go on, please.

3 Let's talk: Test your partner.

Make up questions. What does your partner know?

A: How do the pupils get to the museum?
B: They go by … .
A: What is the number on the … ?
B: It's … .

A: Where do they go first?
B: … .
Go on, please.

1 Don't forget the small words!

A B C D E F

Viele Vokabeln lernst du besser im Zusammenhang, besonders Ausdrücke wie „on foot". So kannst du dir die dazugehörige Präposition (z. B. at, to, by, up, …) besser merken. Schreibe dir Sätze mit diesen Vokabeln auf.

Example: be good at: **I'm good at** football.

be good at: …	on foot: …	get up: …
be at home: …	on skates: …	ask for: …
be married to: …	by bus: …	take out: …
be divorced from: …	by bike: …	*Go on, please.*

2 Find words for the photos.

3 The DLR

under | to (3x) | without | next to | of | at (2x) | from (2x) | in (6x)

Look at the text on the DLR. Put in the missing words.

The DLR is a new train … London. It is a train … a driver. Trains leave Greenwich every ten minutes[1] … Monday … Friday. … busy times there is a train every three minutes. The first train goes … 5:23 … the morning. You can go … Greenwich … the Isle of Dogs. The DLR goes … the River Thames. A lot … people work … East London and live … Greenwich. They use the train … the mornings and … the evenings. Visitors … the Cutty Sark use the DLR, too, because it stops … the river.

[1] minutes ['mɪnɪts] – *Minuten*

1 Questions about Greenwich (Die einfache Gegenwart: Entscheidungsfragen/Kurzantworten → G 16)

Use short answers.

1. Does the number 386 bus go to the Cutty Sark? –
2. Does Terry live in Greenwich? – ☺
3. Does the name 'Cutty Sark' mean short ship? – ☹
4. Does the Foot Tunnel start in Greenwich Park? – ☹
5. Does the Royal Observatory open at ten o'clock? – ☺
6. Does Mrs Taylor work in Bristol? – ☹

2 In Greenwich Park (Die einfache Gegenwart: Entscheidungsfragen/Kurzantworten → G 16)

A boy asks Lisa and Emma a lot of questions. *Put the words in the right order.*

1. you • Italian • Do • or Greek • speak
2. you • in Greenwich • Do • live
3. a lot of • Do • nice places • here • know • you
4. to the Royal Observatory • go • the DLR • Does
5. on foot • Do • go • a lot of visitors • there
6. stop • the Observatory • buses • next to • Do
7. at 9:00 • open • Does • in the morning • it
8. the 24-hour clock • Do • visit • a lot of people

3 Find the questions. (Die einfache Gegenwart: Fragen mit Fragewörtern → G 17)

1. Where … ? – Young people skate in Greenwich Park.
2. When … ? – The Cutty Sark Museum opens at ten o'clock.
3. What … ? – The pupils choose a topic.
4. How … ? – They get to Greenwich by bus.
5. Where … ? – He reads a sign at the Cutty Sark.
6. When … ? – He comes into the café at half past eleven.

4 What do the people answer? (Objektpronomen → G 18)

1. I've got a lot of books here. – Please put … in the cupboard.
2. What do I do with my bag? – Leave … on your desk.
3. Who knows Mrs Taylor? – Lisa knows … .
4. Where can I find Mr Newman? – You can find … in the playground.
5. I don't know where the café is. – We can show … .

Du kannst jetzt

- ✓ deinen Wohnort beschreiben. → *Schreibe fünf Sätze über deinen Wohnort.*
- ✓ über Greenwich sprechen. → *Sage, was dir an Greenwich gefällt/nicht gefällt.*
- ✓ eine Umfrage machen. → *Mache eine Umfrage zu einem beliebigen Thema.*

Unit 5 Shopping in Greenwich

At the shops

sports shop
newsagent
department sto
supermark

1 Match the pictures with the shops.

Picture 1 is a … . Picture 2 is a … . *Go on, please.*

S = small
M = medium
L = large

2 Where can you buy the things in the pictures?

Example: You can buy magazines at the **newsagent** or at the **supermarket**.

1 
2 
3 
4 
5 
6 
7 

8 

9 
10 

3 For my folder: Shops

a) *Copy the grid. Fill in the things from Exercise 2. What else can you buy at the shops?*

sports shop	newsagent	department store	supermarket	…
…	magazines	…	…	…

b) *What other shops do you know? What can you buy there?*

4 Money

In England they have got pounds and pence.
There are 100 pence in a pound.

How much is it? 1. 25p 2. £1.50 3. £3.00 4. 75p 5. £1.99 6. £27

We write:	We say:
£1	a / one pound
£5	five pounds
50p	fifty p
£1.50	one (pound) fifty
£5.30	five (pounds) thirty

5 Let's talk: How much?

A: How much is the bike?
B: It's … .
A: How much are the … ?
B: They're … .

How much **is** the comic?
– **It's** … .
How much **are** the magazines?
– **They're** … .

→ G 20

6 Let's listen: Where are the friends?

1. Terry is in the … .
2. Emma is in … . *Go on, please.*

7 Let's talk: Shopping dialogues

Make dialogues with a partner.

A: Excuse, me. I can't find … . / Where are the … ?
B: It's/They're over there in the window/ near the door/on the shelf.
A: How much is/are the … ?
B: It's … pounds. / They're … p.
A: Have you got this in black/blue …, too?
B: No, I'm sorry, we haven't. / Yes, we have.

Shopping for Sam's party

Sam: OK, Grandma. I think we've got all the things on our list. And there's no chocolate!
Grandma: Very good. We eat too much chocolate. Now what about your birthday? Do you want a cake?
Sam: Well … yes. But can *I* make it this year?
Grandma: Yes, of course. Do you want to have a party?
Sam: Oh yes, Grandma, there's a new burger bar –
Grandma: Sam, I'm sorry. That's too expensive. What about a pizza from Mario's?
Sam: Oh no, Grandma. We don't like Mario's pizzas and they aren't cheap.
Grandma: Well, why don't you all make your favourite pizzas? You and your friends can put all your favourite things on them. How many friends do you want to invite?
Sam: Just three – Terry, Lisa and Emma. Is that OK?
Grandma: Yes, of course it is. Let's get all the things now. Do you want to make a cheese cake?
Sam: No. Can I have a chocolate cake, please?
Grandma: Well … OK, Sam. But only because it's your birthday. Let's go find the chocolate for you.

milk — 2 bottles
eggs — 2 boxes
apples — 1 big bag
tomatoes — 1 bag
lemonade — 1 bottle
cheese — 1 large packet
water — 5 bottles
biscuits — 1 packet
cornflakes — 2 boxes
pencils — 1 box
NO CHOCOLATE!!!

1 The shopping list

What do grandma and Sam want to buy?

Example: They want to buy a packet of …, and a bag of … .

a **packet of** crisps
a **box of** pencils
→ G19

a / two / …	+	packet(s) • box(es) • bag(s) • bottle(s)	+	of	+	apples • biscuits • milk • eggs • lemonade • cheese • cornflakes • tomatoes • water • pencils

2 What else?

Look at the shopping list again. What else can you buy in a supermarket?

Example: You can also buy packets of …, boxes of … .

3 What do they want?

I want an apple.
I want to buy a pizza.

Make sentences about Sam and his grandma. *Example:* Grandma **wants to** talk to Sam.

Grandma Sam	+	wants doesn't want	+	(to)	+	a party. • invite three friends. • make his cake. • go to a burger bar. • buy a pizza from Mario's. • make a cheese cake. • get all the things for the cake. • make a chocolate cake.

4 A present for Sam

What do you know about Sam? What are his hobbies? What's a good present for him?

Terry hasn't got many ideas. Then Emma sees a T-shirt in the sports shop. But it's too expensive.

The friends go to the newsagent. There are a lot of cards there. Emma finds a nice card. But Terry and Lisa want to find a present first.

The friends go back to the department store. What's Terry's idea? What do you think?

5 What hasn't Sam got?

Sam hasn't got +	much many +	money. CDs. posters. chocolate. books. music.

▶ He hasn't got **much homework.**
He hasn't got **many presents.**
→ G20

Example: Sam hasn't got **much** money. Sam hasn't got **many** … .

6 Let's talk: What can we buy?

A: It's …'s birthday on … . What can we buy for him/her?
B: He/She hasn't got much/many … . Let's buy … for him/her.
A: No. That's boring/expensive/not a good idea. Let's get … .
B: OK. How much is it/are they?
A: It's/They're … . *Go on, please.*

Dates

Invitations

1 Who is it from?

a) *Read the invitation and answer the questions.*

Example: What does RSVP mean? – It means 'please answer'.

1. Who is the invitation from?
2. Who does Sam invite to his party?
3. Where is the party?
4. What time is the party?
5. Where does Sam live?
6. Why does Sam write an invitation?

Who? = *Wer?*
What? = *Was?*
When? = *Wann?*
Where? = *Wo?*
Why? = *Warum?*

Why … ?
Because … .

b) *What isn't on Sam's invitation?*
(His address? The date of his party? The time of the party? His name?)

2 The months of the year

a) *Listen and say the months.*

February | July | March | April | January | August | October | November | June | December | May | September

b) *Now say the months in the correct order.*

January, February, … . *Go on, please.*

3 Let's talk: Days in the month

a) *Make a list of the months. How many days are there in the different months?*

Example: January – 31 days

b) *Make a quiz for your partner.*

A: It has got thirty-one days. It has got only three letters.
B: That's May.
A: It has got thirty days. It starts with an 'A'.
B: That's … .

4 Birthdays

a) *Listen and say the numbers.*

b) *Look at Sam's birthday list. When are the birthdays?*

Example: His mum's birthday is on the twenty-first of May.
His dad's birthday is … . *Go on, please.*

Mum	–	21st May
Dad	–	10th December
Grandma	–	15th September
Terry	–	22nd July
Lisa	–	6th November
Emma	–	30th January
Me!	–	3rd March

You say:
on the twenty-first of May
You write:
on 21st May

5 What's the date?

Read and say the dates.

Example: Tue., 23.02. – Tuesday, the twenty-third of February.

1. Fri., 30.12.
2. Wed., 11.05.
3. Sun., 04.07.
4. Thu., 20.10.
5. Sat., 15.09.
6. Mon., 31.01.

6 Let's talk: When's your birthday?

a) *Ask about birthdays in your group. Make a list.*

A: When's your birthday?
B: It's on the … of … . When's your birthday?
C: It's on the … of … . When's … ? *Go on, please.*

b) *Do a class survey.*
How many pupils have got a birthday in January, … ?

7 A birthday calendar

Make a birthday calendar for the pupils in your class.

8 For my folder: A party invitation

Make an invitation to a party. Don't forget your name, your address and the time and date of the party. Here are three ideas.

1. *Write it as a crossword puzzle.*
2. *Blow up a balloon and write on it.*
3. *Use magazine pictures of famous people. They can give the information about the party.*

1st	**first**
2nd	**second**
3rd	**third**
4th	fourth
5th	fifth
6th	sixth
7th	seventh
8th	eig**hth**
9th	ni**nth**
10th	tenth
11th	eleventh
12th	twel**fth**
13th	thirteenth
14th	fourteenth
15th	fifteenth
16th	sixteenth
17th	seventeenth
18th	eighteenth
19th	nineteenth
20th	twentieth
21st	twenty-**first**
22nd	twenty-**second**
23rd	twenty-**third**
30th	thirtieth
31st	thirty-**first**

Mon. = Monday
Tue. = Tuesday
Wed. = Wednesday
Thu. = Thursday
Fri. = Friday
Sat. = Saturday
Sun. = Sunday

Celebrating birthdays

Birthdays are fun

1. I like my birthday. Grandma and I make a big cake. That's fun. My friends come to our flat and we play games and eat a lot of good things. Grandma helps and my dad always gives me a great CD.

2. My birthday is in July. This year I want to have a party in the park and play football. My friends love football. Then I want to go to a burger bar with them. But I hope they don't sing "Happy Birthday"!

3. I love birthdays. I get a lot of cards and presents from my friends and family. I always write a birthday list. My parents don't give me many presents. They often give me money. And I always get a present from my dog, too.

4. I always have a party with my friends. My dad makes the invitations on his computer. My mum often makes a chocolate cake. That's my favourite! And Nasreen goes to her friend's house. That's great!

1 Who says what?

Example: Number 1 is … . Number 2 is … .
Go on, please.

2 Revision: Yes or no?

Example: Does Sam make his cake? – Yes, he does. / No, he doesn't.

1. Does Emma make her cake?
2. Does Sam's dad give him a CD?
3. Does Lisa write invitations?
4. Does Terry want to have a party in the park?
5. Does Sam get money from his parents?
6. Does Emma's sister go to a friend's house?

3 Revision: I, me or my?

Complete the sentences.

1. We haven't got our invitations. Can you give them to …, please?
2. Can you help me, please? I can't find … birthday list.
3. I know them. They always invite us to … parties.
4. His friends always give him cards. … has got twenty this year.
5. Do you like the CD? It's for … for your birthday.
6. She doesn't make her cake. Her mum makes it for … .

▶ I	me	my
you	you	your
he	him	his
she	her	her
we	us	our
you	you	your
they	them	their

→ G 18

4 Let's talk: Birthdays

A: Do you like birthdays?
B: Yes, I do.
A: What do you do?
B: I … .
A: Do you/your friends … ?
Go on, please.

1 Let's listen: Birthday lists

a) *Listen and match the people with one thing on their birthday list.*
You can start like this:
Queen Elizabeth wants … .

Jim | Emma | Ben | Queen Elizabeth

1

2

3

4

b) *Listen again. Answer the questions about the things on the birthday lists.*

1. What's too big for the Queen?
2. What's too small for two people?
3. Where can't Ben use English money?
4. Why is a dog a good thing for Jim's dad?

2 Sounds

a) *Say the sentences.*

[f]	[v]	[w]
Find funny furniture for five fed up friends.	Seven visitors visit the observatory in the evening.	Who wants to work on Wednesday?

b) 1. Without you we forget every face.
2. Every week we watch five films on video.
3. Seventy-four women want to live west of King William Walk.

3 A song: It's your day (Music: K.-H. Böttcher, Lyrics: S. McBride)

Let's sing a song
For you – for you!
Happy birthday,
Happy birthday
To you!

Party time!
It's your day.
Fun and music –
That's OK.

Happy birthday, Sam!

1 Before you read: What do you know about Sam's birthday?

A It's lunchtime. Terry, Lisa and Emma are in the cafeteria. They have got invitations to a school disco. There is only one problem. The disco is today and Sam's birthday party is today, too. They have got his present and Sam is very excited about his party. But the friends really want to go to the disco.

What can they do? "Let's tell him we want to go to the disco," says Terry.

"We can't do that," says Lisa.

"But," says Terry, "I want to go to –"

"Shh!" says Emma, "There's Sam." Sam sits with his friends.

1

2

B "Hi!" says Sam, "Don't forget my party this evening. Five o'clock and don't be late!"

"But *you're* always late," Lisa says and they all laugh. "We're really excited, Sam." An invitation to the disco is on the table. Terry sees it and he kicks Lisa under the table. But Sam sees the invitation. "What's this, Lisa?" Sam asks.

"It's – it's only an invitation to a disco, Sam," says Lisa. She gives Sam the invitation and he reads it.

"Great! A disco!" he says. Then he looks again. "Oh, the third of March. That's too bad. Well, we can dance at my birthday party, too. We can't have a disco, but we can play CDs. And there are a lot of good things to eat."

3

C Emma, Lisa and Terry leave the cafeteria and go into the playground. They aren't very happy. Sam calls his grandma on his mobile. Then Emma comes into the cafeteria again. Sam doesn't see her, but she listens to him.

Oh, no! Sam wants to go to the disco, too! Emma runs into the playground and finds Terry and Lisa. She has got an idea, and she tells her friends about it. They all think it is a very good idea.

D Sam's friends all come to his party at five o'clock. They sing "Happy Birthday" to him and give him his present. There's a funny noise inside the box. What can it be? He opens the box. "An alarm clock?!" Sam says and smiles. Sam and his friends have a good time at the party. They make pizzas, drink lemonade and eat Sam's birthday cake.

4

5

E Two hours later Sam's new alarm clock rings. "What's that?"

"It's your new alarm clock, Sam," says Terry.

"Terry, how do you turn it off?" Sam shouts. Terry turns it off.

Lisa says, "Come on, Sam. It's time to go."

"Go where?" Sam asks.

"Your second birthday present is waiting for you outside," says Emma.

Sam's dad is outside in his car. He says, "Get into the car, kids. It's seven-fifteen. It's time for the school disco!"

"We can go to the disco? What a birthday! Thank you, Grandma!" says Sam.

"Say thank you to your friends, Sam, not to me," says Grandma.

2 Because ...

Example: Why can't the friends go to the disco this evening?
Because Sam's birthday party is this evening, too.

1. Why does Terry kick Lisa?
2. Why aren't the friends very happy?
3. Why does Sam call his grandma?
4. Why does Emma want to find her friends?
5. Why does Sam get a clock for his birthday?
6. Why does Emma say "It's time to go"?

3 Times and dates

Here are six times or dates from the story.
Make questions on the story. Start with 'When ... ?'

1. at lunchtime
2. at 7:30
3. at 5:00
4. Friday, 3rd March
5. after lunch
6. at 7:15

Example: at lunchtime – When do the friends meet?

1 Alphabetical order

▶ Wenn du ein englisches Wort vergessen hast, kannst du das Wort in der Englisch-Deutschen Wortliste auf Seite 169–177 nachschlagen. Hier sind alle Wörter im Buch alphabetisch geordnet. Wenn du z. B. das Wort „money“ nicht kennst, musst du zuerst unter „m“, dann unter „mo“ und weiter unter „mon“ schauen.

a) *Say the alphabet in English.*

b) *Put the words in the right order. Then find them in the word list.*

T-shirt | egg | water | party | ask | pizza | shop | buy | newsagent | pound | cake | expensive | chocolate | shoe | supermarket | money | cheap | apple | CD | boring

2 Letter puzzles

a) *Look at the words in Exercise 1 again. Answer the letter puzzles.*

Example: It has got five letters. It starts with ‘p’ and ends with ‘y’.
– The word is party.

1. It has got nine letters. It starts with ‘n’ and ends with ‘t’. – The word is … .
2. It has got six letters. It starts with ‘t’ and ends with ‘t’.
3. It has got four letters. It starts with ‘s’ and ends with ‘p’.

b) *Make more letter puzzles with a partner..*

3 First letter ideas

Look at the ideas for the word ‘birthday’ on the right. Write more ideas for the words.

1. party
2. present
3. invitation
4. supermarket

B ig party
I nvite friends
R ap music
T hank you
H elp my parents
D raw a map
A re you happy?
Y es, we are.

4 Birthday phrases

What can you say to the people? Match the sentences.

1. It’s your friend’s birthday today.
2. You can’t come to your cousin’s party.
3. Your mum asks: What’s the time?
4. Your teacher asks: What’s the date today?
5. You want to invite a new pupil to your party.
6. You can’t find a present for a friend’s birthday.

a) It’s Tuesday 23rd March.
b) Let’s look in the department store.
c) I’m sorry. We’re in Bristol on 16th February.
d) Happy Birthday!
e) Do you want to come to my party on Saturday?
f) It’s quarter to eight.

1 What do you want for your birthday?

new mobile
play new games
football
play football for England

car
go to disco with Nasreen
euros
visit my friend in Germany

skates
skate in the park with my friends
mouse
put it in my bedroom

*Write sentences about the **things they want** and **why**.*

Example: Lisa wants a **new mobile** because she wants to **play new games**.
Go on, please.

2 'Much' or 'many'? (Mengenangaben mit *much* und *many* → G 20)

a) *Lisa's mum checks the kitchen before Lisa goes shopping. Fill in the right word.*

Mrs Taylor: OK, Lisa. Let's write a list. How … milk have we got?
Lisa: We haven't got … milk, but we've got a lot of eggs. We haven't got … cheese, and there aren't … tomatoes.
Mrs Taylor: How … tomatoes are there?
Lisa: Two and they're very old.
Mrs Taylor: OK. Write them on the list, please. Let's look in the cupboard now. Oh! We've got a lot of chocolate, but we haven't got … cornflakes.
Lisa: What about apples? There aren't … apples here.
Mrs Taylor: OK. And we haven't got … water.
Lisa: There aren't … crisps here. Can we –?
Mrs Taylor: No, we can't. You children eat too … crisps.

b) *Write Lisa's shopping list.*

3 In the shop (Mengenangaben → G 19)

a) *Bottles, packets, bags or boxes? What does Lisa ask for?*

Lisa: Good morning! I want … milk (3 x), … cheese (4 x), … water (1 x), … tomatoes (2 x), … crisps (2 x), and … cornflakes (2x), please.

b) *One thing in Lisa's shopping bag isn't on the list. What is it?*

Du kannst jetzt

- ✓ einkaufen. → *Spiele ein Einkaufsgespräch mit deinem Partner.*
- ✓ Wünsche äußern. → *Schreibe drei Dinge auf, die du haben möchtest und drei Dinge, die du tun möchtest.*
- ✓ über deinen Geburtstag sprechen. → *Sage, wann du Geburtstag hast.*
- ✓ Einladungen schreiben. → *Schreibe eine Einladung zu einer Party.*

Unit 6 Let's go to the country!

An invitation

Rose Tree House

The farm near us

Dear Grace, Ted and Terry,
Our new home in the country is very different from our flat in London. It's so quiet here – you can hear the fish in the river! I often go fishing on Saturdays. Kath sometimes comes with me, but she just plays with the dogs or picks flowers. There's a small river behind the house and there's a farm near us, too. The sheep wake us up every morning. Please come and stay with us soon. Wiltshire is beautiful in the spring. From Friday 13th to Sunday 15th May is OK with us.

Our new address:
Rose Tree House, near Neston, Wiltshire
SN13 9

Love,
Kath, Bob and the dogs

The Jackson family
39 Hither Farm Road
Greenwich
London SE3 8

1 A postcard from Wiltshire

Terry's parents get a postcard from their friends, Kath and Bob.

Read it and write sentences about their friends. What do you know about them?

Example: The sheep wake Kath and Bob up every morning.

Things to write about:

farm, river, invitation, sheep, fish, address

Kath and Bob

2 Let's listen: What about me?

A street in Bath

Match the people with the sentences.

Example: They are in the kitchen. – It's the **Jacksons**.

1. He comes in with a postcard.
2. They've got a new home near Bath.
3. She can visit Bath with Kath.
4. They can go fishing on Saturday.
5. He can go to Bath with his mum.
6. She can call Kath and ask her.
7. She doesn't like cars.
8. They always take Barker for a walk on Saturdays and Sundays.

3 What season of the year is it?

sunny | foggy | hot | rainy | windy | snowy | cold

a) *Match the adjectives with the pictures of the season. Add the months of the year to the seasons.*

Example: Picture 1 – **Autumn** is cold and foggy. **September**, … are in the autumn.

b) *Look at the pictures again. What can children do in the autumn, the summer, the spring and the winter?*

Example: In the autumn they can eat … .

c) *What can you do in the four seasons?*

4 Let's talk: My favourite season

A: What's your favourite season?
B: My favourite season is the … . It's often … .
A: What months don't you like?
B: I don't like … . It can be very … in … .

5 For my folder: The seasons

Where do you live? Write about the seasons there. Draw pictures for the seasons, too.

I live in … .
In the winter it is often very … and … . I (don't) like … because … .
…

What's happening

Friday, 13th May

A lot of people are outside number 39, Hither Farm Road.

> Mr Jackson **is reading**.
> The Jacksons **are packing**.
> → G 21

1. It's 4:00 in the afternoon. The Jacksons are packing for their trip to Wiltshire. Emma and Lisa are carrying a box. Mrs Jackson is putting a cake in the car. Mr Jackson is reading the map. Tiger is sitting on the map. Terry is closing the window. Sam is talking to his dad.

2. It's 4:30 in the afternoon. Mr Jackson and the boys are waiting in the car. Mrs Jackson is closing the door. Mr Jackson is opening the car window. Emma and Lisa are feeding Tiger. Tiger is sitting on the wall. Terry is saying goodbye. Sam is sending a text message.

1 Who is doing what?

> put → putting
> close → closing

Make sentences about the family and friends.

At four o'clock At half past four	+	Terry Emma and Lisa the Jacksons Tiger Sam Mr Jackson Mrs Jackson the boys	+	is are	+	closing … . waiting … . …

Example: At four o'clock Terry **is closing** the window.
At half past four Mr Jackson and the boys **are waiting** … .

2 Question time

Make questions about the pictures on page 80.
Answer the questions.

Example: It's 4:30. **Is** Mrs Jackson read**ing**? – **No, she isn't.**

▶ Is she reading?
– Yes, she is.
– No, she isn't.
→ G 22

1. 4:30 • Mrs Jackson • read
2. 4:00 • Terry • sleep
3. 4:00 • Mr Jackson • open the window
4. 4:30 • Sam • send a text message
5. 4:00 • Emma • play with Tiger
6. 4:30 • Mrs Jackson • sit on map
7. 4:30 • Tiger • send a text message
8. 4:00 • Lisa • eat cake

3 Let's talk: What are they doing?

B: *Look at the pictures again and then close your book.*
A: *Ask questions.*

A: It's 4:30. Are Sam and Terry sitting in the car?
B: Yes, they are.
A: It's 4:00. Are the Jacksons sitting on the wall?
B: No, they aren't.
A: … *Go on, please.*

▶ Are they sleeping?
– Yes, they are.
– No, they aren't.
→ G 22

4 At Rose Tree House

Make answers.

Example: Can you give this cake to Kath, please, Terry?
(I / put on my shoes)
– Just a second. **I'm putting on** my shoes.

1. Can you open the door please, Sam? (I / look for my mobile)
2. Can you help me with this bag, please? (we / carry a big box)
3. Can you take the map, please, Terry? (I / look for my comic)
4. Can I borrow mum's mobile? (she / send a text message)
5. Can dad take that big bag to the bedroom? (he / help Bob)
6. Can we take the dogs for a walk now, Kath? (they / eat)
7. Can the boys go to the river with Bob? (he / talk to Ted)
8. Can you two help Kath, please? (we / put things in our room)

5 A miming game: What am I doing?

Mime an action. Can the others guess what you are doing?

A: OK. What am I doing?
B: Are you shouting?
A: No, I'm not.
C: OK. Are you barking?
A: No. I'm not.
D: Are you singing?
A: Yes, I am. Now it's your turn.

shouting | break-dancing | taking a dog for a walk | skating | singing | dancing | barking | swimming | washing the car

What isn't happening?

Are you joking, Terry?

It's Saturday. Sam and Terry are helping Mr Hunter, the farmer. His farm is near Kath and Bob's house.

Sam: Oh, no! Can you look at this, Terry?
Terry: Hang on! My phone is ringing. Hello?
Emma: Hi, Terry. It's Emma. I'm calling from your kitchen. Lisa and I hope you aren't having fun without us!
Terry: Oh. Hello, Emma!
Emma: What's that noise? Have your friends got pigs?
Terry: No. They're Mr Hunter's pigs. He's a farmer, and Sam and I are helping him. He has got a lot of animals: pigs, cows, sheep –
Emma: Are you joking, Terry? You don't like farms. And it's Saturday afternoon. You and Sam always watch MTV on Saturday afternoons.
Terry: Well, today we aren't watching TV.
Emma: What are you doing?
Terry: We're working. I'm feeding the little baby pigs.
Emma: And what about Sam? Is he feeding them, too?
Terry: No, he isn't. He's checking Mr Hunter's computer. It has got a problem. It's eating his e-mails.
Emma: So you're feeding the pigs, and he's feeding the computer! And what about your mum and dad? Are they feeding the cows?
Terry: No, they aren't, Emma. They aren't here. Mum and Kath are visiting Bath, and Dad and Bob are fishing. Emma … why are you calling?
Emma: Oh, it's Tiger. She isn't eating. She's just sitting on the shed and –
Terry: She's a funny cat, Emma. She often sits there and doesn't eat. Don't worry about her.
Sam: Terry! What are you doing?
Terry: Sorry, Emma. Sam is calling me. Bye!
Emma: OK. Bye, Terry! Have fun on the farm! *Oink-oink!*

1 That's wrong

Read the text. What's wrong with the sentences?

▶ They'**re** eating → They **aren't** eating.
She'**s** eating → She **isn't** eating.

→ G 23

Example: Sam and Terry **are helping** Bob.
That's wrong. They **aren't helping** Bob. They're helping … .

1. Emma is calling Lisa.
2. Terry is feeding the cows.
3. Sam is checking the sheep.
4. Mum and Kath are visiting Bristol.
5. Dad and Bob are swimming.
6. Tiger is sitting in the kitchen.

2 An e-mail for Sam

Hi Sam,
How are you? We hope you're having fun. What are you doing?
Are you fishing? Or are you watching MTV with Terry? I hope you aren't spending your time in front of the TV. Grandma hopes you aren't making work for the Jacksons and she hopes you're helping in the house.
Bye, Dad

What does Sam write to his dad?

Example: Hi Dad! We're OK. I'm having a lot of fun. Today we're helping … .
Terry is … and I'm … . *Go on, please.*

3 Back in Greenwich

Sam and Terry are thinking about home. Are they right?

Example: 1. Tiger **isn't playing** with a mouse. **She's sitting** on the shed.

1

sit • play

2

draw • write

3

play • dance

4

play • walk

5

eat • sleep

6

watch • eat

4 Let's talk: Phone calls

a) *Listen to the dialogue.*

A: Hello?
B: Hi, … . It's … . What are you doing?
A: I'm playing/… . And what about you?
B: I'm … . Can we meet in … at …?
A: Yes. That's a good idea.
B: OK. Bye!
A: Bye!

b) *Phone a partner about Saturday.*

Pointing at things

A lot of rubbish?

Later Terry and Sam are in Mr Hunter's shed. There are a lot of things in there, and there is a lot of rubbish, too. The boys are helping Mr Hunter.

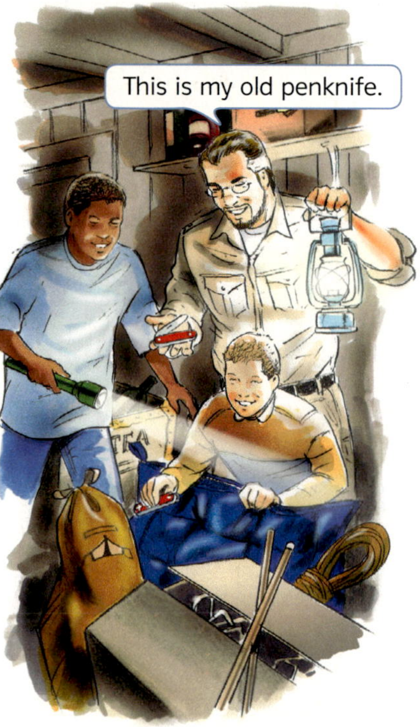

Mr Hunter: Can you take those bottles outside, please, boys? Now, help me with this box here. OK. Let's open it. Can you give me that penknife over there, please, Sam?
Sam: Here you are, Mr Hunter.
Mr Hunter: Thank you, Sam. OK. Let's see what's in this bag. Oh, it's my tent. And there's an old penknife, but it's broken. What about that torch there, Terry? Is it working?
Terry: Yes, it is. And these sleeping bags are new.
Mr Hunter: Do you like camping, Sam?
Sam: I don't know. We haven't got a tent.
Mr Hunter: I've got an idea. Do you want to sleep in the tent tonight?
Sam: Oh yes, Mr Hunter.
Terry: That's a great idea!
Mr Hunter: OK. Let's put these things in Kath and Bob's garden. Then we can ask them when they come home.

1 Answer the questions.

1. Where are Sam and Terry?
2. What are they doing?
3. What do they find with Mr Hunter?
4. Does Sam like camping?
5. Where can they put up the tent?

2 The boys' questions

Put in 'this', 'that', 'these' or 'those'.

1. Where can we put … bottles?
2. What's in … boxes over there?
3. What's in … bag over there?
4. Can we borrow … tent here, please?

▶ here – this/these   over there – that/those
→ G 24

1 Let's listen: Country sounds?

Listen to the sounds. What are they?
Are they town sounds or country sounds?

Example: 1. Those are trains. That's a town sound.
2. Those are pigs. That's a … .
Go on, please.

2 Let's listen: Ten o'clock on Saturday morning

Today Charlie chats on the phone with four young people in his show.

a) *What are Sally, Tim, Paul and Tess doing? Find the right picture.*

Example: 1. Sally is … . That's picture b) … .

1. a) 
Sally

2. a) 
Tim

3. a) 
Paul

4. a) 
Tess

1. b) 

2. b) 

3. b) 

4. b) 

b) *Listen again. Who knows the right answer to the quiz? Where's the information?*

3 A game: Let's say …

A: Let's say it's nine o'clock on Saturday morning. What are you doing?
B: I'm eating breakfast. What are you doing?
C: I'm … . Let's say …
Go on, please.

4 Sounds

Listen and say.

[θ] Don't think of things south of Bath.
[ð] Take these other bags to your brother over there.

5 A song: Leaving town (Music: K.-H. Böttcher, Lyrics: S. McBride)

Get up! We're leaving town.
Summer – the roof is down[1].
Oh, it's a beautiful day.
We're all OK.

We're in the country now.
Look, there's a funny cow!
Oh no, it's really a sheep.
Beep, beep! Beep, beep!

[1] down [daʊn] – *unten*

Noises in the night

1 Before you read: Look at the picture.

What's happening?

A On Saturday Sam and Terry are sleeping in their tent in Kath and Bob's garden. It isn't cold and it isn't raining. They go to bed at eleven o'clock. Soon Sam is sleeping like a baby, but Terry can't sleep. He plays with his mobile. Then he hears noises. He puts on his shoes and his jacket. Then he finds his torch and takes his mobile, and he leaves the tent. Ten minutes later Sam's mobile rings. He wakes up.

B

Sam: Yes, hello.
Terry: Sam. It's Terry. I'm at the river.
Sam: What are you doing there? Are you fishing?
Terry: No! I'm not fishing! Don't be stupid! It's twelve-thirty! I'm watching two men.
Sam: Oh! And what are *they* doing? Are they fishing?
Terry: No, they aren't. They're carrying boxes and bags from their car to the bushes.
Sam: Oh. What's in the boxes?
Terry: I can't see from here. Hang on! They're coming back. They're getting back into the car.
Terry: Listen. Have you got a pen?
Sam: Yes, I'm just getting it. OK.
Terry: The car number is B HE 239. Have you got it?
Sam: Yes. B HE 239.
Terry: Now they're driving away. It's a dark van. Sam, can you come to the river near the bridge? And bring your penknife!
Sam: OK, Terry. Wait for me. I'm looking for my shoes.

C Ten minutes later Sam arrives at the river. He and Terry find the boxes and bags.

Terry: Let's open this big box first, Sam. Have you got your penknife?
Sam: Yes. Wow! Look at this, Terry. Old laptops.
Terry: What about that box over there? Can you open it, too?
Sam: Yes. It's a computer! But it looks broken. It's all rubbish, Terry.
Terry: And what's in those bags near the tree?
Sam: Shh! Listen! I can hear a car.
Terry: They're coming back. Quick – let's hide under the bridge. We can see them from there.

The car stops at the bridge. A man gets out.

D Terry: Dad! What are *you* doing here?
Mr Jackson: What am *I* doing? I'm looking for two boys. Your mum is very worried. What are *you two* doing?

Terry and Sam show him the boxes and the bags. On the way back to their tent they tell Mr Jackson about the noises, the two men, the computers and the van.

Mr Jackson: OK, you two. Back to bed. We can call the police in the morning.

E At 8:00 Mr Jackson phones the police. Later at breakfast, he tells the boys about his phone call.

Mr Jackson: The police are very pleased with you two. They know the two men. They've got a computer shop in Bath. They are already at the police station.
Mrs Jackson: Well, I'm not pleased with you. At least we aren't staying here for a week!
Terry: Oh, Mum. It's great here. Can Sam and I come back in the summer, Kath?
Kath: Of course you can. But please tell us before you leave your tent. Then we can come with you.

1

2

3

4

5

6

2 A puzzle

a) *Add the right sentences to the pictures.*

Terry is watching the men.
Sam is sleeping.
Terry is phoning Sam.
The men are driving away.
Mr Jackson is phoning the police.
Terry is showing his dad the boxes.

b) *Put the pictures in the right order.*

3 Parts of the story

a) *Give each part of the story a title.*

Example: Part A: Terry can't sleep. / Terry leaves the tent. / …
Part B: Sam … .

b) *Choose one part of the story. Act it in class.*

1 Guess the word.

▶ Partnerarbeit kann dir beim Vokabellernen helfen, z. B. ein Ratespiel. Schreibe ein schwieriges Wort auf eine Karte. Dein Partner/Deine Partnerin muss es erraten. Dazu musst du ihm/ihr Hinweise geben.

1.
Nice flowers are ... .
A sunny day is ... .
A picture can be ... .
Answer: beautiful

2.
It's a season.
It's often foggy.
The trees are yellow and red.
Answer: ...

3.
It's old bottles and boxes.
You don't want it.
People leave it in fields and parks.
Answer: ...

4.
It's small.
You can open a box with it. You can pick flowers with it.
Answer: ...

2 A quiz: Make sentences.

Draw six pictures on cards. Show them to your partner. He/She says the word and makes a sentence with it.

3 Plural forms

a) *Look at the pictures. Make two lists.*

Example:

plurals with -s	different plurals
cows	men

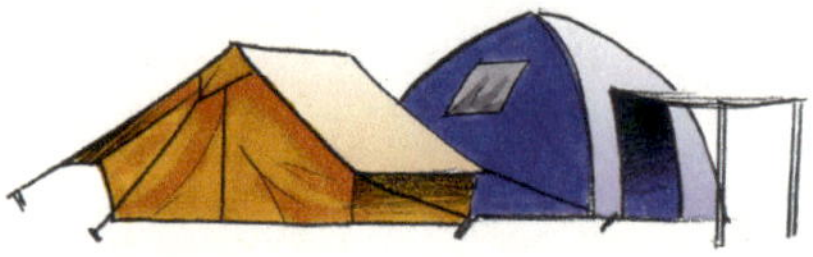

b) *Add more plural forms to your lists.*

1 What are they doing? (Die Verlaufsform der Gegenwart → G21, Verneinung → G23)

1

Terry
Sam
Mr Hunter
Kath
dog

2

Example: In picture one Terry is feeding the pigs. In picture two he isn't … . He's … .

2 What aren't they doing? (Die Verlaufsform der Gegenwart: Verneinung → G23)

Example: 1. They aren't riding bikes.

play | do | go | read | ride

1

2

3

4

5

3 Some days are different. (Die Verlaufsform der Gegenwart: Fragen/Kurzantworten → G22)

It's Sunday morning. What are they doing?

1

2

3

4

Example: 1. Are Ted and Bob working in the garden? No, they aren't. They're … .
2. … watching MTV? … .
3. … talking on the phone? … .
4. … playing the drums? … .

Du kannst jetzt

- ✓ eine Postkarte schreiben. → *Schreibe eine Postkarte an eine Freundin/einen Freund.*
- ✓ über das Wetter sprechen. → *Sage, wie das Wetter heute ist.*
- ✓ sagen, was du gerade tust. → *Sage von drei Mitschülern, was sie gerade tun.*
- ✓ ein Telefongespräch führen. → *Setzt euch Rücken an Rücken und spielt ein Telefongespräch.*

Unit 7 The school year

Big events

The school year always starts in September. Between September and June there are a lot of different events at Thomas Tallis.

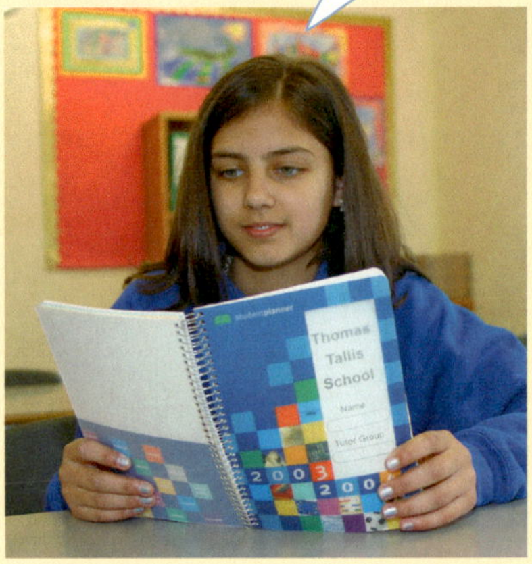

September

1

We make lanterns for the Thames Festival Lantern Procession on the last weekend of September.

December

A lot of pupils act in the school play every year. At the moment we are rehearsing Cats. The songs are great, and we can use make-up and paint our faces.

2

March

3

Every March, Year Seven has a disco. They organize it and sell tickets.

June

4

Sports day is great! We can invite our friends and families to school. It's on the third Saturday in June. Terry is really good at the long jump!

June

5

German pupils from Berlin visit Year Nine pupils in Greenwich. We welcome them the Monday after sports day and show them Greenwich.

July

6

Pupils, teachers and parents help at the summer fair. We collect money for charities and for school projects. You can buy and sell things at different stalls or you can even throw sponges at your friends!

1 When are the events?

Example: The Lantern Procession is **in** … .
Sports day is **on** … . *Go on, please.*

2 The year at Thomas Tallis

Look at the pictures of activities at Thomas Tallis.
Match the pictures with the sentences.

Example: Pupils do different sports. – That's picture number 4.

1. Pupils act in a play for parents, teachers and other pupils.
2. Pupils from Years 7 and 8 make lanterns and walk along the Thames.
3. You can meet new friends, dance and listen to great music.
4. In summer pupils from our partner school come to Thomas Tallis.
5. You can buy and sell things here.

Year Seven disco

3 Let's listen: An idea for a stall

The drama club is talking about their stall for the summer fair.
One word in each sentence is wrong.

Example: The fair is in June. – The word 'June' is wrong.

1. We want to collect a lot of books this year.
2. Our idea is to paint dog faces.
3. We've already got the money.
4. We're all doing different things at the club.
5. Nasreen's class is buying books from 2:00 to 4:30.
6. And the others can make a big map.

4 Let's talk: School events

Choose an event and mime it.
Can the others guess the event?

5 For my folder: Our school year

Compare your school year
with the school year at Thomas Tallis.

Our school year sometimes starts in … . We haven't got a … in September. But we've got a … in … . Our summer fair/sports day/school play is in … .

Describing a scene

Sports day at Thomas Tallis

Today is sports day at Thomas Tallis School. In the picture a lot of pupils are doing different sports. A reporter is watching them. A teacher is timing the runners. Other pupils are waiting for the next race. Parents are watching their children and clapping.

1 Who's doing what?

Match the numbers in the picture with the activities.

Example: run a race – number 3

time the runners
drink water
do the long jump
run a race
sit under a tree
play cricket
throw a ball
eat an ice-cream

2 Describing a picture

a) *Look at the picture. What's the reporter saying?*

Charlie: Good morning. Today **I'm talking** to you from Thomas Tallis School. It's sports day here. At the moment a lot of things **are happening** on the sports field. The girls **are running** a race right now. A teacher … . *Go on, please.*

At the moment Right now Today	I'm talking

→ G 21

b) *Not all the pupils are doing sports. Say what they're doing.*

Example: Three pupils are watching … at the moment. Lisa is … . Other pupils are … . *Go on, please.*

3 Yes, he is.

Look at the picture on page 92 again. Find the right answer.

Example: Is Charlie reporting on sports day? – Yes, he is.

1. Is Terry running a race?
2. Is Lisa doing the long jump?
3. Are the teachers playing football?
4. Are the parents clapping?
5. Is Jade eating an ice-cream?

Yes, he is. ✔ | No, he isn't. | No, she isn't. | Yes, she is. | Yes, they are. | No, they aren't.

> ▶ The teachers **help every year.**
> They **are helping at the moment.**
> → G14, G21

4 Do or doing?

Example: Terry … sports every week. (*do*) – He … the long jump now. (*do*)
Terry does sports every week. – He is doing the long jump now.

1. Sam never … water at home. He … a bottle of water at the moment. (*drink*)
2. The pupils … in the park on Saturdays. This afternoon they … a race. (*run*)
3. Ben often … sports after school. He … cricket right now. (*play*)
4. The parents always … fun at sports day. They … a lot of fun today. (*have*)
5. The reporter sometimes … football on Saturdays. He … a race right now. (*watch*)
6. Pupils often … in the playground. Four pupils … under a tree right now. (*sit*)

5 What's different?

What do the friends often do on Saturday afternoons? What are they doing now?
Example: Terry **often plays** … . **Right now** he **is talking** … .

often
play

right now
talk

always
write

at the moment
run

sometimes
walk

now
throw

6 Let's talk: Sports pictures

Bring in a sports picture. Don't show it to your group.
They ask 'yes/no' questions and guess what's in the picture.

A: Have you got a picture of a man?
B: Yes, I have.
C: Has he got a ball?
B: Yes, he has.
D: Is he playing basketball?
B: Yes, he is.
Go on, please.

Using 'must' and 'needn't'

We must have scones!

All the German classes at Thomas Tallis must welcome the German exchange pupils. What can they do? They are collecting ideas with their teacher.

Mrs Carter: I must talk to you about the German exchange visit. How can we welcome the visitors?
Sam: Miss, what about an English afternoon tea?
Mrs Carter: Yes, Sam. That's a great idea.
Emma: We can make sandwiches – they're easy.
Mrs Carter: Fine. But we must have cakes, too. We can –
Terry: You must ask Sam, Miss. His chocolate cakes are fantastic!
Sam: But it's an Italian recipe.
Mrs Carter: Don't worry, Sam. It needn't be English – as long as it tastes good.
Sam: OK. I can make two chocolate cakes. But we must have scones, too. Afternoon tea isn't afternoon tea without scones.
Mrs Carter: Well, we can all make scones.
Terry: What about tea, Miss? Do German kids drink tea?
Mrs Carter: That's a good question, Terry. You must ask them.
Terry: What – in German, Miss?
Mrs Carter: No, you needn't use German, Terry. They all speak English.

Afternoon tea

1 'Must' or 'needn't'?

We **must** make scones.
We **needn't** make pizza.

Example: The cake **needn't** be English.

The cake The class Terry Sam Mrs Carter	+	must needn't	+	make two chocolate cakes. talk to the class about the exchange. ask the German kids. make scones for the visitors. be English. use German.

2 Let's talk: Afternoon tea

What must you have for an English afternoon tea? Talk to a partner about it.

A: We must have … for our afternoon tea.
B: No, we needn't have … but we must have … .
A: OK. And what about … ?
B: That's right. And we must have …, too.
A: OK. Let's make a list.

1 Things to do

Look at the picture. What things can you do at a summer fair? What about food and drinks? Write a list.

Example:
You can buy lemonade, … .
Go on, please.

2 Let's listen: At the fair

a) *Listen and add more things to your list.*

b) 1. What are the pupils selling?
2. What is Charlie looking for?
3. Who puts water on Charlie's shoes and bag?

c) *Listen again and match the sentences with the right words.*

They are in the playground.
They cost 50p.
Pupils throw them at their friends.
They use the money for new books.
The pupils needn't do it.

book stall | homework | pizza stall | toilets | sponges

3 Let's talk: Different stalls

Choose a stall. Make a poster with prices. Buy and sell things with the other groups.

A: Hello. Can I help you?
B: Yes, how much are your … , please?
A: They're … .
B: OK. Can I have … , please?
A: Yes, of course. Here you are. That's … , please.
B: … *Go on, please.*

4 A poem: The white elephant stall

Oh, Tim, your room is such a mess[1]. There's so much rubbish there!
Why can't you put things in a box and sell them at the fair?
Hey, Mum, that's not a bad idea. They always have a stall
Where people buy all sorts of[2] things – white elephants and all.
So Tim packs all his games and books and puts them in the car.
His mum can take him to the fair and leave him with them there.
At six o'clock she then comes back to take him home for tea.
He's waiting in the playground with *two* boxes and a tree!
She doesn't know what she can do. She says, "Good evening, dear!"
But Tim just smiles, "Don't worry, Mum. I can take them back next year."

[1]such a mess [ˌsʌtʃ‿ə 'mes] – *ein totales Chaos*, [2]all sorts of [ɔːl 'sɔːts‿əv] – *allerlei*

The bloke at the burger stall

A It's 4:00 on the day of the school fair. Emma and Lisa are selling pizzas. A young man comes to the burger stall next to the pizza stall. She knows his face, but she doesn't know who he is.

"Emma, don't look now, but can you see that bloke behind me at the burger stall?" asks Lisa. Emma looks behind Lisa.

"Is he wearing a black cap and a red T-shirt?" asks Emma.

"Yes," says Lisa. "Do you know him?"

"No. He looks like that actor from *Eastenders* – he plays the manager of the supermarket."

"Yes," says Lisa. "That's him. Look, he's buying a burger. Oh, no. He's leaving the hall. Let's follow him!"

"Lisa, we can't just leave the stall," says Emma. "You can go."

"OK. Give me five minutes," says Lisa, and she runs to the door.

B Ten minutes later Lisa comes back to the pizza stall. "So what's his name, Lisa? Have you got his autograph?" asks Emma.

"No," says Lisa. "I can't find him."

"But he must be here in the school. That door goes to the classrooms. I can look with you, but we must find him! Terry's over there at the white elephant stall with Sam. Maybe they can help on the stall," says Emma. They tell Terry and Sam about the young man. The boys think the girls are crazy, but they want to help. Emma and Lisa run out of the hall. They aren't looking, and suddenly they run into a teacher.

C It's Mr Rose. He's in the corridor with a man and a woman. "Hello, Lisa. Hi, Emma," says Mr Rose. "Where's the fire?"

"Sorry, Sir," says Emma. "There's no fire. We're looking for a … a –"

"Boy, Sir," says Lisa. "Er ... we're looking for Lisa's brother, Ben Taylor."

"So *you* are Ben's sister!" says the woman. "Ben is with the German exchange pupils in the music room."

"Lisa, Emma, this is Frau Strobel and this is Herr Konrad. They're here with the German exchange."

"*Guten Tag,*" says Lisa.

"*Hallo, ich heiße Emma.*"

"*Ah, du kannst deutsch!*" says Herr Konrad.

"*Ja, aber nur ein bisschen,*" says Emma.

D The teachers say goodbye and go into the hall. "We can't find him now," says Lisa. "Let's go back to the stall." The two girls are very unhappy.

Sam and Terry are talking to Nasreen. There is a young man with her. Emma and Lisa can see his red T-shirt, but they can't see his face. The two girls walk past Nasreen, and then they see the young man's face. It's the actor from *Eastenders*! "Excuse me," says Lisa. "Can we have your autograph, please?"

"My what?" asks the young man.

"Your autograph," says Lisa. "We know you from *Eastenders* and we –" Terry and Sam look at Nasreen and they all start laughing.

"But he's not from *Eastenders*, Lisa," says Terry. "He's here with the German exchange. His name is Paul Schmidt."

"Oh!" says Lisa.

"*Es tut uns Leid,*" says Emma.

"You needn't speak German, Emma," says Nasreen. "Paul is very good at English."

"Just one question," says Paul. "Who or what are *Eastenders*?"

"That's easy," says Lisa. "It's a TV soap about people in East London."

"I must watch it," says Paul. "Maybe I've got a double in England."

1 Who says what?

Make a list of the people in the story. Match them with the sentences.

Example: **He**'s here with the German exchange. – That's Paul.

1. Just give **me** five minutes.
2. So what's **his** name?
3. So **you** are Ben's sister!
4. **They** are also here with the German exchange.
5. Can **we** have your autograph, please?
6. **You** needn't speak German.

2 Places in the story

What is happening at these places?

At the pizza stall
At the burger stall
Outside the hall

Examples: At the pizza stall Emma and Lisa are … .
At the burger stall the young man … .

1 Words with two meanings

A B C D E F

▶ Manchmal hörst oder liest du ein englisches Wort, das zwei oder mehr verschiedene Bedeutungen im Deutschen hat, z. B. *letter* = „Buchstabe" oder „Brief". Nur wenn du den ganzen Satz hörst oder liest, kannst du wissen, was das Wort bedeutet.
Beispiel: *There are 26 letters in the alphabet. My friend sends me a letter every week.*
Falls eine Bedeutung nicht passt, versuch es mit der anderen Bedeutung.

Look at the underlined words in these sentences.
What do they mean in German?

1. I am in Year Seven.
2. There are twelve months in a year.
3. We always have our tea at six o'clock.
4. I don't like tea with milk.
5. The soap is in the bathroom.
6. My favourite soap is on TV now.
7. You can draw a line here.
8. I must learn my lines for the play.
9. The word is in line 54.

2 Make word stars.

a)

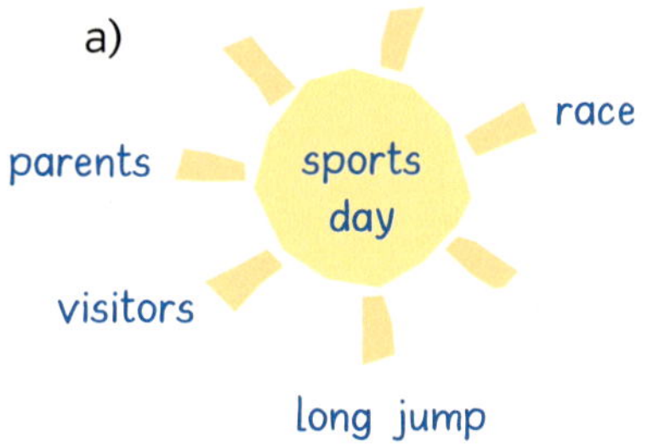

b)

c)

3 A game: The white elephant stall

A: What are you bringing for the white elephant stall?
B: I'm bringing an old German book.
C: I'm bringing an old German book and a big green bottle.
D: I'm bringing an old German book, a big green bottle and a … .
Go on, please.

1 What must and what needn't they do?

Match the pictures with the sentences. What must or needn't these people do?

You must meet my teacher.
We needn't buy all of them.
She must be in a hurry!
I must find the caretaker.
You needn't shout!
You needn't put it in a box.

2 Saturday at the school fair (Adverbien der Häufigkeit → G14 / Die Verlaufsform der Gegenwart → G21)

Choose the right form of the verb and write sentences about the people.

1. On Saturdays Mr Rose often … to town. Today he … to Thomas Tallis. (*go*)
2. On Saturdays Terry often … the breakfast. Today he … pizzas. (*make*)
3. On Saturdays Mrs Carter often … food for the family. Today she … books. (*buy*)
4. On Saturdays Lisa often … a ball for Barker. Today she … sponges. (*throw*)
5. On Saturdays Sam's grandma often … in the café. Today she … in the school hall. (*sit*)

3 Tom's sports day (Die Verlaufsform der Gegenwart → G21 / Verneinung → G23)

What is Tom doing? What isn't he doing?

Example: 1. Tom is doing the long jump. He isn't making tea.

1. do the long jump • make tea
2. swim • wash
3. time the runners • wake up Sam
4. run a race • run away from the cat
5. play cricket • draw a picture

Du kannst jetzt

✓ berichten, was gerade passiert.	→ *Berichte in fünf Sätzen, was gerade im Klassenzimmer passiert.*
✓ sagen, was du machen musst und was du nicht machen musst.	→ *Zähle drei Sachen auf, die du zu Hause machen musst und drei, die du nicht machen musst.*
✓ über dein Schuljahr reden.	→ *Nenne drei Ereignisse in deinem Schuljahr. Sage, was man dabei machen kann.*

Strange stars[1]!

A It's the first day of the school holidays[2]! Nicola is very excited. Tomorrow[3] she wants to visit her grandad in his house in the country. She goes there every summer for two weeks. This year she can go there without her parents. She packs her bag, and Friday morning she and her mum go to the bus station. Her mum says to her, "Give Grandad my love and have fun! But don't take him on an adventure[4] again this year! Remember, he's an old man."

Nicola says, "OK! Bye, Mum!" She sits down for the one-hour trip to Wildcroft. Her grandad lives in a beautiful old house there. He really likes Nicola's visit every year. She's good fun and they laugh a lot together. But sometimes he forgets things, so Nicola calls him the night before she arrives at his house. "Don't forget, Grandad," she tells him on the phone, "my bus arrives tomorrow at one o'clock."

Nicola sits in the bus and thinks about the fun she always has with Grandad. They often go fishing from the bridge in Wildcroft. "Maybe I can sleep in Grandad's tent in the garden this year and watch stars at night through his telescope[5]!" she thinks. Soon she arrives at the bus station in Wildcroft. The bus is only ten minutes late. Nicola looks for Grandad, but she can't see him. She gets off the bus and waits.

Soon she is the only person at the station, but she isn't really worried. She is sure Grandad is on his way. She takes out her mobile and rings his number, but there is no answer. Maybe he is on his way and his old car has got a flat tyre[6] or maybe his watch[7] is broken. She can't be sure, so she opens her book and starts to read. After an hour Nicola starts to worry. "Maybe Grandad is ill[8] and can't come to the station," she thinks. "Well, it's only twenty minutes away, so I can walk to his house. I know the way."

She closes her book and starts to walk. When Nicola arrives at her grandad's house, she sees a newspaper[9] at the door. She looks at the date. "It's today's date," she thinks. "Maybe he's sleeping." She looks through[10] the window, but she doesn't see him. She wants to open the door, but it is locked[11]. Nicola shouts, "Grandad, I'm here! It's me, Nicola!" But there's no answer.

[1]stars [stɑ:z] – *Sterne, Stars,* [2]holidays ['hɒlədeɪz] – *Ferien,* [3]tomorrow [tə'mɒrəʊ] – *morgen,* [4]adventure [əd'ventʃə] – *Abenteuer,* [5]telescope ['telɪskəʊp] – *Fernrohr,* [6]flat tyre [flæt 'taɪə] – *platter Reifen,* [7]watch [wɒtʃ] – *Armbanduhr,* [8]ill [ɪl] – *krank,* [9]newspaper ['nju:speɪpə] – *Zeitung,* [10]through [θru:] – *durch,* [11]it is locked [ɪt‿ɪz 'lɒkt] – *es ist abgeschlossen*

She sees two bottles of milk and thinks, "That's strange. Grandad always collects the milk at breakfast time. Maybe he's at Mrs White's house. He often helps his neighbour[1] in her garden. I can go and see."

But before she goes there, she wants to put the milk in the kitchen. There's always a key[2] to the house in the garden shed, so she goes round[3] the house. His car is there, but the tyres are OK. Then she opens the door of the shed. The key is in the right place under a shelf, but his torch is not there. "That's strange," she thinks. "Why has he got his torch with him? It's a sunny day. And he needn't take a torch to visit Mrs White! She hasn't got a cellar[4]!"

Stop and answer

1. *What happens on Friday morning?*
2. *What clues[5] tell Nicola that Grandad is not at home?*
3. *Why isn't he at home? What do you think? Choose an answer and say why.*
   - *He is at the neighbour's house.*
   - *He is at the bus station.*
   - *He is shopping.*

B Nicola takes the key and goes to the back door[6]. No Wellingtons[7]! Grandad always leaves his Wellingtons there. He only wears them when he is working in the garden or when he goes fishing at the river. "Well, he's not in his garden," Nicola thinks. "He must be fishing. But why must he go fishing now?"

She opens the door. But his fishing things are near the kitchen door. "Well, that's really strange," Nicola thinks. "Then he *is* working in Mrs White's garden. But why take a torch?"

She walks through the house and looks for a note[8] from Grandad. She looks in all the rooms, but there is no note from him. She goes up to the room under the roof. He has got his telescope there. She looks through it. "That's funny – an old house behind a lot of trees." Nicola knows the house – it's Drayton Hall. It's near the river. "Why does Grandad want to look at a house near the river?" she thinks.

She's hungry now, so she goes back downstairs to the kitchen. She makes a big sandwich and eats it. Then she drinks some[9] milk and goes to the door. There's a big box there with apples in it. She puts two in her pocket[10], goes out and locks[11] the door. Ten minutes later she arrives at Mrs White's house. Mrs White is working in her garden.

"Hello, Mrs White!" Nicola shouts. Mrs White doesn't hear very well[12]. "It's me, Nicola!" Mrs White looks at her.

"Who?" she says. And she doesn't see very well.

[1]neighbour ['neɪbə] – *Nachbar(in),* [2]key [kiː] – *Schlüssel,* [3]round [raʊnd] – *um … herum,* [4]cellar ['selə] – *Keller,* [5]clues [kluːz] – *Hinweise,* [6]back door [bæk 'dɔː] – *Hintertür,* [7]Wellingtons ['welɪŋtəns] – *Gummistiefel,* [8]note [nəʊt] – *Notiz,* [9]some [sʌm] – *etwas,* [10]pocket ['pɒkɪt] – *Tasche,* [11]locks [lɒks] – *schließt … ab,* [12]well [wel] – *gut*

"Oh, Nicola! Hello! You're visiting your grandad again. That's nice!" Mrs White says.

"Yes, but he isn't at home. I can't find him. Do you know where he is? Is he here?" Nicola asks.

"Well, no, I don't know where he is. Yesterday[1] evening he gave[2] me some[3] tomatoes from his garden. And he asked[4] me about nude[5] people at Drayton Hall. But I don't know them. Maybe he's there now," says Mrs White.

"OK, thank you, Mrs White," Nicola says loudly[6].

"What?"

"Thank you," Nicola shouts.

"Take me? Oh, no thank you, Nicola. I'm busy today." Nicola smiles and walks away. "Goodbye, Nicola!"

"That's it, then," thinks Nicola. "He's helping the *new* people. I can go to Drayton Hall and find him." She starts to eat one of her apples. Then she sees a young man on the bridge. He's fishing. She doesn't know him. "Maybe he's one of the new neighbours," she thinks. "I can ask him about Grandad." Suddenly a big animal jumps at[7] her.

Stop and answer

1. *Why is Grandad looking at Drayton Hall? What do you think?*
2. *Do you believe[8] Mrs White's information? Why or why not?*
3. *Grandad must be at Drayton Hall. Why? Find two clues.*

C It's just a dog. She knows him. He loves apples, and he wants her apple.

"Jack! Hello! Here, take this apple," Nicola says and gives him the other apple from her pocket.

"Good boy!" a young man shouts. "Come here, Jack!" Nicola looks at him. Jack is Eric's dog, but that can't be Eric. Last

[1]yesterday ['jestədɪ] – *gestern*, [2]gave [geɪv] – *gab*, [3]some [sʌm] – *ein paar*, [4]asked [ɑ:skt] – *fragte*, [5]nude [nju:d] – *nackt*, [6]loudly [laʊdlɪ] – *laut*, [7]jumps at ['dʒʌmps‿ət] – *springt auf*, [8]believe [bɪ'li:v] – *glauben*

summer he was[1] small and this boy is tall[2]. She walks to the bridge. It *is* Eric.

"Hello, Eric," she says.

"Hi, Nicola! How are you? And how's your grandad? I'm sure he's happy to see you."

"Well, maybe he is, but I can't find him," says Nicola. "I think he's at Drayton Hall. I'm on my way there now."

"Can we come with you?" asks Eric, and he throws a ball for Jack.

"Sure," says Nicola, "But what about the fish?"

"Don't worry! It's a good day for the fish and a bad day for me!"

They walk over the bridge and down the road and talk about last year's adventures with Grandad. Soon they arrive at Drayton Hall. Jack starts to run through the trees. "It must be a mouse," says Eric. After a minute or two, they hear him again and run after him.

"Woof, Woof, Woof!" He's barking at a torch near a tree. Nicola looks at it. She can't believe her eyes. There's a purple and green loop[3] on it. She made[4] it for Grandad so that[5] he can hang[6] his torch in the shed. But what's it doing here? And where's Grandad?

"So Grandad was here," Nicola says. "And I saw this house here through his telescope."

"But where is he now?" Eric asks.

"That's a good question," says Nicola.

"And why is his torch in the garden?" asks Eric.

"Let's look round the house," says Nicola. "Maybe Grandad is helping the new neighbours." They walk to the house. Suddenly Jack stops and starts to bark again.

"He can hear a noise," says Eric. Jack runs to a window at the back[7] of the house.

"Look!" shouts Nicola. "It's Grandad! He's at that window." They go to the door, but it's locked. "Let's go round to the front[8] door," says Nicola. "Maybe the neighbours are sleeping."

"They must be very deaf[9]," says Eric, but he runs after Nicola.

[1]was [wəz] – *war,* [2]tall [tɔːl] – *groß,* [3]loop [luːp] – *Schlaufe,* [4]made [meɪd] – *machte,* [5]so that [səʊ ðat] – *damit,* [6]hang [hæŋ] – *(auf)hängen,* [7]back [bæk] – *Rückseite,* [8]front [frʌnt] – *Vorder-,* [9]deaf [def] – *taub*

"Get that dog out of here," shouts a man. "Arrgh!" Then they hear a shot[1].

"Oh, no," says Eric. "Come on, Nicola. The man has got a gun[2]."

Stop and answer

1. *Why does the dog jump at Nicola?*
2. *Who is the young man at the bridge?*
3. *What is happening at the front of the house? What do you think?*

D Eric and Nicola run round to the front of the house. They see about twenty people there. Two of them are policemen[3]. One man is on the ground[4]. He has a gun. His left arm is in Jack's mouth[5]. Two other men are on the ground. They have blood[6] on their shirts, but they are laughing. A big man is shouting at the dog and other people are standing near him. One man has got a big TV camera[7]. "Down boy!" shouts Eric, and Jack runs to him.

The big man looks at Jack. "Is that your dog, young man? Then get him out of here!"

"Sorry," says Nicola. "But we're looking for my grandad. He's –"

"We haven't got your grandad. This is a TV film[8] and there are no grandads in it."

"But he's in your cellar. We saw him. He's at the window and he can't get out. The door is locked."

"Look, Miss, this isn't an afternoon tea party. We're making a film! Not a James Bond film, just a normal crime story[9]. And there isn't a grandad or a cellar in it. We've got a lot to do before it gets dark. We can look for your grandad then. Please go away."

The man behind the camera calls to the big man. "Mr Lean! Look at this! The dog is really good." Mr Lean looks in the camera and smiles.

"Yes," he says. "It is good. We can use it!"

Then he asks Eric, "Listen, young man, can we have your dog for an hour? We can use him for our film."

Nicola wants to scream[10]. "How can you talk about dogs at a time like this? My grandad is locked in your cellar. We must help him."

"OK, Mr Lean" says Eric. "You can have the dog for an hour, but you must help her grandad first."

[1]shot [ʃɒt] – *Schuss,* [2]gun [gʌn] – *Waffe,* [3]policeman [pə'li:smən] – *Polizist,* [4]ground [graʊnd] – *Boden,* [5]mouth [maʊθ] – *Maul,* [6]blood [blʌd] – *Blut,* [7]camera ['kæmərə] – *Kamera,* [8]film [fɪlm] – *Film,* [9]crime story ['kraɪm ˌstɔ:ri] – *Krimi,* [10]scream [skri:m] – *schreien*

Mr Lean looks at his watch. "OK. Bob and Jim, here are the keys to the house. Go with these kids and find Grandad. Then come back here." The two men in police uniform open the front door and go into the house. Jack and the children follow them. They look for the kitchen first. It's at the back of the house. There are three doors in it. Jack starts to bark at the doors.

"Give me the keys, please," says Nicola. They all go over to the white door near the window. But the keys aren't for these doors.

"Oh no," says Eric. "We haven't got the right key."

"Well, it must be in the kitchen then," says Nicola. "Let's think. Where can you put a key to the cellar?" They all look round the kitchen, under the table and behind the cupboards. But there is no key!

Suddenly one of the men says, "Look, it's on the shelf there under the word 'cellar'! Our problem is we make too many crime stories."

"Yes," says Eric. "And our problem is we watch too many." The men laugh. Eric tries the key and it works. They open the door, and they see the stairs[1]. They are very dark.

"There must be a light[2] here," says one of the men. "Yes, here it is." He turns on[3] the light and looks down. He can see a door. "Let's go!" Jack goes first. He stands at the door and barks. Grandad must be behind the door. Suddenly the light goes out[4].

Stop and answer

1. *Who does Jack find at the front of the house?*
2. *What are the people doing there?*
3. *What happens next?*
   - *A man falls down the stairs.*
   - *Grandad opens the door.*
   - *Nicola has an idea.*

E But they are lucky. Nicola has got Grandad's torch in her pocket. She turns it on. "Listen," says Eric. "I can hear a noise." *Knock! Knock! Knock!*

Nicola shouts, "Grandad! It's me, Nicola. Are you OK?" *Knock! Knock! Knock!*

"It's Grandad," shouts Nicola. "And that's Morse Code[5]. I can understand it." She listens again and then says, "He's OK but he wants his breakfast!" They all laugh. Now they must open the door.

They soon find the right key and in one of the rooms in the cellar they find Grandad. He's sitting in a big old chair with a book in his hands. "Nicola," he says, and he hugs[6] her. "And Eric and Jack! How nice!" Then he sees the two policemen. "I'm very glad you are here, too. There are strange people in this house. They've got guns and funny things in boxes. I think they are terrorists[7]. I watched them last night through my telescope. They put a lot of boxes in the house. I'm watching the house this week. My friend Jo is the caretaker here. He's visiting his children in Poland at the moment and I'm keeping an eye on[8] the house."

"OK, Grandad," says Nicola. "You can tell us all about it at home. Let's go!"

"Oh, no, my dear. I can't just go. I'm sure these nice policeman want a report[9]. And I can't walk very well. I fell[10] from the window and hurt[11] my foot."

"Oh, Grandad!" Suddenly Nicola's mobile phone rings. It's her mum. "Yes, Mum," says Nicola. "I'm fine. – I had sandwiches. – Yes, he's fine, too. – He's sitting in a chair with a good book. – No! No adventures! – Yes, OK. – Tomorrow. Bye!" She laughs and says to Grandad, "That was lucky! But let's go home before she rings again."

The two men help Grandad to the outside door. Soon he is sitting on a wall at the

[1]stairs [steəs] – *Treppe,* [2]light [laɪt] – *Licht,* [3]turns on ['tɜ:nz‿ɒn] – *schaltet … ein,* [4]goes out [gəʊz‿aʊt] – *geht aus,* [5]Morse Code [mɔ:s 'kəʊd] – *Morsecode,* [6]hugs [hʌgs] – *umarmt,* [7]terrorists ['terərɪsts] – *Terroristen,* [8]keeping an eye on ['ki:pɪŋ ən‿'aɪ ˌɒn] – *aufpassen auf,* [9]report [rɪ'pɔ:t] – *Bericht,* [10]fell [fel] – *fiel,* [11]hurt [hɜ:t] – *verletzte*

back of the house. "Get the car, Tom," says one of the men. The other man goes to the front of the house and soon comes back in a red car.

"That isn't a police car," says Grandad.

"No, Sir," says Tom. "And we aren't policemen."

"But you've got police uniforms!" says Grandad. He's very confused[1].

"Grandad," says Nicola. "We're going home now. I can make your breakfast and tell you all about it. OK?"

"OK," says Grandad. "But I hope it's a good story." Eric says goodbye, and he goes to the front of the house with Jack. The men put Grandad in the car, and they drive him and Nicola home.

Stop and answer

1. *Grandad is hungry[2]. How does Nicola know this?*
2. *What does Nicola's mum ask her?*
3. *Why is Grandad confused?*

F When they arrive at the house, the nurse, Mrs Martin, is there. She visits Mrs White every day and she often has tea with Grandad. She sees the two policemen. They are helping Grandad into the house. "Oh, dear," she thinks. "One of his adventures!"

"Hello, Mrs Martin," says Nicola. "Don't worry. Come and have some tea and we can explain[3]."

The 'policemen' go back to the house and fifteen minutes later Nicola, Mrs Martin and Grandad are sitting in his living room with their tea. It's four o'clock, but Grandad is eating his breakfast. He wants to know about the policemen. But Nicola has got a lot of questions for him, too. "Tell us your part of the story first," she says. So Grandad tells Nicola and Mrs Martin all about it.

"Well, it's like this. I often watch stars at night. So at nine o'clock I go upstairs. I look through my telescope and wait. It isn't very dark in the summer at nine, and it must be really dark. But I can see lights at Jo's place. That's funny, I think. He's in Poland. I must go and see what's happening. So I go downstairs and put on my Wellingtons. But it isn't cold, so I leave my jacket near the door.

[1]confused [kən'fju:zd] – *durcheinander, verwirrt,* [2]is hungry [ɪz 'hʌŋgri] – *hat Hunger,* [3]explain [ɪk'spleɪn] – *erklären*

I take my torch from the shed because it's nine-thirty and I know it gets dark at ten o'clock. I go through the field at the back of my house and cross the river – near where we always go fishing. I'm walking to the house when I trip[1] and drop[2] my torch. I can't find it, but I don't want to go back home, so I go to the house and look around."

"That's why the torch was near the tree," says Nicola.

"That's right," says Grandad. "And at the front I see a van with a lot of boxes in it. Three men come out and carry the boxes into the house. Suddenly one of the men drops a box, and I can see there are guns in it. 'Be careful[3], Tom. We don't want to shoot[4] anyone[5],' says the big man and laughs. They're terrorists, I think. I must tell the police. The men put the boxes in the house, leave it again and drive away."

"But you don't go back and tell the police. Why not?" asks Nicola.

"Because I want to check the boxes. I don't know what I can tell the police. The front door is locked, but there is a small window in the cellar. It's open. I climb in[6] and look around but it's dark. When I jump down[7], I fall over[8] a chair and hurt my foot. I can't climb out of the window again, so I sit in the chair and wait. And that's where you come in, Nicola."

"And where are the terrorists now, Mr Shaw?" asks the nurse.

"Well, I hope the police have got them," says Grandad.

"No, Grandad. They aren't terrorists. They're actors. They're making a film for TV with Mr Lean," says Nicola. Then she hears the dog. "And one of the stars is here to see you," she says and she goes to the door. Eric is there with Jack. "Come in and have some tea. You must thank Jack, Grandad. He found[9] your torch and you. And Mr Lean gave us the keys only because he liked[10] Jack."

"Well, I like Jack, too. He's a real[11] star. He must come on our next adventure."

"Oh, Grandad, no more adventures, please," says Nicola. "You can watch stars, of course, but please only through your telescope."

Stop and answer

1. *Why does Grandad go to Drayton Hall?*
2. *What happens in the cellar?*
3. *Who is the real star of the story and why?*

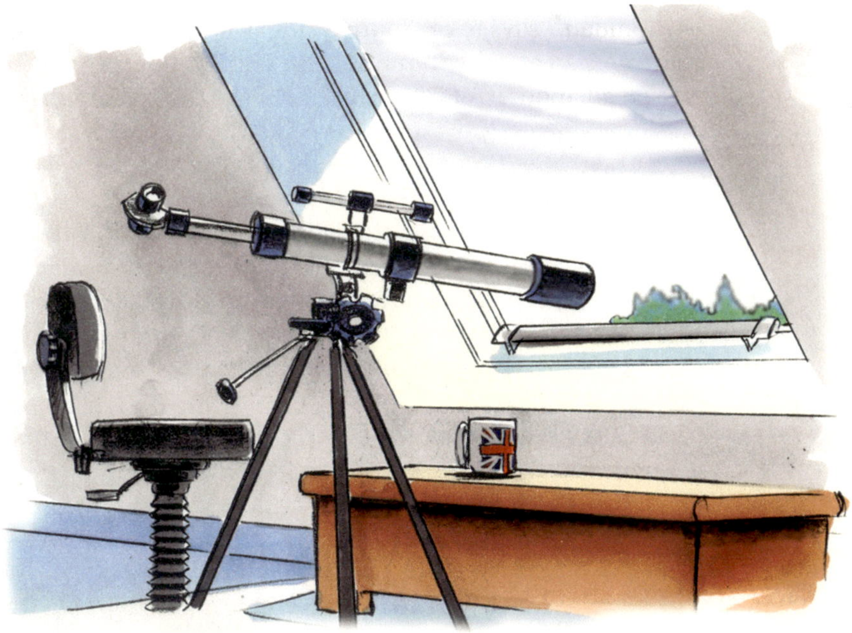

[1]trip [trɪp] – *stolpere,* [2]drops [drɒps] – *lässt fallen,* [3]Be careful [bi: 'keəfl] – *Sei vorsichtig, Pass auf,* [4]shoot [ʃu:t] – *erschießen,* [5]not … anyone [nɒt 'enɪwʌn] – *niemand,* [6]climb in ['klaɪm‿ɪn] – *steige hinein,* [7]jump down [dʒump 'daʊn] – *springe hinunter,* [8]fall over ['fɔ:l‿əʊvə] – *falle über etw., stolpere,* [9]found [faʊnd] – *fand,* [10]liked [laɪkt] – *mochte,* [11]real [rɪəl] – *echter*

Turn[1] again, Whittington!

1 Dick Whittington
2 Blacky
3 Barny Forge
4 Sissy Forge, his daughter[2]
5 The bells[3] of Bow Church
6 Lady Anne Fitzwarren
7 Alice Fitzwarren, her daughter
8 George Buckingham
9 Stouty Burke
10 Two pickpockets[4]

Storyteller[5] 1: My friends, come listen to our play. The place is London, not today. But 1380, let us say. It tells of Dick and of his cat. He makes a fortune[6] out of that, and soon he wears the Lord Mayor's[7] hat[8].

Scene[9] One

Storyteller 2: We are in the country near London. A man with a horse stops near a poor[10] house.
Sissy Forge: Good morning, Sir[11]. What can I do for you?
Buckingham: Can you tell me the way to London, please?
Sissy: Yes, Sir. But it isn't easy to find. Dick can show you the way. Dick! Dick!
Dick: I'm coming! What's up, Sissy?
Sissy: Can you show this man the road to London? He doesn't know the way.
Dick: Yes, of course. Follow me, Sir. *(They walk together for a short time.)* They say London is beautiful and there's gold[12] in the streets – is that right, Sir?
Buckingham: Well, there isn't much gold in the streets – just a lot of rubbish.
Dick: We're here, Sir. Go over the river, and the road to London is behind those trees.
Buckingham: Thank you, Dick! *(throws him a gold coin)* That's for your help.
Dick: Wow! A gold coin[13]! Thank you! Bye! *(sings)*
Barny Forge: Hey, Dick! What are you doing? Why aren't you working? What about the pigs? I'm fed up with you. Go and pack your things and leave!
Dick: But, but – where can I go, Mr Forge? I haven't got a family now.
Barny: That's your problem!

[1]turn [tɜːn] – *dreh dich um,* [2]daughter ['dɔːtə] – *Tochter,* [3]bells [belz] – *Glocken,* [4]pickpocket ['pɪkˌpɒkɪt] – *Taschendieb,* [5]storyteller ['stɔːriˌtelə] – *Geschichtenerzähler,* [6]fortune ['fɔːtʃuːn] – *Vermögen,* [7]Lord Mayor [lɔːd 'meə] – *Oberbürgermeister,* [8]hat [hæt] – *Hut,* [9]scene [siːn] – *Szene,* [10]poor [pɔː] – *arm,* [11]Sir [sɜː] – *mein Herr,* [12]gold [gəʊld] – *Gold,* [13]coin [kɔɪn] – *Münze*

Scene Two

Storyteller 1: Two days later Dick arrives in London. He takes out his gold coin, but suddenly –
1st pickpocket: Stupid idiot!
2nd pickpocket: Sorry. We're in a hurry.
Dick: Wait! Give me my gold coin!
Pickpockets: We haven't got your gold coin!
Stouty Burke: What's up? Who here has got a gold coin?
Dick: They've got it. But it's my coin.
2nd pickpocket: We're poor boys. We haven't got a gold coin.
Stouty Burke: Show me your hands[1].
1st pickpocket: See! He's right!
Stouty Burke: *(to the second pickpocket)* Now your pockets. Aha! A gold coin! That's funny. You haven't got a gold coin? What's this then? *(gives the coin to Dick)* Here you are, boy.
2nd pickpocket: But we're hungry[2].
Stouty Burke: Well, here's an apple for you.
Pickpockets: Thank you. Bye.
Dick: How can I thank you, Sir?
Stouty Burke: Well, you can come and help me in the kitchen. I work for a very important[3] family and tonight I'm cooking[4] for the Lord Mayor.
Dick: The Lord who?
Stouty Burke: The Lord Mayor of London. He's a very rich[5] and very important man.
Dick: Oh! Then I want to be Lord Mayor one day!
Stouty Burke: What? You? With one gold coin! *(laughs)* Come on!

Scene Three

Storyteller 2: That night Dick sleeps in Stouty's kitchen with a lot of mice. The next morning he comes back from shopping with four big bags.
Cat: Meow! Meow!
Dick: *(looks in one of the bags)* Oh, it's a little black cat! Hello! What's your name?
Cat: Meow! Meow! Meow!
Dick: Hey! Where are you going? Are you hungry?
Cat: Purr[6]! Purr!
Dick: What's that in your mouth? Oh, it's a big mouse. Clever[7] cat. You can stay here and help us in the kitchen. But I can't call you 'Cat'. What about 'Blacky'?
Cat: Purr! Purr!!

Scene Four

Storyteller 1: One day Stouty Burke goes home to his family. A new cook comes. He doesn't like Dick and he doesn't like cats. Dick is very unhappy. He leaves the house.

[1]hands [hændz] – *Hände*, [2]we're hungry [wɪə 'hʌŋgri] – *wir haben Hunger*, [3]important [ɪm'pɔ:tənt] – *wichtig*, [4]I'm cooking [kʊkɪŋ] – *ich koche*, [5]rich [rɪtʃ] – *reich*, [6]Purr! [pɜ:] – *Schnurr!*, [7]clever ['klevə] – *klug*

Scene Five

Storyteller 2: The next morning Dick and Blacky are sleeping in a field near a big church. It's 12:00, and the bells start ringing. Dick wakes up.

Dick: Listen, Blacky! The bells are talking. What are they saying?

Bells: Turn again, Whittington, Lord Mayor of London! Turn again, Whittington, Lord Mayor of London! Turn again, Whittington, Lord Mayor of London!

Dick: Come on, Blacky! I want to be Lord Mayor and a Lord Mayor doesn't run away from problems! Let's go back and tell Lady Fitzwarren about the cook.

Scene Six

Storyteller 1: Lady Fitzwarren is in the living room with Alice and her brother, George.

Lady Fitzwarren: *(standing on a chair)* Ah! Ah! There's a mouse! It wants the cake!

Buckingham: Oh, Anne! I'm glad[1] you don't see the mice on my ship.

Lady Fitzwarren: Please, George, catch[2] it!

Dick: Just a minute! Catch it, Blacky! Good cat! Bring it here!

Lady Fitzwarren: Oh! Thank you, Dick. And thank you, Blacky.

Blacky: Purr! Purr!

Buckingham: Dick? I know you. You showed me the road to London.

Dick: Yes, Sir.

Buckingham: Can I buy your cat for my ship? Here are three gold coins for her.

Blacky: Meow! Meow! Meow!

Dick: Sorry, Sir, but Blacky is my friend. I can't sell her to you.

Buckingham: Well, can I borrow her? There are a lot of mice on my ship. They eat the silk[3]. You can have a gold coin for every ten mice she catches.

Blacky: Purr! Purr!!

Dick: Well, Blacky likes the idea. You can take her, but please bring her back to me.

Buckingham: Fine. Now let's all eat this cake.

Scene Seven

Storyteller 2: Stouty Burke soon comes back, and Dick is very happy. One day they go to town with Alice. A beautiful coach[4] passes[5] them on the road.

Dick: Wow! What a big coach! I want to ride in a big coach like that.

Stouty: That isn't for people like you and me, Dick. That's the Lord Mayor's coach.

[1]I'm glad [glæd] – *ich bin froh (darüber),* [2]catch [kætʃ] – *fangen,* [3]silk [sɪlk] – *Seide,* [4]coach [kəʊtʃ] – *Kutsche,* [5]passes ['pɑːsɪz] – *fährt vorbei*

Dick: Then I want to be Lord Mayor one day, too.
Alice: You? But you can't even[1] read and write.
Dick: I know. But I want to learn. Hey! Watch out[2]!
Alice: *(Dick pushes Alice away[3])* Arrgh!
Stouty: Are you OK, Miss?
Alice: Yes! That was[4] terrible!
Stouty: Can you get up?
Alice: Yes. Thank you, Dick. You saved my life[5]!

Scene Eight

Storyteller 1: Stouty and Dick bring Alice to her mum. Lady Fitzwarren has got a visitor.
Lady Fitzwarren: Come in! Ah, hello children! Hello, Mr Burke.
Buckingham: Alice! What –?
Alice: Hello, Uncle George! Mum, a coach came down[6] the road. I didn't see[7] it, but Dick did[8] and he pushed[9] me out of the way and saved my life.
Lady Fitzwarren: Oh, Dick, how can we thank you?
Alice: I've got an idea, Mum. Dick wants to learn to read and write. Can we teach him?
Lady Fitzwarren: Is that right, Dick?
Dick: Yes, it is, Lady Fitzwarren.
Lady Fitzwarren: Then let me talk to Lord Fitzwarren. But first my brother wants to speak to you.
Buckingham: Hello, young man. *(gives Dick a bag and a box)* Here's your cat. And your gold coins are in this bag.
Dick: Blacky! Hello!
Blacky: Purr! Purr! Purr!!
Dick: *(looks in the bag)* But there are a lot of gold coins here.
Buckingham: Blacky caught[10] a lot of mice. And I can sell my silk now for a lot of money. You can put your money in a bank[11], Dick. And one day you can buy a house.
Dick: No. Please buy silk and sell it for me. Blacky can protect[12] it.
Buckingham: OK, Dick.

Storyteller 2: And this is where our story ends, of Dick and Blacky and their friends, of how a boy whose luck was down[13], became[14] Lord Mayor of London Town.

[1](not) even ['i:vən] – *nicht einmal,* [2]Watch out! [ˌwɒtʃ 'aʊt] – *Vorsicht!,* [3]pushes … away [pʊʃɪz ə'weɪ] – *stößt … zur Seite,* [4]was [wɒz] – *war,* [5]saved my life [ˌseɪvd maɪ 'laɪf] – *hast mir das Leben gerettet,* [6]came down [ˌkeɪm 'daʊn] – *fuhr … herunter,* [7]didn't see ['dɪdənt ˌsi:] – *sah … nicht,* [8]did (see) [dɪd] – *sah,* [9]pushed [pʊʃt] – *stieß,* [10]caught [kɔ:t] – *fing,* [11]bank [bæŋk] – *Bank,* [12]protect [prə'tekt] – *schützen,* [13]whose luck was down [hu:z ˌlʌk wɒz 'daʊn] – *der kein Glück hatte,* [14]became [bɪ'keɪm] – *wurde*

Pets[1]

1 A rap: Family pets

a) *Look at the pictures of the animals in the rap.*
Find the right word on the cards and say the rap.

There's a  in our family,
A  too.
A  in the garden
And a  – he's blue.
We haven't got a 

Or a  or a 
But there's a bed in the kitchen
Where the  can sleep.
There on the sofa you can see my .
He isn't very happy – the  is in the house.

sheep | rabbit[3] | horse | pig | guinea pig[2] | mouse | fish | cat | budgie[4] | dog

b) *Listen to the rap. Have you got the right words?*

c) *What animals hasn't the family got?*

2 Pets survey

a) *Who in your group has got a pet? Do a survey.*
Start like this:

A: Have you got a pet?
B: Yes, I have. / No, … .
A: What have you got?
B: I've got a …/two … .
A: What's his/her name? / What are their names?
B: … *Go on, please.*

pupil's name	pet	pet's name
…	…	…

b) *Read your survey to the class. Start like this:*
… people in our group have got a … .
… people haven't got a pet. Favourite names are … .

c) *Collect all the information from b). How many budgies/cats/… are there in your class?*
How many people haven't got a pet?

[1]pets [pets] – *Haustiere,* [2]guinea pig ['gɪni ˌpɪg] – *Meerschweinchen,* [3]rabbit ['ræbɪt] – *Kaninchen,* [4]budgie ['bʌdʒi] – *Wellensittich*

3 Information about pets

Read the texts. Find one good thing and one bad thing about each animal.

1. Before you choose a dog, think about your home and your family. Do you want a big dog or a small dog? Big dogs like a big garden and long walks[1]. And they eat a lot! Small dogs can be great fun but they sometimes bark a lot. All dogs can learn tricks, but you must start when they are young.

2. A lot of young people want to have a horse. They see them in pictures or on TV and they are so beautiful. But horses are very expensive. You must have a lot of time for them, too. You must ride them every day. You can't just do your homework or go to the disco and forget your horse.

3. A lot of people don't want to have a dog, but they want to cuddle[2] their animal. They often choose a cat as[3] a pet. You can't leave a dog in the house every day, but you needn't stay with a cat. Just give it food, water and a nice bed, and play with it when you come home. But don't forget: Cats like to bring home mice!

4. A budgie is a good pet for an only child, an old person or for a family. They like people, but you must spend time with them. They can be good friends, and it is fun to watch them and listen to their songs. But they can mean a lot of work because they make a terrible mess[4].

5. A lot of people give a baby rabbit to their children in the spring. Rabbits look so nice, and the children want to cuddle them. But small children often mean stress[5] to rabbits. They are quiet animals and they like a quiet life[6]. But keep your rabbit away[7] from the wires[8] to your computer or TV. Rabbits eat everything[9]!

6. Guinea pigs are good pets for families. They don't bite[10] or bark, but they can't do tricks. They like people, and they don't have a problem with young children. You must give them a big cage[11] and good food every day. But don't always leave them in their cage. They like to run round[12] the room.

4 Pet posters

Work with a partner. You're one of these pets. You're looking for a nice home. Make a poster. What's your name? How old are you? Say why you're a nice pet.

My name is Snoopy.

I'm four months old.

I like nice people and long walks.

I don't like cats.

I want good food.

I don't want a cat in the house.

I'm a nice pet because I don't bark much, but I can do a lot of tricks.

[1]long walks [lɒŋ 'wɔ:ks] – *lange Spaziergänge,* [2]cuddle ['kʌdl] – *knuddeln,* [3]as [æz] – *als,* [4]mess [mes] – *Schweinerei,* [5]stress [stres] – *Stress,* [6]life [laɪf] – *Leben,* [7]keep … away [ki:p ə'weɪ] – *halte … fern,* [8]wires [waɪəz] – *Kabel,* [9]everything ['evriθɪŋ] – *alles,* [10]bite [baɪt] – *beißen,* [11]cage [keɪdʒ] – *Käfig,* [12]round [raʊnd] – *um … herum*

Around[1] the year

Boxing Day

Boxing Day is the day after Christmas Day. But it is not a day when people throw away boxes from their Christmas presents. And it is not a day when the family watches boxing[2] on TV. The boxes in the name 'Boxing Day' are presents. But they aren't Christmas presents. They are presents from rich[3] people to poor[4] people. Boxing Day is a very old tradition[5] in England, but today people don't give things only to poor people. They sometimes give money to the postman[6] or the milkman. Other people play games or run in a special[7] race. A lot of people visit friends and neighbours[8].

A present for the postman

Remember, remember, the fifth of November!

Guy Fawkes Day

It's 5th November, 1605: Guy Fawkes and his friends try to blow up[9] the Houses of Parliament in London. The King's[10] men catch[11] them and kill[12] them. Today, children carry their 'guys' through[13] the streets on this day. When it is dark, they burn[14] their guys and there are a lot of fireworks[15].

[1]around [ə'raʊnd] – *durch,* [2]boxing ['bɒksɪŋ] – *Boxkampf,* [3]rich [rɪtʃ] – *reich,* [4]poor [pɔ:] – *arm,* [5]tradition [trə'dɪʃn] – *Tradition,* [6]postman ['pəʊstmən] – *Briefträger,* [7]special [speʃl] – *besonderen,* [8]neighbours ['neɪbəz] – *Nachbarn,* [9]blow up [bləʊ 'ʌp] – *in die Luft jagen,* [10]king [kɪŋ] – *König,* [11]catch [kætʃ] – *fassen,* [12]kill [kɪl] – *töten,* [13]through [θru:] – *durch,* [14]burn [bɜ:n] – *verbrennen,* [15]fireworks ['faɪəwɜ:ks] – *Feuerwerk,* [16]Christmas ['krɪstməs] – *Weihnachten,* [17]Halloween [ˌhæləʊ'i:n] – *Halloween*

Pancake[1] Day

Pancake Day is on Shrove Tuesday[2], about four weeks before Easter. A lot of people make pancakes and eat them. In some parts of England, Pancake Day is a day for fun. They have pancake races in their towns. They usually wear an apron[3] and a hat[4]. They have a frying pan[5] with a pancake in it. They must toss[6] the pancake three times[7]. It can bring bad luck if the pancake falls on the ground[8].

A race at the Houses of Parliament

Red Nose[9] Day

On this day in March, a lot of people in England put on a red nose and do something funny for charity. Seventy per cent[10] of schools in England take part[11]. The pupils sing, dance or tell jokes and their friends and family give them money. Famous people collect money, too. They want to make people laugh[12] and to help others. The money goes to poor people in England and in other countries. Red Nose Day is an English idea, but you can find it in many countries now.

Lenny Henry and Robbie Williams

1 Special[13] days in your country

What special days do you know? Make a calendar with these days.
What do you and your friends and family do on these days?

[1]pancake ['pænkeɪk] – *Pfannkuchen,* [2]Shrove Tuesday [ˌʃrəʊv 'tju:zdeɪ] – *Faschingsdienstag,* [3]apron ['eɪprən] – *Schürze,* [4]hat [hæt] – *Hut,* [5]frying pan ['fraɪɪŋ ˌpæn] – *Bratpfanne,* [6]toss [tɒs] – *(durch Hochwerfen) wenden,* [7]three times [ˌθri: 'taɪmz] – *dreimal,* [8]falls on the ground [ˌfɔ:lz ɒn ðə 'graʊnd] – *fällt hinunter,* [9]nose [nəʊz] – *Nase,* [10]per cent [pɜ: 'sent] – *Prozent,* [11]take part [teɪk 'pa:t] – *nehmen teil,* [12]make people laugh [ˌmeɪk pi:pl 'la:f] – *Leute zum Lachen bringen,* [13]special ['speʃəl] – *besondere,* [14]Valentine's Day ['væləntaɪnz ˌdeɪ] – *Valentinstag,* [15]Easter [i:stə] – *Ostern*

Mediation and communication

Nicht alle Menschen beherrschen die gleichen Fremdsprachen. Manchmal kommt es zu Begegnungen, bei denen zwei oder mehrere Gesprächspartner miteinander reden möchten oder auch müssen, von denen aber einer beispielsweise nicht Englisch spricht. Dann benötigen sie einen Helfer, der für sie die Informationen, um die es geht, ins Englische oder aus dem Englischen übermittelt. Wir nennen so etwas deshalb auch Sprachmitteln oder Mediation.
In solche Situationen kannst auch du geraten – ob nun während des Urlaubs im Ausland oder in deinem Heimatort mit Englisch sprechenden Reisenden. Deshalb erhältst du auf den folgenden Seiten einige Tipps, die dir helfen werden, Situationen dieser Art zu meistern.

Unit 1 All about Suzanne

Tipp: In der Alltagsunterhaltung benutzen wir häufig feststehende Wendungen. Du musst also nicht mehr überlegen, welche Wörter du für eine Übersetzung benötigst, sondern dich einfach an die gesamte Wendung erinnern.

Situation: Suzanne, ein Mädchen aus Großbritannien, ist bei euch zu Hause zu Besuch. Dein Opa ist auch da und hat viele Fragen an Suzanne. Hilf ihnen.

Match the questions and answers and act the story with two partners.

Wie heißt du?
Woher kommst du?
Wo liegt Greenwich?
Wie alt bist du?
Was heißt „Auf Wiedersehen“ auf Englisch?
Danke.

I'm from Greenwich.
I'm eleven.
My name is Suzanne.
It's 'Goodbye'.
You're welcome.
Greenwich is in London.

Unit 2 What can they say?

Tipp: Manche Wendungen musst du dir besonders gut einprägen, denn man kann ihren Sinn aus den einzelnen Wörtern nicht mehr ableiten.

Situation: Welche Wendungen brauchst du in diesen Situationen? Wähle aus den folgenden Wendungen passende für die abgebildeten Situationen aus

Keep out!

Sort it out with her.

You're in big trouble!

Hurry up!

Barker, you stupid dog!

What's up?

Unit 3 An interview[1]

Tipp: Beim Übertragen eines deutschen Satzes in die englische Sprache gibt es meistens mehrere Ausdrucksmöglichkeiten. Wenn dir ein Wort nicht einfällt, dann überlege, ob du ein anderes mit ähnlicher Bedeutung kennst oder ob du den Satz umstellen kannst, um die Schwierigkeit zu umgehen.

Situation: Deutsche Schüler machen eine Umfrage darüber, was englische Schüler in ihrer Freizeit alles tun. Übertrage diese Fragen für eine Freundin.

Frage für sie ein englisches Mädchen:
- ob sie singen und tanzen kann.
- ob sie Fahrrad fahren kann.
- ob Basketball und Hockey schrecklich sind.
- ob der Computerklub am Montag ist.
- ob der Sportklub gut ist.
- welche Klubs es an der Schule gibt.
- wie ihr Lieblingsklub heißt.
- was man im Klub alles tun kann.
- wann die Klubveranstaltungen sind.
- wo die Veranstaltungen stattfinden.

[1]interview ['ɪntəvju:] – *Interview*

Unit 4 A brochure[1]

Tipp: Oft findest du auf Broschüren Texte, von denen du nicht alles verstehst. Das macht nichts. Du kannst die wichtigsten Informationen oft entnehmen, ohne die Einzelwörter zu kennen.
Hier sind dafür noch einige Tricks.

- *Konzentriere dich auf die Überschrift und zum Text gehörende Bilder, um leichter herauszufinden, worum es im Text geht.*
- *Achte auch auf Wörter, deren Schreibung deutschen Wörtern gleicht oder ähnelt und die du so erraten kannst.*
- *Achte beim Lesen besonders auf Eigennamen von Ländern, Flüssen, Museen, auf Zahlenangaben, Daten, Jahreszahlen etc., weil sie dir viele Informationen geben.*
- *Was sagt dir die Aufmachung des Textes? Wofür ist er bestimmt?*

Situation: Du schaust dir mit einem Freund/einer Freundin, der/die kein Englisch versteht, diese Bilder und Texte an. Erkläre ihm/ihr, worum es hier geht. Hier sind ein paar Fragen, die dir helfen sollen:

1. *Worum geht es hier?*
2. *Was ist das?*
3. *Wo befindet es sich?*
4. *Welchem Zweck dient es?*

The Thames Barrier
Visitors to London can see a lot of interesting places. One of them is the Thames Barrier. It is not a tunnel or a bridge. It is on the river near Greenwich. The barrier keeps sea water out of London. You can visit it by boat or by train. They can open the barrier for river traffic. Ships can go into London or leave it every day. There is a museum there with a model of the barrier. It shows you how they open and close it.

[1]brochure ['brəʊʃə] – *Broschüre*

Unit 5 Shopping

Tipp: Wenn dir ein Wort nicht einfällt, kannst du dir auch helfen, indem du es umschreibst, also erläuterst. Du kannst z. B. erklären, wo sich das Bezeichnete befindet, wozu man es braucht, wie es aussieht.

Situation: Du darfst deine Oma auf eine Reise nach London begleiten. An einem freien Nachmittag freut ihr euch auf einen gemeinsamen Einkaufsbummel. Du hast versprochen, deiner Oma zu helfen, denn sie spricht kein Englisch. Ihr schaut euch Kleidung an. Wie bewältigst du diese kleine Einkaufssituation?

Grandma: Frage bitte den Verkäufer, ob sie diese gelben T-Shirts auch in Blau haben.
You: …
The man: No, we haven't. I'm sorry. But we've got other very nice T-shirts in blue. Look.
You: …
Grandma: Haben sie die in Größe M?
You: …
The man: Yes, we have. They are over there on the shelf.
You: …
Grandma: Sehr schön. Frage, wie viel eins kostet.
You: …
The man: It is £9.95.
You: …
Grandma: Das ist nicht teuer. OK.
You: …
The man: Anything else?
You: …
Grandma: Nein, danke. Das ist alles. Bitte sehr. *(sie bezahlt)*
You: …
The man: Thank you and bye.
You: …

Unit 6 A picture postcard from …

Tipp: Wenn du für jemanden einen Text aus dem Englischen ins Deutsche übersetzt, beachte folgendes:
- Wichtig ist, dass der Inhalt vollständig übertragen wird. Dabei kann gelegentlich das eine oder andere Wort weggelassen werden.
- Für feststehende Wendungen solltest du gute deutsche Übersetzungen finden.
- Achte auch auf grammatische Erscheinungen, die es im Deutschen nicht gibt und für die du gute Übersetzungen finden musst (*present progressive*, Kurzantworten).
- Die Wortstellung im englischen Satz kann vom Deutschen abweichen.

Situation: Du bekommst eine Karte aus Somerset. Dein kleiner Bruder kann kein Englisch und ist neugierig, was dort geschrieben steht. Finde eine gute Übersetzung. Einige Stellen, auf die du besonders achten solltest, sind markiert.

Hi Paul,
I'm staying in a little place near Wells at the moment. You can see it on the map. I'm staying with a friend from my old school. We're sitting in her garden now. I'm eating a big cheese sandwich! It's great. Somerset cheese is very famous.
What about you? Are you having a good time? You can write to me at the address on this postcard. Bye for now.
Love,
Suzanne

Hi!
Wie du weißt, gibt es überall im Leben Regeln. Manchmal ist das auch ganz gut so. Stell dir z. B. mal vor, was auf den Straßen los wäre, wenn jeder machen würde, was er will.

Die Regeln, nach denen eine Sprache funktioniert, heißen Grammatik. Auf den folgenden Seiten habe ich für dich die wichtigsten Regeln der englischen Grammatik zusammengestellt. Du kannst hier nachschlagen, wenn:

- du bei einer Aufgabe im Unterricht oder zu Hause unsicher bist
- du etwas vergessen hast oder genauer wissen willst
- du dich auf die Klassenarbeit vorbereitest.

Jedes Kapitel hat eine dicke Überschrift, die dir sagt, um welches Thema es geht. Danach folgen ein kurzer Merksatz und viele Übersichten. Sie zeigen dir, wozu du diese Formen brauchst und wie diese Formen gebildet werden.

Weiterhin solltest du unbedingt auf dieses Symbol achten:

Vorsicht Falle!

Hier wird immer auf besondere Schwierigkeiten hingewiesen. Aber keine Angst, ich werde dir natürlich auch mit Rat und Tat zur Seite stehen!
Wenn du trotzdem einmal einen Begriff nicht mehr weißt, kannst du einfach auf Seite 139 nachschlagen. Dort findest du eine Übersicht der wichtigsten grammatischen Begriffe mit einem Beispiel dazu und der Angabe, in welchem Grammatikpunkt du mehr darüber lesen kannst.

G1 Personalpronomen — *Personal pronouns*

Die Personalpronomen werden auch persönliche **FÜR**wörter genannt, weil sie FÜR Personen, FÜR Tiere oder FÜR Gegenstände stehen.

I	*ich*	**I**'m a mouse.
you	*du*	**You**'re twelve.
he	*er*	**He**'s from Istanbul.
she	*sie*	**She**'s my teacher.
it	*es*	**It**'s a big school.
we	*wir*	**We**'re in the right classroom.
you	*ihr/Sie*	**You**'re lucky, you two.
they	*sie*	**They**'re new here.

He steht immer für eine männliche Person! *She* steht immer für eine weibliche Person! Für Tiere, deren Namen man kennt, verwendet man *he* oder *she*!

Für Sachen sagst du im Englischen immer *it*! Auch für Tiere, deren Namen man nicht kennt, sagt man *it*! *I* wird immer groß geschrieben.

G 2 Die Formen des Verbs *be*

Forms of the verb 'be'

Das Verb ***be*** brauchst du, wenn du Aussagen zu Personen oder Gegenständen machen willst. Genau wie im Deutschen das Verb „sein" (bin, bist, sind, seid) ändert sich im Englischen das Verb ***be*** auch jeweils nach der Person. Dabei kann ***be*** in Lang- oder Kurzformen auftreten. Beim Schreiben verwendet man meist die Langform, beim Sprechen die Kurzform.

Long forms

I	**am**	*ich bin*	I **am** new in Greenwich.
you	**are**	*du bist*	You **are** late, Sam.
he	**is**	*er ist*	He **is** eleven.
she	**is**	*sie ist*	She **is** from Bristol.
it	**is**	*es ist*	It **is** a big school.
we	**are**	*wir sind*	We **are** at Thomas Tallis.
you	**are**	*ihr seid / Sie sind*	You **are** here.
they	**are**	*sie sind*	They **are** my friends.

Short forms

I'**m**	*ich bin*	I'**m** new in Greenwich.
you'**re**	*du bist*	You'**re** late, Sam.
he'**s**	*er ist*	He'**s** eleven.
she'**s**	*sie ist*	She'**s** from Bristol.
it'**s**	*es ist*	It'**s** a big school.
we'**re**	*wir sind*	We'**re** at Thomas Tallis.
you'**re**	*ihr seid / Sie sind*	You'**re** here.
they'**re**	*sie sind*	They'**re** my friends.

Wenn du Englisch sprichst, kannst du einen Buchstaben der Langform verschlucken, um schneller und flüssiger zu sprechen. Das sind dann die Kurzformen von *be*. Wenn man diese Kurzformen nun aufschreiben will, (z. B. ein Gespräch), setzt man ein Apostroph ('), um zu zeigen, dass etwas weggefallen ist.

G 3 Pluralformen *Plural forms*

Plural heißt Mehrzahl. Die Pluralformen der meisten Substantive werden im Englischen gebildet, indem man ein ***-s*** an das Wort anhängt.

Singular (Einzahl)	Plural (Mehrzahl)	Sound
a book	five book**s**	[s]
a dog	two dog**s**	[z]
a sandwich	three sandwich**es**	[ɪz]

Bei manchen Substantiven wird ***-es*** angehängt, wenn die Aussprache sonst Probleme bereiten würde. Diese Formen musst du einfach mitlernen. Sie stehen im Vokabular.

G 4 Die Verneinung des Verbs *be* *Negation of the verb 'be'*

Wenn du einen Satz verneinen willst, setzt du ***not*** nach ***am***, ***is*** und ***are*** ein. In der gesprochenen und der geschriebenen Sprache werden hier meist Kurzformen verwendet.

I	**am not** **'m not**	*ich bin nicht*	I'm **not** new in Greenwich.
you	**are not** **aren't**	*du bist nicht*	You **aren't** late, Sam.
he	**is not** **isn't**	*er ist nicht*	He **isn't** eleven.
she	**is not** **isn't**	*sie ist nicht*	She **isn't** from Bristol.
it	**is not** **isn't**	*es ist nicht*	It **isn't** a big school.
we	**are not** **aren't**	*wir sind nicht*	We **aren't** at Thomas Tallis.
you	**are not** **aren't**	*ihr seid nicht / Sie sind nicht*	You **aren't** in my class.
they	**are not** **aren't**	*sie sind nicht*	They **aren't** my friends.

Die verneinte Kurzform von *I am* ist ***I'm not***.

G 5 *be* in Fragen/Kurzantworten — *Questions/short answers with be*

Wenn du mit ***be*** eine Frage stellen willst, beginnst du den Satz mit ***Am*** **…**, ***Is*** **…** oder ***Are*** **…**. Wenn du auf eine Frage antwortest, können „***Yes.***“ oder „***No.***“ allein manchmal etwas unhöflich klingen. Deshalb antwortet man meistens mit einem verkürzten Satz, einer so genannten Kurzantwort, in der man die Form von ***be*** aus der Frage und das Personalpronomen noch anfügt, z. B. „Ja, ich bin.“ oder „Nein, sie sind nicht.“.

Fragen

Am I late?	**Am I …?**	*Bin ich … ?*
Are you from Greenwich?	**Are you …?**	*Bist du … ?*
Is he at Thomas Tallis?	**Is he …?**	*Ist er … ?*
Is she from Bristol?	**Is she …?**	*Ist sie … ?*
Is it in your bag?	**Is it …?**	*Ist es … ?*
Are we late?	**Are we …?**	*Sind wir … ?*
Are you new in Greenwich?	**Are you …?**	*Seid ihr … ? / Sind Sie … ?*
Are they in your class?	**Are they …?**	*Sind sie … ?*

Kurzantworten

Yes, **I am.**		No, **I'm not.**	
Yes, **you are.**		No, **you aren't.**	
Yes, **he is.**		No, **he isn't.**	
Yes, **she is.**	*Ja!*	No, **she isn't.**	*Nein!*
Yes, **it is.**		No, **it isn't.**	
Yes, **we are.**		No, **we aren't.**	
Yes, **you are.**		No, **you aren't.**	
Yes, **they are.**		No, **they aren't.**	

G 6 Fragen mit Fragewörtern — *Questions with question words*

Fragewörter sind Wörter wie ***Who*** … ? ***What*** … ? ***Where*** … ? und ***How*** … ? (Wer … ? Was … ? Wo … ? Wie … ?). Fragewörter stehen immer am Anfang der Frage.

Who are you?	– I'm Tom.
How old are you?	– I'm one.
Where are you from?	– I'm from Greenwich.
What's on the table?	– A book.

G 7 Besitzangaben mit -'s — *The possessive form with -'s*

Wenn du sagen willst, wem etwas gehört, hängst du einfach **-'s** an den Namen oder die Person: *Terry's cat*. Wenn schon ein **-s** am Ende des Wortes ist, setzt du das Apostroph einfach dahinter: *my parents' garden*.

Emma's sister isn't very nice.	***Emmas*** *Schwester ist nicht sehr nett.*
The **Taylors'** house is in Pond Road.	*Das Haus der* ***Familie Taylor*** *ist in der Pond Road.*

Beispiel: My brother's house. → *ein Bruder (besitzt ein Haus alleine: das Haus meines Bruders.)*

My brothers' house. → *zwei oder mehrere Brüder (besitzen ein Haus zusammen: das Haus meiner Brüder.)*

G 8 Besitzangaben *mit have got/has got* — *The possessive form with have got/has got*

Wenn man sagen will, dass jemand etwas **besitzt** oder dass etwas zu einem Gegenstand gehört, benutzt man ***have got/has got***. Es gibt auch wie bei *be* Kurz- und Langformen.

Long forms	Short forms		
I **have got …**/	I**'ve got …**	*ich habe …*	I **have got** a new book.
you **have got …**/	you**'ve got …**	*du hast …*	You **have got** a cool T-shirt.
he **has got …** /	he**'s got …**	*er hat …*	He **has got** a new ball.
she **has got …** /	she**'s got …**	*sie hat …*	She **has got** a problem.
it **has got …** /	it**'s got …**	*es hat …*	It **has got** blue doors.
we **have got …**/	we**'ve got …**	*wir haben …*	We **have got** a cafeteria in the school.
you **have got …**/	you**'ve got …**	*ihr habt …*	You **have got** a nice teacher.
they **have got …**/	they**'ve got …**	*sie haben …*	They **have got** a new flat.

In der gesprochenen Sprache und in manchen Texten findest du statt *have got*/*has got* die Kurzform -*'**ve got**/-'**s got***.
Beispiel: I've got a new T-shirt. She's got a book.

G 9 *have got/has got:* Verneinung — *have got/has got: Negation*

Wenn man sagen will, dass jemand etwas **nicht besitzt** oder dass etwas nicht zu einem Gegenstand gehört, benutzt man ***haven't got/hasn't got***.

Bei *he*, *she* und *it* heißt es natürlich wieder ***hasn't got!***

I **haven't got …**	*ich habe kein …*	I **haven't got** a new book.
you **haven't got …**	*du hast kein …*	You **haven't got** a cool T-shirt.
he **hasn't got …**	*er hat kein …*	He **hasn't got** a new ball.
she **hasn't got …**	*sie hat kein …*	She **hasn't got** a problem.
it **hasn't got …**	*es hat kein …*	It **hasn't got** blue doors.
we **haven't got …**	*wir haben kein …*	We **haven't got** a cafeteria in the school.
you **haven't got …**	*ihr habt kein …*	You **haven't got** a nice teacher.
they **haven't got …**	*sie haben kein …*	They **haven't got** a new flat.

In seltenen Fällen findest du in Texten auch *have not got* und *has not got.*

G 10 *have got/has got:* Fragen und Kurzantworten — *have got/has got: Questions and short answers*

Wenn man fragen will, ob jemand etwas besitzt oder ob etwas zu einem Gegenstand gehört, muss man den Fragesatz mit ***Have*** … oder ***Has*** … beginnen. Für die Antworten gibt es auch hier wieder Kurzformen.

Fragen

Have I **got** a new book?	**Have** I **got** …?	*Habe ich …?*
Have you **got** a pencil?	**Have** you **got** …?	*Hast du …?*
Has he **got** a new ball?	**Has** he **got** …?	*Hat er …?*
Has she **got** a problem?	**Has** she **got** …?	*Hat sie …?*
Has it **got** blue doors?	**Has** it **got** …?	*Hat es …?*
Have we **got** a cafeteria in the school?	**Have** we **got** …?	*Haben wir …?*
Have you **got** a computer?	**Have** you **got** …?	*Habt ihr/Haben Sie …?*
Have they **got** a new flat?	**Have** they **got** …?	*Haben sie …?*

Kurzantworten

🙂		☹	
Yes, I **have.**	*Ja!*	No, I **haven't.**	*Nein!*
Yes, you **have.**		No, you **haven't.**	
Yes, he **has.**		No, he **hasn't.**	
Yes, she **has.**		No, she **hasn't.**	
Yes, it **has.**		No, it **hasn't.**	
Yes, we **have.**		No, we **haven't.**	
Yes, you **have.**		No, you **haven't.**	
Yes, they **have.**		No, they **haven't.**	

G 11 Das Verb *can/can't* — *The verb 'can/can't'*

Mit dem Verb ***can*** kannst du sagen, was du **machen kannst** und was du **machen darfst**. Mit ***can't*** sagst du, was du **nicht machen kannst** oder **darfst**. Es gibt nur die Formen ***can*** und ***can't*** für alle Personen. Die Form ***can*** bildest und verwendest du wie im Deutschen.

I **can** read English texts.		*Ich **kann** englische Texte lesen.*	
She **can** read my comics.		*Sie **darf** meine Comics lesen.*	
We **can** play football.		*Wir **können** Fußball spielen.*	
I **can't** write this word.		*Ich **kann** dieses Wort **nicht** schreiben.*	
She **can't** eat my chocolate.		*Sie **darf** meine Schokolade **nicht** essen.*	
We **can't** ride a horse.		*Wir **können nicht** reiten.*	
Can Sam play the drums?	– Yes, he **can.**	***Kann** Sam Schlagzeug spielen?*	*– Ja!*
	– No, he **can't.**		*– Nein!*
Can you come over?	– Yes, I **can.**	***Darfst** du zu mir rüber kommen?*	*– Ja!*
	– No, I **can't.**		*– Nein!*

Manchmal wird in der geschriebenen Sprache *cannot* statt *can't* verwendet.

G 12 Der Imperativ *The imperative*

Mit dieser Form gibst du **Befehle**, z. B. *Go! Listen!* Beachte aber, dass im englischen Satz aus Gründen der Höflichkeit das Wort ***please*** nicht fehlen sollte. Es steht oft am Ende des Satzes. Mit ***don't*** kannst du etwas verbieten, z. B. *Don't go! Don't talk!* Die Form ändert sich nicht, egal wie viele und welche Leute du ansprichst!

	Put	your bags in my room, please.	*Stellt eure Taschen bitte in mein Zimmer.*
	Bring	your T-shirts, please.	*Bringt bitte eure T-shirts mit.*
	Help	your children with their homework, please.	*Helfen Sie bitte Ihren Kindern bei den Hausaufgaben.*
Don't	**be**	late!	*Kommt bitte nicht zu spät.*
Don't	**bring**	your mobiles.	*Bringt bitte nicht eure Handys (mit her).*
Don't	**do**	the homework for your children, please!	*Machen Sie bitte nicht die Hausaufgaben für Ihre Kinder!*

Don't als Verneinung steht im Englischen immer vor dem Verb. Im Deutschen ist es umgekehrt.
Beispiel: **Don't** go, please! – *Geh* ***nicht****!*

G13 Die einfache Gegenwart — *The simple present*

Mit dem ***simple present*** kannst du ausdrücken, was du **regelmäßig tust**. Du kannst damit auch **Tatsachen** wiedergeben.

I	**play**	music.	*Ich spiele Musik.*
You	**play**	music.	*Du spielst Musik.*
He/She/It	**plays**	music.	*Er/Sie/Es spielt Musik.*
We	**play**	music.	*Wir spielen Musik.*
You	**play**	music.	*Ihr spielt Musik.*
They	**play**	music.	*Sie spielen Musik.*

An die meisten Verben wird bei *he, she, it* ein *-s* angehängt. Es gibt aber auch Ausnahmen. Die musst du einfach lernen.

Beispiele: do → do**es**, finish → finish**es**, wash → wash**es**, watch → watch**es**.

Achtung! Aussprache! She **plays** [z] football.
She **watches** [ɪz] a dog.

G14 Adverbien der Häufigkeit — *Adverbs of frequency*

Wörter wie „immer" – ***always***, „oft" – ***often***, „manchmal" – ***sometimes***, oder „niemals" – ***never*** heißen **Häufigkeitsadverbien**. Damit kannst du ausdrücken, wie häufig etwas passiert.
Diese stehen immer vor dem Verb.

I	sometimes	**eat**	crisps.	*Ich*	***esse***	*manchmal*	*Kartoffelchips.*
We	always	**watch**	MTV.	*Wir*	***sehen***	*immer*	*MTV.*
Tiger	often	**sits**	on the roof.	*Tiger*	***sitzt***	*oft*	*auf dem Dach.*
Emma	never	**plays**	football.	*Emma*	***spielt***	*nie*	*Fußball.*

Vorsicht bei *be* und *can*.
Beispiele: We **are** often in the playground.
We **can** always swim at the club after school.

G 15 Die einfache Gegenwart: Verneinung — *The simple present: Negation*

Wenn du einen Satz **verneinen** willst, setzt du das Hilfsverb ***don't*** oder ***doesn't*** vor das Verb.

I	**don't eat**	chocolate in class.	*Ich esse **keine** Schokolade im Unterricht.*
You	**don't shout**	in class.	*Du schreist **nicht** im Unterricht.*
He	**doesn't do**	his homework.	*Er macht seine Hausaufgaben **nicht**.*
She	**doesn't like**	Mondays.	*Montag **mag** sie **nicht**.*
It	**doesn't start**	here.	*Es fängt hier **nicht** an.*
We	**don't know**	the answer.	*Wir wissen die Antwort **nicht**.*
You	**don't sit**	on a sofa.	*Ihr sitzt / Sie sitzen **nicht** auf einem Sofa.*
They	**don't listen**	to the teacher.	*Sie hören dem Lehrer **nicht** zu.*

Wenn du Sätze mit *he* oder *she* verneinst, so wandert das *-s* vom Vollverb hin zu *doesn't*.
Beispiel: He play**s** football.
↓
He doe**s**n't play basketball.

G16 Die einfache Gegenwart: Entscheidungsfragen/Kurzantworten

The simple present: Questions/short answers

Entscheidungsfragen sind Fragen, die du mit „Ja!" oder „Nein!" beantworten musst. Im Englischen beginnen sie oft mit ***Do*** … oder ***Does*** … (vgl. auch G 5).

Fragen

Do	I **know** you?	***Kenne** ich dich?*
Do	you **live** in London?	***Wohnst** du in London?*
Does	he **work** in London?	***Arbeitet** er in London?*
Does	she **go** to London by bus?	***Fährt** sie mit dem Bus nach London?*
Does	it **stop** here?	***Hält** er hier an?*
Do	we **take** the train or the car?	***Fahren** wir mit dem Auto oder mit dem Zug?*
Do	you **like** your new school in London?	***Mögt** ihr eure/**Mögen** Sie Ihre neue Schule in London?*
Do	they **have** friends in London?	***Haben** sie Freunde in London?*

Kurzantworten

Yes, I **do**.		No, I **don't**.	
Yes, you **do**.		No, you **don't**.	
Yes, he **does**.		No, he **doesn't**.	
Yes, she **does**.	*Ja!*	No, she **doesn't**.	*Nein!*
Yes, we **do**.		No, we **don't**.	
Yes, you **do**.		No, you **don't**.	
Yes, they **do**.		No, they **don't**.	

Beispiel: He likes chocolate.

Does he **like** chocolate?

G 17 Die einfache Gegenwart: Fragen mit Fragewörtern — *The simple present: Questions with question words*

Wenn du nach etwas Bestimmtem fragen möchtest, setzt du das **Fragewort** ganz an den Anfang noch vor ***do/does.***

When	**does**	the museum open?	***Wann*** *macht das Museum auf?*
How	**do**	they get to the Cutty Sark?	***Wie*** *kommen sie zur Cutty Sark?*
Where	**do**	we meet?	***Wo*** *treffen wir uns?*
What	**does**	she write on her worksheet?	***Was*** *schreibt sie auf ihren Arbeitsbogen?*

Wenn im Satz Formen von *be, have/has got, can* vorkommen, können die Fragewörter ohne ***do/does*** direkt vor diesen Wörtern stehen.

Beispiele: **Who are** you?
When have you got time?
How can you say that?

G 18 Objektpronomen — *Object pronouns*

Wörter wie „mich/mir", „dich/dir", „ihn/ihm", … heißen Objektpronomen. Im Englischen gibt es jeweils nur eine Form: ***me, you, him, her, it, us, you, them.***

Can you help **me**?	*Kannst du* ***mir*** *bitte helfen?*
I can see **you**.	*Ich kann* ***dich*** *sehen.*
Do you know **him**?	*Kennst du* ***ihn****?*
I meet **her** every morning.	*Ich treffe* ***sie*** *jeden Morgen.*
Say **it** again, please.	*Sage* ***es*** *bitte noch einmal.*
Can you tell **us** the way, please?	*Können Sie* ***uns*** *bitte sagen, wie wir dorthin kommen?*
Can I take **you** boys home?	*Kann ich* ***euch*** *Jungs nach Hause bringen?*
You can ask **them**.	*Du kannst* ***sie*** *fragen.*

Im Englischen steht das Objektpronomen immer direkt **nach** dem Vollverb.
Beispiel: Can you **see him**? *Kannst du ihn sehen?*

G 19 Mengenangaben — *Expressions of quantity*

Im Englischen werden Mengenangaben zusammen mit dem Wort ***of*** gemacht.

a	**bottle(s)**	**of**	lemonade
two	**packet(s)**		crisps
five	**box(es)**		pencils
nine	**bag(s)**		apples

G 20 Mengenangaben mit *a lot of, much* und *many* — *Expressions with a lot of, much and many*

Mit ***a lot of*** kannst du „**viel**" und „**viele**" ins Englische übersetzen. In Verneinungen verwendest du ***not much*** (nicht viel) und ***not many*** (nicht viele). „Wie viel?" und „Wie viele?" werden immer mit ***How much?*** und ***How many?*** übersetzt.

A lot of children like crisps.	*Viele Kinder mögen Kartoffelchips.*
There is **a lot of** milk here.	*Es gibt hier viel Milch.*
I have**n't** got **much** time.	*Ich habe nicht viel Zeit.*
There are**n't many** apples here.	*Es gibt nicht viele Äpfel hier.*

Many findest du manchmal mit Pluralformen ohne *not*:
Beispiel: Many people work in London but don't live here.
Hier heißt *many* „etliche" oder „viele verschiedene".

G 21 Die Verlaufsform der Gegenwart — *The present progressive*

Wenn du sagen willst, was du **gerade tust**, verwendest du im Englischen das ***present progressive***. Diese Form gibt es im Deutschen nicht. Oft wird „gerade", „im Moment" oder „jetzt" bei der Übersetzung eingefügt: *She's doing* her homework. Sie macht gerade ihre Hausaufgaben.

I'**m**	eat**ing**	crisps.	*Ich esse **gerade** Kartoffelchips.*
You'**re**	clos**ing**	the window.	*Du schließt **gerade** das Fenster.*
He'**s**	sleep**ing**	on the sofa.	*Er schläft **im Moment** auf dem Sofa.*
She'**s**	sing**ing**	a song.	*Sie singt **gerade** ein Lied.*
It'**s**	rain**ing**	now.	*Es regnet **gerade**.*
We'**re**	play**ing**	cards.	*Wir spielen **im Moment** Karten.*
You'**re**	mak**ing**	too much noise.	*Ihr macht **gerade** zu viel Lärm.*
They'**re**	danc**ing**	on the table.	*Sie tanzen **jetzt** auf dem Tisch.*

Vorsicht beim Schreiben!
Ein stummes *-e* am Ende des Verbs entfällt.
Bei manchen Verben verdoppelt sich der letzte Buchstabe.

make	+	**ing**	=	making
skate	+	**ing**	=	skating
dance	+	**ing**	=	dancing
sit	+	**ing**	=	sitting
get	+	**ing**	=	getting
put	+	**ing**	=	putting

G 22 Die Verlaufsform der Gegenwart: Fragen/Kurzantworten

The present progressive: Questions/short answers

Wenn du im ***present progressive*** eine Frage stellen willst, beginnst du die Frage mit ***Am …***, ***Is …*** oder ***Are …***. Wenn du auf eine Frage antwortest, können ***Yes.*** oder ***No.*** allein manchmal etwas unhöflich klingen. Deshalb antwortest du meistens mit einem verkürzten Satz, einer so genannten Kurzantwort.

Fragen

Am I using the right computer?	*Benutze ich gerade den richtigen Computer?*
Are you having problems?	*Hast du gerade Probleme?*
Is he looking for his mobile?	*Sucht er jetzt sein Handy?*
Is she taking Mark to school?	*Bringt sie gerade Mark in die Schule?*
Is it raining?	*Regnet es gerade?*
Are we making too much noise?	*Machen wir im Moment zu viel Lärm?*
Are you having fun?	*Habt ihr Spaß dabei?*
Are they eating the flowers?	*Fressen sie gerade die Blumen?*

Kurzantworten

Yes, **I am.**		No, **I'm not.**	
Yes, **you are.**		No, **you aren't.**	
Yes, **he is.**		No, **he isn't.**	
Yes, **she is.**	*Ja.*	No, **she isn't.**	*Nein.*
Yes, **it is.**		No, **it isn't.**	
Yes, **we are.**		No, **we aren't.**	
Yes, **you are.**		No, **you aren't.**	
Yes, **they are.**		No, **they aren't.**	

Manche Verben haben keine *present progressive*-Form. Da musst du die *simple present*-Form verwenden, z. B. *can, have got, mean, want to.*

Beispiele:	I can help you now.	*Ich kann dir jetzt helfen.*
	We have got a lot to do.	*Wir haben gerade viel zu tun.*
	What do you mean?	*Was meinst du damit?*
	Where does he want to go?	*Wo will er hinfahren?*

G 23 Die Verlaufsform der Gegenwart: Verneinung

The present progressive: Negation

Wenn du die Verlaufsform der Gegenwart verneinen willst, verneinst du einfach die Form des Verbs ***be***. Die ***-ing***-Form bleibt unverändert.

I **am not** /	I **'m not**	jok**ing**.	*Ich scherze nicht.*
You **are not** /	You **aren't**	watch**ing** TV.	*Du siehst gerade nicht fern.*
He **is not** /	He **isn't**	draw**ing** a picture.	*Er malt gerade kein Bild.*
She **is not** /	She **isn't**	help**ing** him.	*Sie hilft ihm nicht.*
It **is not** /	It **isn't**	rain**ing** now.	*Es regnet im Moment nicht.*
We **are not** /	We **aren't**	leav**ing** the bags here.	*Wir lassen die Taschen nicht hier.*
You **are not** /	You **aren't**	listen**ing**!	*Ihr hört nicht zu!*
They **are not** /	They **aren't**	eat**ing** the flowers.	*Sie fressen die Blumen nicht.*

Die Kurzformen *you're not, he's not, …* hörst du auch, vor allem in der gesprochenen Sprache.

G 24 This/that – *these/those*

This verwendest du für Dinge, die in deiner Nähe sind. – ***This*** *book* ***here***. Für Dinge, die weiter entfernt sind, verwendest du ***that***. – ***That*** *house* ***over there***. ***These*** und ***those*** sind die Pluralformen.

Einzahl	Mehrzahl	Signalwort	
this	these	here	*das/dies(e) hier*
that	those	over there	*das/die dort*

Stehen diese Wörter vor einer Form von *be*, wird wegen des Sprechflusses *that* immer mit der Kurzform gebraucht:
Beispiel: **That's** my old box.
Aber: **This is** my new tent and **these/those are** my sleeping bags.

Grammatical terms

(Lateinisch) / Deutsch	Englisch	Englisches Beispiel
Adverb / Umstandswort **G14**	adverb	always, often, sometimes, never
Apostroph **G7**	apostrophe	I'm, you're, here's
Besitzangaben mit *have got/has got* **G8**	possessive form with have got/has got	You have got a cool T-shirt.
Besitzangaben mit *-'s* **G7**	possessive form with -'s	Emma's sister, the Taylors' house
hinweisende Fürwörter	demonstrative pronouns	this, that, these, those
Entscheidungsfragen **G16**	'yes/no'-questions	Do you like computers?
Frage **G5, G6, G10, G17, G22**	question	What's your name? Are you Tom?
Fragewort **G6, G17**	question word	Who? What? When? Where? How?
Häufigkeitsadverb **G14**	adverb of frequency	always, often, sometimes, never
Hilfsverb **G8, G11, G12, G15–17, G21–23**	auxiliary	be, have got, do, can
Imperativ / Befehlsform **G12**	imperative	Don't talk! Listen, please.
Infinitiv / Grundform des Verbs	infinitive	to do, to go, to see
Konsonant / Mitlaut **G21**	consonant	b, d, k, l, r, n
Kurzantwort **G5, G10, G16, G22**	short answer	Yes, I am. No, he isn't.
Kurzform **G2, G4, G8**	short form	I'm, we're, she's got
Langform **G2, G4, G8**	long form	I am, we are, she has got
Mengenangaben **G19, G20**	expressions of quantity	a lot of, much, many, a bottle of
Objektpronomen **G18**	object pronoun	me, you, him, her, it, us, them
Personalpronomen / persönliches Fürwort **G1, G5**	personal pronoun	I, you, he, she, it, we, you, they
Plural / Mehrzahl **G3, G20, G24**	plural	girls, children, books
Possessivbegleiter / besitzanzeigendes Fürwort	possessive pronoun	my, your, his, her, its, our, your, their
Präsens / einfache Gegenwart **G13, G15–17**	simple present	I live in Greenwich.
Singular / Einzahl **G3, G24**	singular	a girl, a boy, a book
Substantiv / Hauptwort **G3**	noun	book, dog, sandwich
Verb / Tätigkeitswort **G2, G11–13, G15–17, G21–23**	verb	to be, to go, to do, to write
Verlaufsform der Gegenwart **G21–G23**	present progressive	We are having a party.
Verneinung **G4, G9, G15, G23**	negation	I'm not finding this easy.
Vokal / Selbstlaut	vowel	a, e, i, o, u
Vollverb **G18**	verb	to go, to do, to write

Vocabulary

Auf den folgenden Seiten findest du alle neuen englischen Wörter und Ausdrücke. Sie stehen in der Reihenfolge, wie sie im Buch vorkommen.
Diese Wortliste ist in drei Spalten aufgeteilt:

- Links stehen die englischen Wörter und Sätze.
- In der Mitte werden sie übersetzt.
- Rechts findest du Beispiele, Erklärungen und Tipps, die dir beim Lernen helfen.

Die fett gedruckten Wörter musst du lernen. Normal gedruckte Wörter solltest du wiedererkennen, wenn du sie hörst oder liest.
Gleich nach jedem neuen englischen Wort steht die Lautschrift in eckigen Klammern. Sie zeigt dir, wie das neue Wort ausgesprochen wird. Wie du diese Lautzeichen liest, siehst du unten.

Englische Laute

Mitlaute

[b]	bed	[p]	picture
[d]	day	[r]	red
[ð]	the	[s]	six
[f]	family	[ʃ]	she
[g]	go	[t]	ten
[ŋ]	morning	[tʃ]	lunch
[h]	house	[v]	video
[j]	you	[w]	we, one
[k]	can, milk	[z]	easy
[l]	letter	[ʒ]	revision
[m]	man	[dʒ]	page
[n]	no	[θ]	thank you

Selbstlaute

[ɑ:]	car
[æ]	apple
[e]	pen
[ə]	again
[ɜ:]	girl
[ʌ]	but
[ɪ]	it
[i]	happy
[i:]	teacher
[ɒ]	dog
[ɔ:]	ball
[ʊ]	book
[u]	January
[u:]	too, two

Doppellaute

[aɪ]	I, my
[aʊ]	now, mouse
[eɪ]	name, they
[eə]	there, pair
[ɪə]	here, idea
[əʊ]	hello
[ɔɪ]	boy
[ʊə]	sure

[:] der vorangehende Laut ist lang, z. B. *you* [ju:] [ˈ] die folgende Silbe wird betont, z. B. *hello* [heˈləʊ]

Tipps zum Vokabellernen findest du in den Kästen zu Beginn jeder *unit* sowie auf den *wordwise*-Seiten.
Am Ende der *units* kannst du nützliche Ausdrücke für deinen *folder* sammeln, mit denen du dich auf Englisch verständigen kannst.
Es gibt auch noch *word games*. Dies sind kleine Aufgaben, Rätsel und Wortspiele, in denen du die neuen Wörter üben kannst.

Auf das *vocabulary* folgt das *dictionary*, eine alphabetische Wortliste aller englischen Wörter in dem Buch. Wenn du ein Wort nicht verstehst, kannst du es hier nachschlagen.

Abkürzungen und Zeichen

pl	Plural, Mehrzahl	!	Achtung!
sing	Singular, Einzahl	↔	ist das Gegenteil von
10	Auf dieser Seite kommen die Wörter vor.	→	ist verwandt mit
		=	entspricht

! *Homework* hat keine Mehrzahl.
old ↔ new
teach → teacher
Dear Sam = Lieber Sam

Unit 1 Thomas Tallis School

Lerntipp: So geht's los.

Mit dem Lernen fängst du so an: Lies dir das englische Wort, die deutsche Übersetzung und das, was in der rechten Spalte dazu steht, genau durch. Danach deckst du die mittlere und die rechte Spalte ab. Weißt du noch, was das englische Wort auf deutsch heißt?
Du kannst natürlich auch die linke Spalte abdecken und versuchen, ob du das englische Wort noch weißt.
Auch das Aufschreiben und das laute Vorsagen der englischen Wörter helfen dir beim Lernen.

10	**Hello!** [heˈləʊ]	Hallo! →	
	I'm [aɪm]	ich bin	
	I [aɪ]	ich →	! *I* schreibst du immer groß.
	My name is .... [maɪ ˈneɪm‿ɪz]	Ich heiße	
	my [maɪ]	mein/meine	
	name [neɪm]	Name →	! Merk dir bei *name:* Hauptwörter schreibst du immer klein.
	is [ɪz]	ist	
	eleven [ɪˈlevn]	elf	
	from [frɒm]	aus, von	
	in [ɪn]	in, auf; herein	
	new [nju:]	neu →	
	school [sku:l]	Schule	
	year [jɪə]	Jahr, Jahrgangsstufe	
	seven [sevn]	sieben →	I'm in Year *Seven.*
	Hi! [haɪ]	Hi!	
	twelve [twelv]	zwölf	
	a, an [ə; ən]	ein/eine →	! Vor a, e, i, o, u wird *a* zu *an.*
	pupil [ˈpju:pl]	Schüler/Schülerin →	! *Pupil* heißt „Schülerin" oder „Schüler".
	at [æt; ət]	in, auf, bei, an →	Lisa is a pupil *at* Thomas Tallis School.
	too [tu:]	auch →	! Satzstellung: I'm from Greenwich, *too.*
	Let's .... [lets]	Lasst uns	
	to **talk** [tɔ:k]	sprechen, reden →	Das *to* vor dem Verb brauchst du nicht zu lernen.
	ten [ten]	zehn	
	five [faɪv]	fünf	
	mouse [maʊs]	Maus →	
	one [wʌn]	eins; ein/eine	
11	**What's your name?** [ˌwɒts jə ˈneɪm]	Wie heißt du? →	! *'s* ist eine Abkürzung von *is.*
	what [wɒt]	was	
	your [jɔ:]	dein/deine, euer/eure, Ihr/Ihre	
	Where are you from? [ˌweər‿ə jə ˈfrɒm]	Woher kommst du?	

where [weə]	wo, wohin →	
are [ɑː]	bist, seid, sind	
you [juː; jə]	du, ihr, Sie	
How old are you? [haʊ‿ˈəʊld‿ɑː juː]	Wie alt bist du?	
how [haʊ]	wie	
old [əʊld]	alt →	*old* ↔ new
to **listen** [ˈlɪsn]	zuhören, anhören →	Achtung Aussprache! Das „t" ist stumm.
phone number [ˈfəʊn ˌnʌmbə]	Telefonnummer →	What's your *phone number*?
phone [fəʊn]	Telefon →	*Phone* ist kurz für *telephone*.
number [ˈnʌmbə]	Nummer, Zahl	
and [ænd]	und →	Lisa *and* Terry are new at TTS.
to write [raɪt]	schreiben	
the [ðə; ði]	der/die/das →	! Vor a, e, i, o, u sprichst du *the* so: [ði].
home [həʊm]	Zuhause, Heim; nach Hause	
mobile [ˈməʊbaɪl]	Handy, Mobiltelefon →	! Handy heißt auf Englisch *mobile*.

Numbers 1–12

1	**one** [wʌn]	5	**five** [faɪv]	9	**nine** [naɪn]
2	**two** [tuː]	6	**six** [sɪks]	10	**ten** [ten]
3	**three** [θriː]	7	**seven** [ˈsevn]	11	**eleven** [ɪˈlevn]
4	**four** [fɔː]	8	**eight** [eɪt]	12	**twelve** [twelv]

to **say** [seɪ]	sagen, sprechen →	*Say* hello.
or [ɔː]	oder	
English [ˈɪŋglɪʃ]	englisch →	! *I'm English.* = „Ich bin Engländer." oder „Ich bin Engländerin."
for [fɔː]	für →	! Gleiche Aussprache: *for* - four
folder [ˈfəʊldə]	Ordner, Mappe	
to **make** [meɪk]	machen, tun	
poster [ˈpəʊstə]	Poster, Plakat →	Let's make a *poster*.

Language

12	**sport** [spɔːt]	Sport	
	it [ɪt]	es	
	big [bɪg]	groß →	BIG
	here [hɪə]	hier →	Hello, I'm *here*.
	he [hiː]	er	
	this [ðɪs]	dies; diese/dieser/dieses →	*This* is Emma.
	she [ʃiː]	sie →	*she* ↔ he
	yes [jes]	ja	
	to **look** [lʊk]	sehen, schauen, aussehen	
	Mrs [ˈmɪsɪz]	Frau (*Anrede*)	
	teacher [ˈtiːtʃə]	Lehrer/Lehrerin →	
	favourite [ˈfeɪvrɪt]	Lieblings- →	Mrs Carter is my *favourite* teacher.
	football [ˈfʊtbɔːl]	Fußball	

	goal [gəʊl]	Tor, Ziel	
	no [nəʊ]	nein, nicht; kein/keine →	yes ↔ *no*
	shoe [ʃu:]	Schuh →	Achtung Schreibung!
	sorry ['sɒri]	Tut mir Leid. Entschuldigung. →	I'm *sorry.*
	that [ðæt]	das, jenes	
	OK [əʊ'keɪ]	OK →	That's *OK.*
	thank you ['θæŋk‿ju:]	danke	
	Mr ['mɪstə]	Herr *(Anrede)*	
	caretaker ['keəteɪkə]	Hausmeister/Hausmeisterin →	Mr Newman 
	nice [naɪs]	nett →	Mrs Carter is *nice.*
13	example ['ɪgza:mpl]	Beispiel	
	Go on, please. ['gəʊ‿ɒn pli:z]	Mach/Macht bitte weiter.	
	sentence ['sentənts]	Satz	
	to match [mætʃ]	zuordnen, zusammenfügen	
	tip [tɪp]	Tipp	
	quiz [kwɪz]	Quiz, Rätsel	
	right [raɪt]	richtig, korrekt →	That's *right.*
	about [ə'baʊt]	über	
14	**school bag** ['sku:l bæg]	Schultasche, Schulranzen →	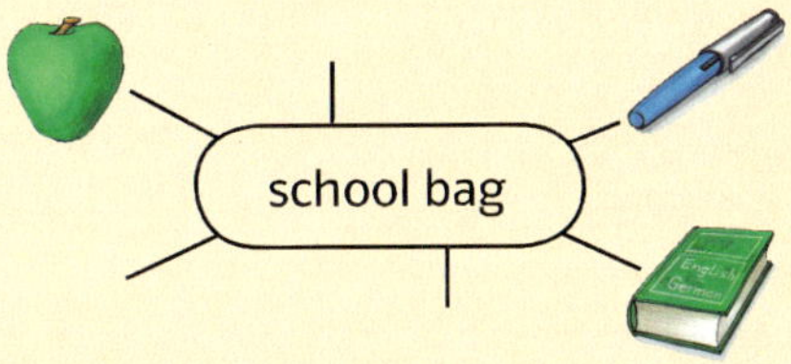
	bag [bæg]	Tasche, Tüte	
	to copy ['kɒpi]	abschreiben, kopieren	
	grid [grɪd]	Gitter, Tabelle	
	into ['ɪntə]	in; in … hinein	
	exercise book ['eksəsaɪz ˌbʊk]	Heft, Übungsheft →	Achtung Schreibung!
	to fill in [fɪl‿'ɪn]	ausfüllen, einsetzen	
	pencil case ['pensl ˌkeɪs]	Mäppchen	
	pen [pen]	Füller	
	pencil ['pensl]	Bleistift →	*pencil* → pencil case
	rubber ['rʌbə]	Radiergummi	
	ruler ['ru:lə]	Lineal	
	book [bʊk]	Buch	
	sandwich ['sænwɪdʒ]	Sandwich, belegtes Brot →	Mmm, a *sandwich.* 
	apple ['æpl]	Apfel	
	to look at ['lʊk‿ət]	ansehen	
	on [ɒn]	auf, an →	What's the name *on* the bag?
	picture ['pɪktʃə]	Bild →	What's in the *picture*?

Numbers 13–100

13	**thirteen** [θɜ:'ti:n]	20	**twenty** ['twenti]	40	**forty** ['fɔ:ti]
14	**fourteen** [fɔ:'ti:n]	21	**twenty-one** ['twenti'wʌn]	50	**fifty** ['fɪfti]
15	**fifteen** [fɪf'ti:n]	22	**twenty-two** ['twenti'tu:]	60	**sixty** ['sɪksti]
16	**sixteen** [sɪks'ti:n]	23	**twenty-three** ['twenti'θri:]	70	**seventy** ['sevnti]
17	**seventeen** [sevn'ti:n]	24	**twenty-four** ['twenti'fɔ:]	80	**eighty** ['eɪti]
18	**eighteen** [eɪ'ti:n]	…		90	**ninety** ['naɪnti]
19	**nineteen** [naɪn'ti:n]	30	**thirty** ['θɜ:ti]	100	**one hundred** [wʌn'hʌndrəd]

	to **play** [pleɪ]	spielen →	Let's *play*.
	all [ɔ:l]	alle/alles; ganz	
	with [wɪð]	mit	
15	sound [saʊnd]	Ton, Geräusch, Klang	
	alphabet ['ælfəbet]	Alphabet, Abc →	the *alphabet*

The alphabet

a [eɪ]	**e** [i:]	**i** [aɪ]	**m** [em]	**q** [kju:]	**u** [ju:]	**y** [waɪ]
b [bi:]	**f** [ef]	**j** [dʒeɪ]	**n** [en]	**r** [ɑ:]	**v** [vi:]	**z** [zed]
c [si:]	**g** [dʒi:]	**k** [keɪ]	**o** [əʊ]	**s** [es]	**w** ['dʌblju:]	
d [di:]	**h** [eɪtʃ]	**l** [el]	**p** [pi:]	**t** [ti:]	**x** [eks]	

	rap [ræp]	Rap	
	lesson ['lesn]	Unterrichtsstunde →	English *lessons* are OK.
	to **shout** [ʃaʊt]	schreien, rufen	
	to **clap** [klæp]	klatschen	
	to **do** [du:]	machen, tun →	Let's *do* a rap. = Lasst uns rappen.
	word [wɜ:d]	Wort	
	to read [ri:d]	lesen	
	to spell [spel]	buchstabieren	
	puzzle ['pʌzl]	Rätsel, Puzzle	
	partner ['pɑ:tnə]	Partner/Partnerin →	You're my *partner.*
	letter ['letə]	Buchstabe, Brief →	L-E-T-T-E-R-S and a *letter*
16	**we** [wi:]	wir	
	classroom ['klɑ:srʊm]	Klassenzimmer	
	class [klɑ:s]	Schulklasse, Klasse	
	room [ru:m]	Zimmer, Raum, Platz	
	sure [ʃʊə]	sicher →	Are you *sure*?
	who [hu:]	wer →	*Who*'s Sam? – He's my friend.
	friend [frend]	Freund/Freundin	
	always ['ɔ:lweɪz]	immer, ständig	
	late [leɪt]	spät, zu spät, verspätet →	He's always *late*.
	you're lucky ['jʊə'lʌki]	du hast Glück	
	lucky ['lʌki]	glücklich	
	not [nɒt]	nicht →	I'm *not* from Greenwich.
	they [ðeɪ]	sie *(Mehrzahl)*	
	What's up? [ˌwɒts‿'ʌp]	Was ist los?	
	bye [baɪ]	tschüss →	
	Good Morning! ['gʊd 'mɔ:nɪŋ]	Guten Morgen!	
	good [gʊd]	gut	
	morning ['mɔ:nɪŋ]	Morgen, Vormittag	
	boy [bɔɪ]	Junge	
	girl [gɜ:l]	Mädchen →	a *girl* and a *boy*
	wrong [rɒŋ]	falsch →	right ↔ *wrong*
	people ['pi:pl]	Leute, Menschen	
	long form ['lɒŋ fɔ:m]	Langform	
17	question ['kwestʃn]	Frage	

	answer ['ɑ:ntsə]	Antwort	
	game [geɪm]	Spiel	
	German ['dʒɜ:mən]	deutsch; Deutsche/ Deutscher →	! Nationalitäten schreibst du immer groß.
18	**playground** ['pleɪgraʊnd]	Schulhof, Spielplatz →	The pupils are in the *playground*.
	table ['teɪbl]	Tisch	
	lunch [lʌntʃ]	Mittagessen →	The sandwich is for my *lunch*.
	behind [bɪ'haɪnd]	hinter	
	door [dɔ:]	Tür	
	under ['ʌndə]	unter →	on ↔ *under*
	chair [tʃeə]	Stuhl	
	crisp [krɪsp]	Kartoffelchip	
	cupboard ['kʌbəd]	Küchenschrank, Schrank →	Achtung Schreibung!
	chocolate ['tʃɒklət]	Schokolade →	Achtung Schreibung!
	window ['wɪndəʊ]	Fenster	
	board [bɔ:d]	Tafel, Wandtafel →	
	desk [desk]	Schreibtisch	
	wall [wɔ:l]	Wand, Mauer	
	to point [pɔɪnt]	zeigen	
19	phrase [freɪz]	Redewendung, Ausdruck	
	to **sit down** [sɪt 'daʊn]	sich setzen, sich hinsetzen	
	please [pli:z]	bitte →	Sit down, *please*.
	can [kæn]	können, dürfen	
	to **open** ['əʊpən]	öffnen, aufmachen →	Can we *open* the window?
	of course [əv 'kɔ:s]	natürlich, selbstverständlich →	Can you say the abc? – *Of course* I can!
	page [peɪdʒ]	Seite →	Open your books at *page* 11, please.
	exercise ['eksəsaɪz]	Übung, Aufgabe →	We're on page 19, *exercise* 6.
	homework ['həʊmwɜ:k]	Hausaufgabe/ Hausaufgaben →	! *Homework* hat keine Mehrzahl.
	You're welcome. [jʊə 'welkəm]	Bitte sehr!, Gern geschehen! →	
	goodbye [gʊd'baɪ]	auf Wiedersehen	
	to **go** [gəʊ]	gehen	
	to [tʊ; tə]	zu, nach, bis	
	toilet ['tɔɪlɪt]	Toilette →	Can I go to the *toilet*, please?
	lunchtime ['lʌntʃtaɪm]	Mittag, Mittagszeit →	lunch → *lunchtime*

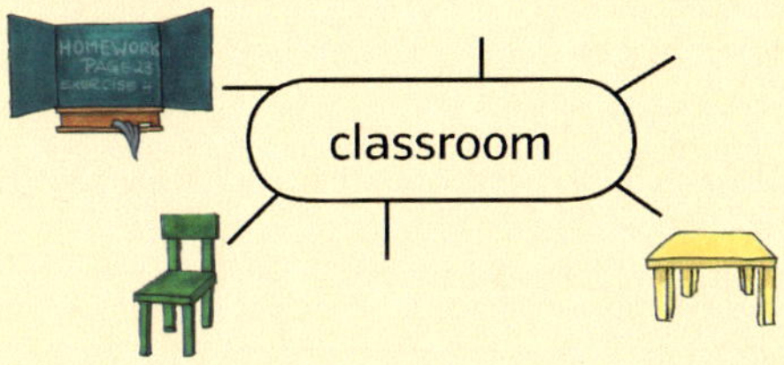

Story

20	**problem** ['prɒbləm]	Problem, Schwierigkeit →	No *problem*!
	cafeteria [ˌkæfə'tɪəriə]	Cafeteria	
	cool [ku:l]	cool, prima →	School is *cool*!
	joke [dʒəʊk]	Witz	
	easy ['i:zi]	einfach, leicht →	
	boring ['bɔ:rɪŋ]	langweilig →	Your joke is *boring*.
	very ['veri]	sehr →	You are *very* nice.
	now [naʊ]	jetzt, nun →	Lisa is in the playground *now*.
	Here you are! ['hɪə ju:‿ɑ:]	Bitte schön!	

	I'm good at ... ['aɪm gʊd‿ət]	ich bin gut in ... →
	ball [bɔ:l]	Ball
	tree [tri:]	Baum →
21	**idiot** ['ɪdɪət]	Idiot, Dummkopf
	story ['stɔ:ri]	Geschichte, Erzählung →
	order ['ɔ:də]	Reihenfolge, Ordnung
	to sort [sɔ:t]	sortieren
	to act [ækt]	spielen (Theater)
	group [gru:p]	Gruppe
	then [ðen]	dann
22	word star ['wɜ:d stɑ:]	Wortstern
	pair [peə]	Paar
	to find [faɪnd]	finden
	adjective ['ædʒəktɪv]	Adjektiv, Eigenschaftswort
23	to **be** [bi:]	sein

I'm good at football.

This is a good *story*.

For my folder: Hello

Schreibe alle Ausdrücke *(phrases)*, die du zum Thema Begrüßung gelernt hast, auf ein Blatt Papier. Lege es in deinem *English folder* ab. Lass dahinter Platz für weitere *phrases*, damit du deine Redemittelsammlung im Laufe des Schuljahres ergänzen kannst.
So kannst du anfangen. Schreibe noch mehr Ausdrücke dazu.

Begrüßung
Hi!
My name is ...
...

Word game

Manchmal hörst oder liest du ein englisches Wort, das sich ähnlich anhört oder schreibt wie ein deutsches Wort. Manche kennst du schon, z. B. *computer*, *skateboard*, *T-shirt*. Diese Wörter haben die gleiche Bedeutung im Englischen und im Deutschen. Schau dir folgende neue englische Wörter an und ordne sie den deutschen Wörtern zu.

hand	Kostüm
finger	Lampe
paper	Eis
costume	Hand
glass	Papier
hair	Glas
ice	Finger
lamp	Haar

Link-up A Home sweet home

24	**sweet** [swi:t]	süß
	purple ['pɜ:pl]	lila, violett
	yellow ['jeləʊ]	gelb →
	black [blæk]	schwarz
	white [waɪt]	weiß
	red [red]	rot
	green [gri:n]	grün

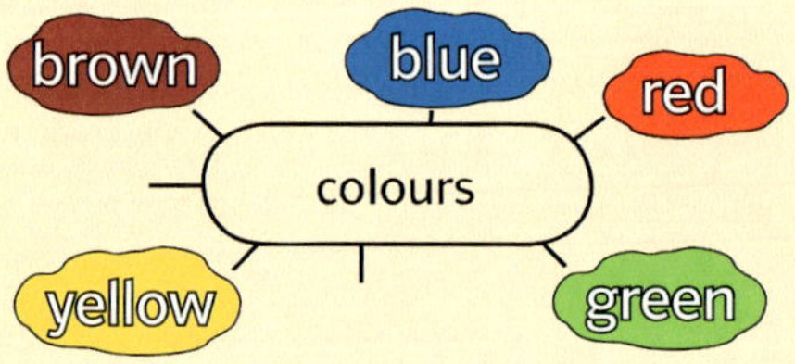

	pink [pɪŋk]	pink, rosa
	blue [blu:]	blau
	brown [braʊn]	braun
	card [kɑ:d]	Karte
	per [pɜ:]	pro
	bedroom ['bedrʊm]	Schlafzimmer →
	living room ['lɪvɪŋ rʊm]	Wohnzimmer →
	kitchen ['kɪtʃɪn]	Küche
	dining room ['daɪnɪŋ rʊm]	Esszimmer, Speisesaal
	bathroom ['bɑ:θrʊm]	Bad, Badezimmer →
	to show [ʃəʊ]	zeigen
	colour ['kʌlə]	Farbe →
	to ask [ɑ:sk]	fragen
	to close [kləʊz]	schließen, zumachen
	to answer ['ɑ:ntsə]	antworten, beantworten
25	rhyme [raɪm]	Reim
	bed [bed]	Bett
	tiny ['taɪni]	winzig
	sofa ['səʊfə]	Sofa, Couch →
	funny ['fʌni]	komisch, lustig
	house [haʊs]	Haus
	TV [ˌti:'vi:]	Fernsehen, Fernseher
	computer [ˌkəm'pju:tə]	Computer
	furniture ['fɜ:nɪtʃə]	Möbel →
	dream [dri:m]	Traum →
	to draw [drɔ:]	zeichnen
	to put [pʊt]	setzen, stellen, legen
	his [hɪz]	sein/seine
	family ['fæmli]	Familie →
	brother ['brʌðə]	Bruder
	mum [mʌm]	Mama, Mutti
	sister ['sɪstə]	Schwester
	grandad ['grændæd]	Opa
	dad [dæd]	Papa, Vati
	grandma ['grændmɑ:]	Oma

a *bedroom* 

! Du schreibst *bedroom* und *bathroom*, aber *living room* und *dining room*.

a *bathroom* 

What's your favourite *colour*?

! *Furniture* hat keine Mehrzahl.
My *dream* house is yellow.

Unit 2 At home in Greenwich

Lerntipp: Dein Arbeitsplatz

Am besten lernst du die Vokabeln in Ruhe zu Hause. Setze dich nach Möglichkeit immer an den gleichen Arbeitsplatz. Versuche einen Platz zu finden, an dem du möglichst ungestört arbeiten kannst. Lege dir schon vor dem Lernen alles zurecht, was du dafür brauchst: dein Schreibzeug, deine Hefte und Bücher.

26	**at home** [ət 'həʊm]	zu Hause →	Terry is *at home*.
	parents ['peərənts]	Eltern →	mum and dad = *parents*
	half-sister ['hɑ:fˌsɪstə]	Halbschwester	
	so [səʊ]	so, also, deshalb	
	her [hɜ:]	ihr/ihre; sie →	*Her* parents are OK.
	stepdad ['stepdæd]	Stiefvater	
	manager ['mænɪdʒə]	Manager/Managerin →	My mum is a *manager*.
	shop [ʃɒp]	Laden, Geschäft →	Let's go to the computer *shop*.
	our ['aʊə]	unser/unsere	
	flat [flæt]	Wohnung	
	over ['əʊvə]	über →	The flat is *over* the shop.
	small [smɔ:l]	klein →	*small* ↔ big
	but [bʌt]	aber	
	great [greɪt]	großartig, toll	
	game [geɪm]	Spiel →	Let's play a computer *game*.
	there [ðeə]	dort, da	
	only child ['əʊnli ˌtʃaɪld]	Einzelkind →	Terry is an *only child*.
	child, children *(pl)* [tʃaɪld, 'tʃɪldrən]	Kind →	! one *child* – two *children*
	cat [kæt]	Katze →	a *cat* 
	place [pleɪs]	Platz, Stelle, Ort	
	roof [ru:f]	Dach	
	of [ɒv; əv]	von	
	shed [ʃed]	Schuppen	
	garden ['gɑ:dn]	Garten	
	drums [drʌmz]	Schlagzeug →	Can you play the *drums*?
	Keep out! [ki:p‿'aʊt]	Eintritt verboten!	
	sign [saɪn]	Schild, Zeichen	
	only ['əʊnli]	nur, bloß, erst →	The apple is *only* for Tom. He's *only* one.
	tiger ['taɪgə]	Tiger	
27	**dog** [dɒg]	Hund →	a *dog* 
	text [tekst]	Text	
	to **come over** [kʌm‿'əʊvə]	herüberkommen	
	again [ə'gen]	wieder	
	thing [θɪŋ]	Sache, Ding	
	to **add** [æd]	hinzufügen	
	upstairs [ʌp'steəz]	oben, im oberen Stock	
	downstairs [daʊn'steəz]	unten, im unteren Stock →	upstairs ↔ *downstairs*

Language

28	**married to** ['mærid tə]	verheiratet mit →	Tim is *married to* Maria.
	divorced from [dɪ'vɔ:st frəm]	geschieden von →	David is *divorced from* Elena.
	aunt [ɑ:nt]	Tante →	! Als Name schreibst du *aunt* groß, z. B.: *Aunt* Maria.
	uncle ['ʌŋkl]	Onkel	
	cousin ['kʌzn]	Cousin/Cousine →	Susan is my *cousin*.
	family tree ['fæmli tri:]	Familienstammbaum	
	on the right [ɒn ðə 'raɪt]	rechts →	David is *on* his mum's *right*.
	on the left [ɒn ðə 'left]	links →	*on the left* ↔ on the right
	next to ['nekst tə]	neben	
29	**well** [wel]	also, na ja, nun gut →	*Well*, my family's name is Pilch.
	Polish ['pəʊlɪʃ]	polnisch →	! Nationalitäten schreibst du groß!
	England ['ɪŋglənd]	England →	London is in *England*.
	Greece [gri:s]	Griechenland	
	Greek [gri:k]	griechisch; Grieche/Griechin →	*Greek* → Greece
	Italian [ɪ'tæliən]	italienisch; Italiener/Italienerin →	Achtung Schreibung!
	Italy ['ɪtəli]	Italien →	Italian → *Italy*
	today [tə'deɪ]	heute →	He's at school *today*.
	country, countries *(pl)* ['kʌntri, 'kʌntriz]	Land →	! one *country* – two *countries*
	people ['pi:pl]	Leute, Menschen	
	Poland ['pəʊlənd]	Polen	
	language ['læŋgwɪdʒ]	Sprache	
	flag [flæg]	Flagge, Fahne →	
	Russia ['rʌʃə]	Russland	
	Russian ['rʌʃn]	russisch; Russe/Russin	
	Turkey ['tɜ:ki]	Türkei	
	Turkish ['tɜ:kɪʃ]	türkisch	
	Germany ['dʒɜ:məni]	Deutschland	
	more [mɔ:]	mehr →	Can you say *more*?
30	**trouble** [trʌbl]	Schwierigkeiten, Ärger →	You're in *trouble*.
	to **have got** [hæv 'gɒt]	besitzen, haben	
	their [ðeə]	ihr/ihre →	! Gleiche Aussprache: *their* – they're.

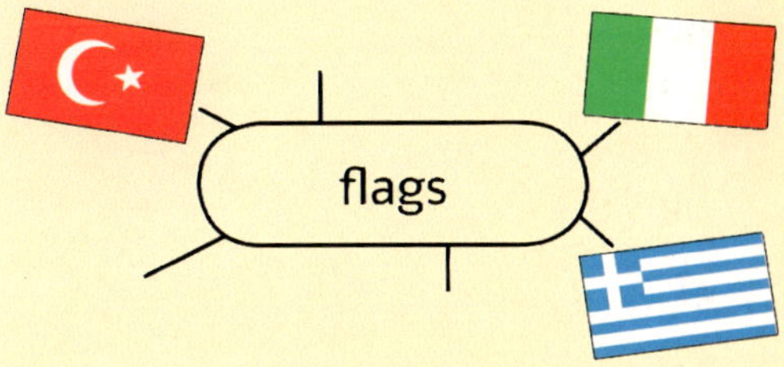

My, your, his, her, our, their

Mit diesen Wörtern kannst du Besitzverhältnisse ausdrücken:

my	mein/meine	***My*** brother and ***my*** parents are in the garden.
your	dein/deine, euer/eure, Ihr/Ihre	***Your*** friends are nice. ***Your*** teacher is OK.
his	sein/seine	***His*** drums are in ***his*** shed.
her	ihr/ihre	***Her*** sisters are in ***her*** grandma's house.
our	unser/unsere	***Our*** flat is over ***our*** shop.
their	ihr/ihre	***Their*** uncle and ***their*** cousins are from Greece.

	wardrobe ['wɔ:drəʊb]	Kleiderschrank, Garderobe	
	a lot of [ə 'lɒt‿əv]	viel/viele, eine Menge →	I've got *a lot of* friends.
	time [taɪm]	Zeit →	She hasn't got a lot of *time*.
	outside [aʊt'saɪd]	außerhalb, draußen, nach draußen →	The pupils are *outside*.
	to **be in a hurry** [bi: ɪn‿ə 'hʌri]	es eilig haben →	She's *in a hurry*.
	T-shirt ['ti:ʃɜ:t]	T-Shirt	
	What about ...? [wɒt‿ə'baʊt]	Was ist mit ...? Wie wäre es mit ...? →	
	Hurry up! [ˌhʌri‿'ʌp]	Beeil dich! →	You're late. *Hurry up!*
	shelf, shelves *(pl)* [ʃelf; ʃelvz]	Regal, Regalbrett →	! one *shelf* – two *shelves*
	second ['seknd]	Sekunde	
	mark [mɑ:k]	Fleck	
	later ['leɪtə]	später	
	Discman ['dɪskmən]	Discman →	a *Discman*
	just [dʒʌst]	nur, gerade, einfach	
	because [bɪ'kɒz]	weil →	I'm in a hurry *because* I'm late.
	to **sort out** ['sɔ:t‿aʊt]	klären (*ein Problem*), regeln →	*Sort* it *out* with your sister.
31	to test [test]	testen, prüfen	
	question ['kwestʃn]	Frage →	
32	different ['dɪfrnt]	anders, verschieden	
	there is [ðer‿'ɪz]	da ist, es gibt →	! *There is* wird oft mit *there's* abgekürzt.
	there are [ðer‿'ɑ:]	da sind, es gibt →	*There are* two apples on the table.
	closed [kləʊzd]	zu, geschlossen	
	revision [rɪ'vɪʒn]	Wiederholung	
	I spy with my little eye something beginning with ... [aɪ 'spaɪ wɪð maɪ 'lɪtl aɪ 'sʌmθɪŋ bɪ'gɪnɪŋ wɪð]	Ich sehe was, was du nicht siehst, das fängt mit ... an.	

Chats with Charlie

33	**radio show** ['reɪdiəʊ ˌʃəʊ]	Radiosendung	
	radio ['reɪdiəʊ]	Radio	
	show [ʃəʊ]	Show, Sendung, Schau	
	chat [tʃæt]	Geplauder, Unterhaltung	
	to **chat** [tʃæt]	sich unterhalten →	to *chat* → a chat
	topic ['tɒpɪk]	Thema →	What's the *topic* today?
	to **phone** [fəʊn]	anrufen, telefonieren →	to *phone* → a phone
	to **come** [kʌm]	kommen	
	studio ['stju:diəʊ]	Studio	
	happy ['hæpi]	glücklich, froh	
	to **see** [si:]	sehen →	
	before [bɪ'fɔ:]	vor; bevor	
	magazine [mægə'zi:n]	Zeitschrift, Magazin →	I've got a lot of football *magazines*.
	when [wen]	wenn, als; wann	

unhappy [ʌnˈhæpi]	unglücklich →	happy ↔ *unhappy*
to **sing** [sɪŋ]	singen →	to *sing*
song [sɒŋ]	Lied	
DJ [ˌdiːˈdʒeɪ]	DJ	

Story

34 **ghost** [gəʊst]	Geist, Gespenst	
Saturday [ˈsætədeɪ]	Samstag →	! *Saturday* schreibst du groß.
afternoon [ˌɑːftəˈnuːn]	Nachmittag	
laptop [ˈlæptɒp]	Laptop →	A *laptop* is a computer.
busy [ˈbɪzi]	beschäftigt, ausgefüllt →	Achtung Aussprache!
music [ˈmjuːzɪk]	Musik →	Achtung Aussprache!
project [ˈprɒdʒekt]	Projekt →	I'm busy with the school *project*.
really [ˈrɪəli]	wirklich →	This magazine is *really* boring.
slow [sləʊ]	langsam →	Your computer is really *slow*.
to **be fed up** [biː ˌfed‿ˈʌp]	die Nase voll haben →	He's *fed up*.
to **help** [help]	helfen →	Can I *help* you?
to **borrow** [ˈbɒrəʊ]	borgen, leihen →	Can I *borrow* your football magazine?
hour [ˈaʊə]	Stunde →	! Du sagst: *an hour*.
to **finish** [ˈfɪnɪʃ]	beenden, erledigen, aufhören	
knock [nɒk]	Klopfen, Schlag →	There is a *knock* on the door. = Es klopft.
help [help]	Hilfe	
to **be good with ...** [biː ˈgʊd wɪð]	gut mit ... umgehen können →	I'm *good with* computers.
already [ɔːlˈredi]	schon	
dark [dɑːk]	dunkel →	It is already *dark* outside.
35 **spooky** [ˈspuːki]	unheimlich →	Ghosts are *spooky*.
strange [streɪndʒ]	merkwürdig, seltsam	
noise [nɔɪz]	Geräusch, Lärm	
wind [wɪnd]	Wind	
to **take home** [ˌteɪk ˈhəʊm]	nach Hause bringen →	I can *take* you *home*.
suddenly [ˈsʌdnli]	plötzlich, auf einmal	
terrible [ˈterəbl]	schrecklich, furchtbar	
scared [skeəd]	verängstigt →	Emma and Terry are *scared*.
eye [aɪ]	Auge	
stupid [ˈstjuːpɪd]	dumm, blöd	
Come on. [kʌm‿ˈɒn]	Komm./Kommt. →	*Come on*. Let's go.
a bit [ə ˈbɪt]	ein bisschen	
to use [juːz]	benutzen, verwenden	

For my folder: Problems

Ergänze deine *phrases* zum Thema Begrüßung mit *This is my family…, My mum is …, I've got a brother…, Our flat is …* .
Du findest bestimmt noch mehr!
In Unit 2 hast du gelernt, wie man über Probleme spricht und was man sagen kann, wenn man sich streitet. Schreibe die Ausdrücke auf ein neues Blatt Papier, das du in deinen *folder* legst. Lass auch hier wieder Platz für Ergänzungen.

Probleme/Streit
That's a big problem.
It's boring at home.
You're in big trouble!
…

Word game

NAME-ELEVEN-NEW-WHAT-TEACHER … Kannst du die Wortkette fortsetzen? Du kannst allein weiterspielen oder mit anderen. Wenn es nicht mehr weitergeht, fang einfach eine neue Kette an.

NAME-ELEVEN-NEW-WHAT-TEACHER …

Link-up B Hobbyland

38	**hobby, hobbies** *(pl)* ['hɒbi; 'hɒbiz]	Hobby →
	land [lænd]	Land
	to **skate** [skeɪt]	Inlineskates fahren, skaten
	to **break-dance** ['breɪkdɑ:nts]	Breakdance tanzen
	to **swim** [swɪm]	schwimmen →
	to **ride** [raɪd]	fahren, reiten
	bike [baɪk]	Fahrrad →
	to **draw** [drɔ:]	zeichnen →
	to **collect** [kə'lekt]	sammeln
	to **swap** [swɒp]	tauschen →
	card [kɑ:d]	Karte
	to **read** [ri:d]	lesen →
	comic ['kɒmɪk]	Comic, Comicheft
	to **watch** [wɒtʃ]	ansehen, beobachten
	video ['vɪdiəʊ]	Video
	horse [hɔ:s]	Pferd →
	list [lɪst]	Liste
	to write down ['raɪt ˌdaʊn]	aufschreiben
	to check [tʃek]	überprüfen
	to correct [kə'rekt]	korrigieren, verbessern
	together [tə'geðə]	zusammen, miteinander →
	then [ðen]	dann →
	to **teach** [ti:tʃ]	lehren →
	you [ju:]	dich, dir, Sie, Ihnen, euch →
	idea [aɪ'dɪə]	Idee, Einfall →

! one *hobby* – two *hobbies*

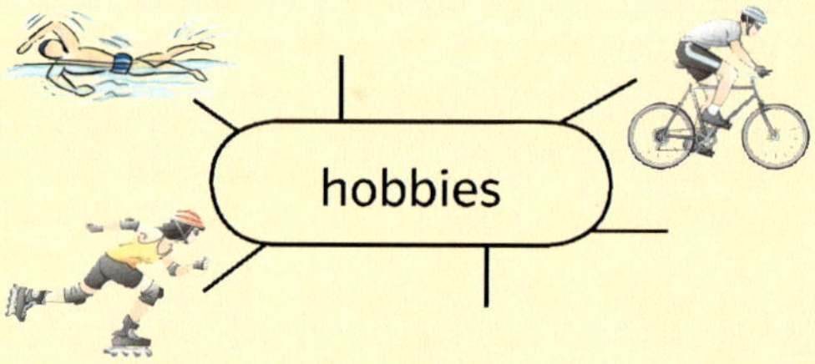

I ride my *bike*. You ride your *bike*.
Let's *draw* a picture.

to *read*

You can ride a bike or you can ride a *horse*.

You can play *together*.
Sing a song, *then* play a game.
to *teach* → teacher
I can teach *you*.

	me [miː]	mich, mir	
	club [klʌb]	Klub, Verein, Arbeitsgemeinschaft →	Let's go to the computer *club*.
39	**week** [wiːk]	Woche	

Days of the week

Monday ['mʌndeɪ]	Montag	**Thursday** ['θɜːzdeɪ]	Donnerstag	**Sunday** ['sʌndeɪ]	Sonntag
Tuesday ['tjuːzdeɪ]	Dienstag	**Friday** ['fraɪdeɪ]	Freitag		
Wednesday ['wenzdeɪ]	Mittwoch	**Saturday** ['sætədeɪ]	Samstag		

on Mondays [ɒn 'mʌndeɪz]	montags →	I skate *on Mondays*. I read on Tuesdays.
plan [plæn]	Plan	
day [deɪ]	Tag →	There are seven *days* in a week.
after ['ɑːftə]	nach →	The children go home *after* school.
before [bɪ'fɔː]	vor; bevor →	*before* ↔ after

Unit 3 Free time

Lerntipp: Mach dir eine Vokabelkartei.

Das Lernen geht einfacher mit einer Vokabelkartei. Dazu brauchst du einen Karton mit zwei Fächern und Karteikarten. Vorn auf die Karte schreibst du das englische Wort. Du kannst auch ein Bild dazu malen. Hinten auf die Karte schreibst du das deutsche Wort. Die fertigen Karten stellst du in das vordere Fach deines Kartons. Zum Lernen nimmst du eine Karte nach der anderen heraus und prüfst, ob du die Übersetzung auf der anderen Seite noch weißt. Wenn du ein Wort gut kannst, stellst du die Karte ins hintere Fach.

40	**free** [friː]	frei →	Have you got a lot of *free* time?
	to **learn** [lɜːn]	lernen	
	to **rap** [ræp]	rappen →	
	gym [dʒɪm]	Turnhalle	
	basketball ['bɑːskɪtbɔːl]	Basketball	
	badminton ['bædmɪntən]	Badminton, Federball	
	volleyball ['vɒlibɔːl]	Volleyball	
	cooking ['kʊkɪŋ]	Kochen, Koch- →	Who's in the *cooking* club?
	park [pɑːk]	Park	
	about [ə'baʊt]	über →	What can you say *about* your new school?
	trick [trɪk]	Trick, Streich	
	o'clock [ə'klɒk]	Uhr (*Zeitangabe*) →	It's six *o'clock*.
	half past (two) ['hɑːf pɑːst]	halb (drei) →	In English it is *half past two*. Auf Deutsch sagt man halb drei dazu.
	every ['evri]	jede/jeder/jedes	
	drama ['drɑːmə]	Theater, Drama	
	to **dance** [dɑːnts]	tanzen	
	thing [θɪŋ]	Sache, Ding →	A book is a good *thing*.
	hall [hɔːl]	Halle, Saal, Flur →	A *hall* is a very big room.
41	**fun** [fʌn]	Spaß	
	town [taʊn]	Stadt	

Language

42	**He is on his way to ....** [ˌhiː ɪz ɒn hɪz ˈweɪ tə]	Er ist auf dem Weg zu .... →	Lisa *is on* her *way to* school.
	way [weɪ]	Weg →	I'm on my *way* home.
	Excuse me! [ɪkˈskjuːz mi]	Entschuldigung!	
	What's the time, please? [ˌwɒts ðə ˈtaɪm pliːz]	Wie viel Uhr ist es, bitte? →	
	quarter past [ˈkwɔːtə pɑːst]	Viertel nach	
	quarter to [ˈkwɔːtə tə]	Viertel vor	
	dialogue [ˈdaɪəlɒg]	Gespräch	
	to **take out** [teɪk‿ˈaʊt]	herausnehmen	
	to **take** [teɪk]	nehmen, mitnehmen, bringen →	to *take* → to take out → to take home
	out [aʊt]	außerhalb, heraus, draußen →	*out* → outside
	oven [ˈʌvn]	Backofen	
	to **stop** [stɒp]	aufhören, aufhören mit, anhalten →	*Stop* the music!
	to **put** [pʊt]	setzen, stellen, legen	
	to **walk the dog** [wɔːk ðə ˈdɒg]	mit dem Hund spazieren gehen →	Lisa *walks* Barker.
	back [bæk]	zurück →	Come *back* here, Barker!
43	**rule** [ruːl]	Regel, Vorschrift	
	to **write** [raɪt]	schreiben	
	to **bring** [brɪŋ]	bringen, mitbringen →	
	to **leave** [liːv]	lassen, verlassen, abfahren	
	line [laɪn]	Zeile, Text, Linie →	Learn your *lines* at home.
	to **smile** [smaɪl]	lächeln	
	to **be fun** [biː ˈfʌn]	Spaß machen →	Clubs at Thomas Tallis *are fun*.
44	**e-mail** [ˈiːmeɪl]	E-Mail →	! Statt *e-mail* heißt es oft nur *mail*.
	dear [dɪə]	lieb →	! *Dear* Sam = Lieber Sam (*im Brief*)
	to **ask** [ɑːsk]	fragen	
	to **like** [laɪk]	mögen, gern haben	
	uniform [ˈjuːnɪfɔːm]	Uniform →	school *uniforms*
	shirt [ʃɜːt]	Hemd →	*shirt* → T-shirt
	long [lɒŋ]	lang	
	to **start** [stɑːt]	anfangen, starten →	We *start* school at 8:40.
	most [məʊst]	das meiste, die meisten →	! *most* people = die meisten Leute
	to **get** [get]	kommen, bekommen, besorgen →	How can I *get* to the museum?
	normal [ˈnɔːml]	normal	
	to **get up** [get‿ˈʌp]	aufstehen →	I *get up* at 7:45.
	to **wash** [wɒʃ]	sich waschen, waschen	
	often [ˈɒfn]	oft →	I *often* go to the football club.
	to **dress** [dres]	sich anziehen →	I *dress* at eight o'clock.
	into [ˈɪntə]	in; in ... hinein →	I go *into* the kitchen.
	to **eat** [iːt]	essen, fressen	
	breakfast [ˈbrekfəst]	Frühstück	
	to **have supper** [hæv ˈsʌpə]	zu Abend essen →	The Brooks *have supper* at seven o'clock.
	supper [ˈsʌpə]	Abendessen →	breakfast, lunch, *supper*

	sometimes ['sʌmtaɪmz]	manchmal →	I *sometimes* go to the rap club.
	never ['nevə]	nie, niemals →	I *never* go to the all sports club.
	kid [kɪd]	Kind →	You can say 'child' or '*kid*'.
	to **love** [lʌv]	lieben, gern mögen	
	night [naɪt]	Nacht	
45	to **meet** [mi:t]	treffen, sich treffen →	
	young [jʌŋ]	jung	
	mice *(pl)* [maɪs]	Mäuse →	! one mouse – two *mice*
	to **wear** [weə]	anhaben, tragen →	English pupils *wear* a school uniform.
	to **live** [lɪv]	wohnen, leben →	Emma and Nasreen *live* in a flat.
	weekend [ˌwi:k'end]	Wochenende	
46	**early** ['ɜ:li]	früh	
	to **sleep** [sli:p]	schlafen →	

Chats with Charlie

47	**night nurse** ['naɪt nɜ:s]	Nachtschwester →	Anna is a *night nurse*.
	nurse [nɜ:s]	Krankenschwester, Krankenpfleger	
	work [wɜ:k]	Arbeit	
	in the morning [ˌɪn ðə 'mɔ:nɪŋ]	morgens, am Morgen, vormittags	
	in the evening [ˌɪn ði: 'i:vnɪŋ]	abends, am Abend →	We eat supper at six o'clock *in the evening*.
	evening ['i:vnɪŋ]	Abend →	*evening* ↔ morning
	in the afternoon [ˌɪn ði: ˌɑ:ftə'nu:n]	nachmittags, am Nachmittag	

Story

48	to **wake up** [weɪk‿'ʌp]	aufwecken, aufwachen →	
	face [feɪs]	Gesicht	
	to **bark** [bɑ:k]	bellen	
	to **run away** [rʌn‿ə'weɪ]	wegrennen	
	to **run** [rʌn]	rennen, laufen →	Let's *run* to the tree and back.
	away [ə'weɪ]	weg →	Don't run *away*, Barker.
	café ['kæfeɪ]	Café	
	to **sit** [sɪt]	sitzen	
	to **come in** [kʌm‿'ɪn]	hereinkommen →	Can I *come in*?
	to **work** [wɜ:k]	arbeiten, funktionieren	

Bringen

Dafür gibt es auf Englisch zwei Wörter:

*I can **take** you home.* — Ich kann dich nach Hause **bringen**. (= hinbringen)

*Can you **bring** me the ball, please?* — Kannst du mir bitte den Ball **bringen**? (= herbringen)

to **get lost** [get 'lɒst]	verloren gehen, sich verirren →	My cat sometimes *gets lost* in the park.

	to **call** [kɔ:l]	rufen, anrufen, nennen	
	to **find** [faɪnd]	finden	
	again [ə'gen]	wieder →	He's late *again*.
49	**out of** ['aʊt‿əv]	aus … heraus →	We often go *out of* town on Sundays.
	car [kɑ:]	Auto →	a *car* 
	in front of [ɪn 'frʌnt‿əv]	vor	
	to **throw** [θrəʊ]	werfen	
	dog-tired [ˌdɒg 'taɪəd]	hundemüde	
	to **think** ['θɪŋk]	denken	
	to **tell** [tel]	erzählen, sagen →	Can you *tell* me a story?
	to **remember** [rɪ'membə]	sich erinnern, sich erinnern an, sich merken	
50	**all** [ɔ:l]	alle/alles; ganz →	*All* children from 5 to 16 go to school.

For my folder: Let's …

Schreibe alle Ausdrücke, mit denen du Vorschläge machen und darauf reagieren kannst, auf ein Blatt Papier. Lege es in deinen *English folder.*

Vorschläge	Anworten
Let's go to the … club.	*OK, that's cool.*
Learn to …	*That's a stupid idea.*
…	…

Word game

Eins der Wörter gehört nicht in die Gruppe. Kannst du es finden?

1. *sometimes – often – where – never*
2. *breakfast – supper – lunch – eat*
3. *mice – cats – kid – children*
4. *boring – night – evening – afternoon*
5. *mum – dad – sister – aunt*
6. *teach – take – talk – table*

Link-up C In town

52	**map** [mæp]	Stadtplan, Landkarte →	Look at the *map* in your book.
	museum [mju:'zi:əm]	Museum	
	road [rəʊd]	Straße, Landstraße →	Is this the *road* to London?
	street [stri:t]	Straße →	Don't play in the *street*.

Straße

*I'm in the **street**.* — Mit **street** meinst du eine Straße mit Häusern **in einem Ort**.

*Is this the **road** to Berlin?* — Mit **road** meinst du eine Verkehrsstraße **außerhalb eines Orts**.

river ['rɪvə]	Fluss →	
bridge [brɪdʒ]	Brücke	
department store [dɪ'pɑ:tmənt stɔ:]	Kaufhaus	
supermarket ['su:pəˌmɑ:kɪt]	Supermarkt	

newsagent ['nju:sˌeɪdʒənt]	Zeitschriftenhändler/ Zeitschriftenhändlerin	
church [tʃɜ:tʃ]	Kirche →	
bus stop ['bʌs ˌstɒp]	Bushaltestelle	
bus, buses *(pl)* [bʌs; 'bʌsɪz]	Bus	
stop [stɒp]	Halt, Haltestelle	
information centre [ɪnfə'meɪʃn ˌsentə]	Informationszentrum	
information [ˌɪnfə'meɪʃn]	Information/Informationen →	I've got a lot of *information* about London.
centre ['sentə]	Zentrum, Mittelpunkt →	This bus goes to the town *centre*.
Go left. [gəʊ 'left]	Biege nach links ab.	
Go right. [gəʊ 'raɪt]	Biege nach rechts ab. →	
53 **Go down …** ['gəʊ daʊn]	Geh … entlang.	
to **close** [kləʊz]	schließen, zumachen →	to open ↔ to *close*
near [nɪə]	in der Nähe von, nahe →	The café is *near* the supermarket.

Unit 4 Greenwich Project Week

Lerntipp: Dreimal fünf Minuten

Du behältst die neuen Wörter besser, wenn du sie dreimal fünf Minuten lang lernst. Zuerst schaust du sie dir fünf Minuten an, nach einer halben Stunde wiederholst du sie, und am Ende deiner Hausaufgaben überprüfst du sie nochmal fünf Minuten lang. Das bringt mehr als eine halbe Stunde.

54 out and about ['aʊt‿nd‿ə'baʊt]	unterwegs	
skateboard ['skeɪtbɔ:d]	Skateboard	
skates *(pl)* [skeɪts]	Inlineskates	
foot, feet *(pl)* [fʊt; fi:t]	Fuß →	! one *foot* – two *feet*
tunnel ['tʌnl]	Tunnel, Unterführung	
to **walk** [wɔ:k]	gehen, laufen →	
to **use** [ju:z]	benutzen, verwenden →	
east [i:st]	Osten	
west [west]	Westen	
famous ['feɪməs]	berühmt →	This place is very *famous*.
ship [ʃɪp]	Schiff →	The Cutty Sark is a famous *ship*.
train [treɪn]	Zug	
without [wɪ'ðaʊt]	ohne →	You can't write *without* a pen.
driver ['draɪvə]	Fahrer/Fahrerin	
clock [klɒk]	Uhr	
group [gru:p]	Gruppe	
to **choose** [tʃu:z]	wählen, auswählen	
to **want**, to **want to** ['wɒnt tə]	wollen, mögen →	I *want* skates. I *want to* skate.
to complete [kəm'pli:t]	vervollständigen	
first [fɜ:st]	zuerst; erste/erster/erstes →	I want to go *first*.
to **visit** ['vɪzɪt]	besuchen, besichtigen	

55 **right** [raɪt] – rechter/rechte/rechtes; rechts
left [left] – linke/linker/linkes; links →
to **mean** [mi:n] – bedeuten, meinen →
short [ʃɔ:t] – kurz →
than [ðæn] – als
north [nɔ:θ] – Norden
south [saʊθ] – Süden →
visitor ['vɪzɪtə] – Besucher/Besucherin

left ↔ right
GMT *means* Greenwich Mean Time.
short ↔ long

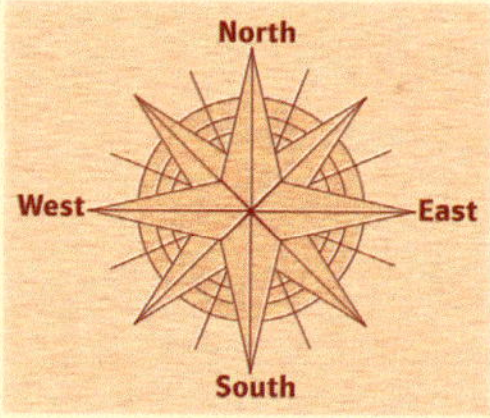

Language

56 **survey** ['sɜ:veɪ] – Umfrage
57 **transport** ['træntspɔ:t] – Transport →
by bike [baɪ 'baɪk] – mit dem Fahrrad →
on foot [ɒn 'fʊt] – zu Fuß →

Achtung Aussprache!
Sam goes to school *by bike*.
to go *on foot* = to walk

by und *on*

by bike	mit dem Fahrrad	***by bus***	mit dem Bus	***on foot***	zu Fuß
by car	mit dem Auto	***by train***	mit dem Zug	***on skates***	mit Inlineskates

58 to **know** [nəʊ] – wissen, kennen →
answer ['ɑ:ntsə] – Antwort
to put in [pʊt‿'ɪn] – einsetzen
worksheet ['wɜ:kʃi:t] – Arbeitsblatt
59 to **get off** [get‿'ɒf] – aussteigen aus →
60 to **forget** [fə'get] – vergessen →
them [ðem] – sie, ihnen →
folder ['fəʊldə] – Ordner, Mappe
to **stay** [steɪ] – bleiben
to **give** [gɪv] – geben, schenken →
us [ʌs] – uns
to **ask for** ['ɑ:sk fə] – fragen nach, bitten um →
him [hɪm] – ihn, ihm →
to **thank** [θæŋk] – danken →
to **spell** [spel] – buchstabieren →
to try [traɪ] – versuchen, probieren

You *know* a lot of English words now.
Where do we *get off* the bus?
Don't *forget* your worksheets!
I see *them*. Let's play with *them*.
to *give*

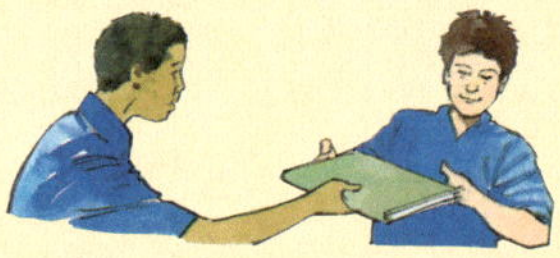

You can *ask* her *for* the answers.
Can you see *him*?
thank you → *to thank*
Spell 'Tom'. – T-O-M.

Chats with Charlie

61 to go up [gəʊ‿'ʌp] – hinaufgehen
to go down [gəʊ 'daʊn] – hinuntergehen

Story

62 **hours** ['aʊəz] – Öffnungszeiten →
to **speak** [spi:k] – sprechen →
man, men *(pl)* [mæn; men] – Mann →

Can I *speak* to Terry, please?
! one *man* – two *men*

	woman, women *(pl)* [ˈwʊmən; ˈwɪmɪn]	Frau →
	cold [kəʊld]	kalt
	to **rain** [reɪn]	regnen
	to **make up** [meɪk‿ˈʌp]	erfinden, sich ausdenken
	to **find out** [faɪnd‿ˈaʊt]	herausfinden
63	**Good luck!** [ˌɡʊd ˈlʌk]	Viel Glück!
	luck [lʌk]	Glück →
	bad luck [ˌbæd ˈlʌk]	Pech →
	timeline [ˈtaɪmlaɪn]	Zeitleiste
64	photo [ˈfəʊtəʊ]	Foto
	missing [ˈmɪsɪŋ]	fehlend
65	to **show** [ʃəʊ]	zeigen

! one *woman* – two *women*

luck → lucky → be lucky
bad luck ↔ luck

For my folder: Information

Stell dir vor, du bist in einer fremden Stadt. Was gibt es dort? Wo ist es? Wie kommst du dorthin? Schreibe alle Fragen und möglichen Antworten dazu auf ein Blatt für deinen *English folder.*

Fragen	Antworten
Excuse me, I'm a visitor here. What can I do in … ?	*You can … here.*
Can you tell me the way to … ?	*Go down …*
How do I … ?	…
…	

Word game

Schreibe die fehlenden Buchstaben der nebenstehenden Wörter auf einen Zettel. In der richtigen Reihenfolge ergeben sie den Namen einer englischen Stadt.
Du kannst selber ähnliche Rätsel für deine Freunde machen. Dazu überlegst du dir zuerst ein englisches Lösungswort und suchst dir dann die passenden englischen Vokabeln.

ti_er	s_ared	h_lp
ga_den	_oise	borro_
top_c	_our	sudd_nly

Unit 5 Shopping in Greenwich

Lerntipp: Wiederholung mit der Vokabelkartei

Hast du schon eine Vokabelkartei angelegt? Dann sind sicher schon ganz viele Karten im hinteren Fach. Schau dir diese Karten alle paar Wochen nochmal an. Wenn du ein Wort nicht mehr kannst, stellst du die Karte wieder ins vordere Fach und lernst sie nochmal.

	shopping [ˈʃɒpɪŋ]	Einkaufen, Einkauf →
	How much is ... ? [ˌhaʊ ˈmʌtʃ‿ɪz]	Wie viel kostet ... ? →
	How much are ... ? [ˌhaʊ ˈmʌtʃ‿ɑː]	Wie viel kosten ... ?
	much [mʌtʃ]	viel
	pound [paʊnd]	Pfund (*Währung*) →
	anything [ˈeniθɪŋ]	etwas, irgendetwas
	else [els]	sonst, noch →
	cap [kæp]	Kappe, Mütze
	too [tuː]	zu →
	large [lɑːdʒ]	groß, riesig
	medium [ˈmiːdiəm]	mittel →
	over there [ˌəʊvə ˈðeə]	da drüben →
	sports shop [ˈspɔːts ʃɒp]	Sportgeschäft
	to **buy** [baɪ]	kaufen
67	other [ˈʌðə]	andere/anderer/anderes
	money [ˈmʌni]	Geld →
	pence *(pl)* [pents]	Pence (*Währung*) →

Let's go *shopping* at the supermarket.

! one pound = £1

Anything *else*?

I'm sorry but this T-shirt is *too* big.

S = small, M = *medium*, L = large
Your things are *over there*.

English *money*
! five *pence* = 5p

Language

68	**party** [ˈpɑːti]	Party, Feier
	list [lɪst]	Liste
	birthday [ˈbɜːθdeɪ]	Geburtstag →
	cake [keɪk]	Kuchen
	to **have a party** [ˌhæv‿ə ˈpɑːti]	eine Party feiern →
	to **have** [hæv]	haben →
	burger bar [ˈbɜːɡə ˌbɑː]	Fastfood-Restaurant
	burger [ˈbɜːɡə]	Hamburger →
	expensive [ɪkˈspentsɪv]	teuer
	pizza [ˈpiːtsə]	Pizza
	cheap [tʃiːp]	billig →
	how many [haʊ ˈmeni]	wie viele →
	many [ˈmeni]	viele →
	to **invite** [ɪnˈvaɪt]	einladen
	cheese [tʃiːz]	Käse
	milk [mɪlk]	Milch →
	bottle [ˈbɒtl]	Flasche
	egg [eɡ]	Ei

I want to *have a party* for my birthday.

! Do you *have*? = Have you got?

I want a *burger* for lunch.

cheap ↔ expensive
How many books do you have?
! *many* friends – much money

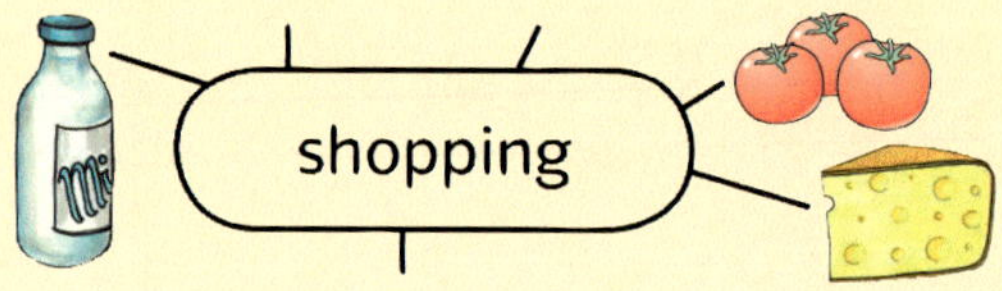

box, boxes *(pl)* [bɒks; 'bɒksɪz]	Kiste, Schachtel, Kasten →	! one *box* – two *boxes*
tomato, tomatoes *(pl)* [tə'mɑːtəʊ; tə'mɑːtəʊz]	Tomate →	! one *tomato* – two *tomatoes*
lemonade [ˌlemə'neɪd]	Limonade	
packet ['pækɪt]	Päckchen, Paket →	A *packet* of cheese, please.
water ['wɔːtə]	Wasser	
biscuit ['bɪskɪt]	Keks →	! *'Biscuit'* heißt nicht „Biskuit".
cornflakes ['kɔːnfleɪks]	Cornflakes	
also ['ɔːlsəʊ]	auch →	You can *also* buy apples here.

Wie viel?

How much ... ?	Wie viel ... ?	***a bag of*** *apples*	eine Tüte Äpfel
How many ... ?	Wie viele ... ?	***a bottle of*** *water*	eine Flasche Wasser
a lot of *money/books*	viel Geld/viele Bücher	***a box of*** *eggs*	eine Schachtel Eier
a packet of *cheese*	ein Päckchen Käse	***no*** *chocolate*	keine Schokolade

69	**present** ['preznt]	Geschenk →	This is your birthday *present*.
	to **wait** [weɪt]	warten →	Can you *wait*, please?
	next [nekst]	nächste/nächster/nächstes	
	minute ['mɪnɪt]	Minute	
	CD [ˌsiː'diː]	CD →	a *CD* 
70	**invitation** [ˌɪnvɪ'teɪʃn]	Einladung	
	date [deɪt]	Datum →	What's the *date* today?
	third [θɜːd]	dritte/dritter/drittes →	The party is on the *third* of March.
	March [mɑːtʃ]	März →	! Monatsnamen schreibst du groß.
	See you! ['siː jə]	Bis dann! Bis ... →	Bye. *See you* then! *See you* later!
	RSVP [ˌɑː es viː 'piː]	um Antwort wird gebeten →	You can write *RSVP* in an invitation.
	why [waɪ]	warum →	*Why* ...? – Because ...
	address [ə'dres]	Adresse →	Achtung Schreibung!
	month [mʌnθ]	Monat →	day, week, *month*, year

Months

January ['dʒænjʊri]	Januar	**July** [dʒʊ'laɪ]	Juli
February ['februri]	Februar	**August** ['ɔːgəst]	August
March [mɑːtʃ]	März	**September** [sep'tembə]	September
April ['eɪprl]	April	**October** [ɒk'təʊbə]	Oktober
May [meɪ]	Mai	**November** [nəʊ'vembə]	November
June [dʒuːn]	Juni	**December** [dɪ'sembə]	Dezember

71	**calendar** ['kæləndə]	Kalender →	All the dates are in a *calendar*.
	crossword (puzzle) ['krɒswɜːd 'pʌzl]	Kreuzworträtsel	
	to blow up ['bləʊ‿ʌp]	aufblasen	
	balloon [bə'luːn]	Luftballon	

Numbers

first [fɜ:st]	erste (-r/-s)	**fourteenth** [fɔ:'ti:nθ]	vierzehnte (-r/-s)
second ['seknd]	zweite (-r/-s)	**fifteenth** [fɪf'ti:nθ]	fünfzehnte (-r/-s)
third [θɜ:d]	dritte (-r/-s)	**sixteenth** [sɪks'ti:nθ]	sechzehnte (-r/-s)
fourth [fɔ:θ]	vierte (-r/-s)	**seventeenth** [sevn'ti:nθ]	siebzehnte (-r/-s)
fifth [fɪfθ]	fünfte (-r/-s)	**eighteenth** [eɪ'ti:nθ]	achzehnte (-r/-s)
sixth [sɪksθ]	sechste (-r/-s)	**nineteenth** [naɪn'ti:nθ]	neunzehnte (-r/-s)
seventh ['sevnθ]	siebte (-r/-s)	**twentieth** ['twentiɪθ]	zwanzigste (-r/-s)
eighth [eɪtθ]	achte (-r/-s)	**twenty-first** [ˌtwenti'fɜ:st]	einundzwanzigste (-r/-s)
ninth [naɪnθ]	neunte (-r/-s)	**twenty-second** [ˌtwenti'seknd]	zweiundzwanzigste (-r/-s)
tenth [tenθ]	zehnte (-r/-s)	**twenty-third** [ˌtwenti'θɜ:d]	dreiundzwanzigste (-r/-s)
eleventh [ɪ'levnθ]	elfte (-r/-s)	...	...
twelfth [twelfθ]	zwölfte (-r/-s)	**thirtieth** ['θɜ:tiəθ]	dreißigste (-r/-s)
thirteenth [θɜ:'ti:nθ]	dreizehnte (-r/-s)	**thirty-first** [ˌθɜ:ti'fɜ:st]	einunddreißigste (-r/-s)

72 to **hope** [həʊp] — hoffen → — I *hope* he likes our present.

Chats with Charlie

73 like [laɪk] — wie

euro ['jʊərəʊ] — Euro (*Währung*) → — How many *euros* have you got?

observatory [əb'zɜ:vətri] — Observatorium, Sternwarte

Story

74 **disco** ['dɪskəʊ] — Disko

excited [ɪk'saɪtɪd] — aufgeregt → — Sam is very *excited* about his party.

to **sit with** ['sɪt wɪθ] — sich setzen zu → — He *sits with* his friends.

to **laugh** [lɑ:f] — lachen → — Achtung Schreibung!

to **kick** [kɪk] — treten

bad [bæd] — schlecht → — *bad* ↔ good

75 **inside** [ɪn'saɪd] — innen, drin, nach drinnen → — *inside* ↔ outside

alarm clock [ə'lɑ:m ˌklɒk] — Wecker

to **have a good time** [ˌhæv‿ə gʊd 'taɪm] — sich amüsieren

to **drink** [drɪŋk] — trinken

to **ring** [rɪŋ] — klingeln

to **turn off** ['tɜ:n‿ɒf] — abschalten, ausschalten →

to **get into** [get‿'ɪntə] — einsteigen in

76 alphabetical [ˌælfə'betɪkl] — alphabetisch

to **end** [end] — enden → — The word 'May' *ends* with the letter 'y'.

For my folder: Shopping

Du möchtest einkaufen. Was sagst du? Was sagt der Verkäufer/die Verkäuferin? Schreibe alle Ausdrücke, die du beim Einkaufen verwenden kannst, auf ein Blatt Papier für deinen *folder.*

Kunde/Kundin
How much is … ?
Excuse me. This T-shirt/… is too small/too … .
Have you got it in … ?
Where are … ?
…

Verkäufer/Verkäuferin
It's … .

Yes, … / No, …
…

Word game

Schreibe die nebenstehenden Wörter auf Karten.
Lege alle Karten mit der Schrift nach unten. Versuche Gegensatzpaare aufzudecken. Wenn du ein Paar gefunden hast, darfst du die beiden Karten behalten.
Wenn du mit Freunden/Freundinnnen spielst, kannst du das Spiel erweitern: Ihr dürft das Kartenpaar erst dann behalten, wenn ihr mit den beiden Wörtern Sätze gebildet habt, z. B.:
*I've got a **small** dog. – He lives in a **big** house.*

big – right – good – white – short – old – black – new – long – bad – small – wrong

Unit 6 Let's go to the country!

Lerntipp: Gemeinsam lernen

Damit du die Vokabeln richtig gut behältst, kannst du sie mit deinen Freunden/Freundinnen zusammen wiederholen. Nehmt euch in regelmäßigen Abständen Vokabeln aus einer früheren Unit vor. Ihr könnt sie euch gegenseitig durcheinander abfragen oder ein Spiel damit machen.

78	**in the country** [ˌɪn ðə ˈkʌntri]	auf dem Land →	*They live in the country.*
	different [ˈdɪfrnt]	anders, verschieden	
	quiet [ˈkwaɪət]	ruhig, still, leise →	Can you be *quiet*, please?
	to **hear** [hɪə]	hören →	Can you *hear* me?
	fish, **fish** *(pl)* [fɪʃ]	Fisch/Fische →	! one *fish* – five *fish*
	fishing [ˈfɪʃɪŋ]	Angeln, Fischen →	I often go *fishing*.
	to **pick** [pɪk]	pflücken, auswählen	
	flower [ˈflaʊə]	Blume	
	farm [fɑːm]	Bauernhof, Farm →	
	sheep, sheep *(pl)* [ʃiːp]	Schaf/Schafe →	! one *sheep* – a lot of *sheep*
	to **stay with** [ˈsteɪ wɪð]	wohnen bei →	Please come and *stay with* us.
	soon [suːn]	bald →	See you *soon*.

	beautiful ['bju:tɪfl]	schön, wunderschön →	Achtung Schreibung!
	spring [sprɪŋ]	Frühling	
	is OK with us [ɪz‿əʊ'keɪ wɪð‿ʌs]	ist uns recht →	Monday *is OK with us*.
	love [lʌv]	Herzliche Grüße *(am Briefende)*; Liebe →	You can write *'Love, … '* and your name in a letter or in an e-mail.
	postcard ['pəʊstkɑ:d]	Postkarte	
79	**season** ['si:zn]	Jahreszeit, Saison →	
	sunny ['sʌni]	sonnig	
	foggy ['fɒgi]	neblig	
	hot [hɒt]	heiß	
	rainy ['reɪni]	regnerisch, verregnet	
	windy ['wɪndi]	windig	
	snowy ['snəʊi]	verschneit	
	autumn ['ɔ:təm]	Herbst	
	summer ['sʌmə]	Sommer	
	winter ['wɪntə]	Winter	

Language

80	to **pack** [pæk]	packen →	*pack* → packet
	trip [trɪp]	Ausflug, Reise →	The Jacksons are on a *trip* to Wiltshire.
	to **carry** ['kæri]	tragen	
	to **feed** [fi:d]	füttern →	
	to **send** [send]	schicken	
	text message ['tekst ˌmesɪdʒ]	SMS →	! SMS heißt auf Englisch *text message*.
81	to **put on** [pʊt‿'ɒn]	anziehen, aufsetzen →	! I'm *putting on* my shoes. I'm *looking for* my pen.
	to **look for** ['lʊk fə]	suchen →	
	miming ['maɪmɪŋ]	Pantomime	
	to mime [maɪm]	pantomimisch darstellen	
	action ['ækʃn]	Handlung, Aktion	
	to guess [ges]	raten, vermuten	

Schreibweisen bei der *-ing*-Form

to read	***reading***	*to come*	***coming***	*to get*	***getting***
to pack	***packing***	*to take*	***taking***	*to put*	***putting***
to see	***seeing***	*to have*	***having***	*to run*	***running***
to be	***being***	*to make*	***making***	*to sit*	***sitting***

82	to **joke** [dʒəʊk]	scherzen, Witze machen →	Are you *joking*?
	farmer ['fɑ:mə]	Bauer, Bäuerin, Landwirt/Landwirtin →	*farmer* → farm
	to **look at** ['lʊk‿ət]	ansehen →	*Look at* Barker!
	Hang on! ['hæŋ‿ɒn]	Moment mal! Warte mal!	
	to **have fun** [ˌhæv 'fʌn]	Spaß haben, sich amüsieren	
	pig [pɪg]	Schwein	

animal ['ænɪml]	Tier →	
cow [kaʊ]	Kuh	
little [lɪtl]	klein	
baby, babies *(pl)* ['beɪbi; 'beɪbiz]	Baby, Säugling →	! one *baby* – ten *babies*
to **check** [tʃek]	überprüfen	
to **worry** ['wʌri]	sich Sorgen machen →	
Have fun! [ˌhæv 'fʌn]	Viel Spaß!	
83 **How are you?** [ˌhaʊ‿'ɑː juː]	Wie geht es dir/Ihnen/ euch?	
to **spend** [spend]	verbringen, ausgeben →	You can *spend* money or time.
We're OK. [ˌwɪər‿əʊ'keɪ]	Es geht uns gut. →	How are you? – *I'm OK.*
to be right [biː 'raɪt]	Recht haben	
call [kɔːl]	Anruf	
84 **rubbish** ['rʌbɪʃ]	Abfall, Abfälle, Müll →	There is a lot of *rubbish* in the shed.
those [ðəʊz]	diese dort, jene	
penknife, penknives *(pl)* ['pennaɪf; 'pennaɪvz]	Taschenmesser →	! one *penknife* – five *penknives*
tent [tent]	Zelt	
broken ['brəʊkn]	kaputt, zerbrochen, gebrochen →	
torch, torches *(pl)* [tɔːtʃ; 'tɔːtʃɪz]	Taschenlampe, Fackel →	! one *torch* – two *torches*

Besondere Pluralformen

family	*famil**ies***	*fish*	***fish***	*penknife*	*penkni**ves***	*woman*	***women***
baby	*bab**ies***	*sheep*	***sheep***	*shelf*	*shel**ves***	*man*	***men***
country	*countr**ies***					*child*	***children***
hobby	*hobb**ies***					*mouse*	***mice***
tomato	*tomato**es***					*foot*	***feet***
torch	*torch**es***						

these [ðiːz]	diese, diese hier →	*These* books are new, those are old.
sleeping bag ['sliːpɪŋ ˌbæg]	Schlafsack →	sleep → *sleeping bag*
camping ['kæmpɪŋ]	Camping, Zelten →	Do you like *camping*?
tonight [tə'naɪt]	heute Abend, heute Nacht →	this evening = *tonight*
to **put up** [pʊt‿'ʌp]	aufstellen, aufbauen →	Where can we *put up* the tent?

Chats with Charlie

85 **sound** [saʊnd]	Ton, Geräusch, Klang	

Story

86 to **happen** ['hæpn]	geschehen, passieren →	What's *happening* in the story?
like [laɪk]	wie →	He's sleeping *like* a baby.
jacket ['dʒækɪt]	Jacke →	It's cold. Put on your *jacket*.

	bush, bushes *(pl)* [bʊʃ; bʊʃɪz]	Busch, Strauch →	*bushes*, trees, garden, park
	to **drive** [draɪv]	fahren	
	van [væn]	Lieferwagen →	a *van* 
	to **wait for** ['weɪt fɔ:]	warten auf	
	to **arrive** [ə'raɪv]	ankommen	
	quick [kwɪk]	schnell →	*Quick*! We haven't got much time.
	to **hide** [haɪd]	verstecken, sich verstecken	
	to **get out** [get‿'aʊt]	aussteigen →	The man *gets out* of the car.
87	to **be worried** ['wʌrid]	besorgt sein, beunruhigt sein →	to worry → to be *worried*
	police [pə'li:s]	Polizei →	! The *police* **are** coming.
	to **be pleased with** [bi: 'pli:zd wɪð]	zufrieden sein mit →	I'm very *pleased with* you.
	station ['steɪʃn]	Wache, Station, Bahnhof →	They are at the police *station*.
	at least [ət 'li:st]	wenigstens, mindestens →	*At least* it isn't raining.
	part [pɑ:t]	Teil	
	each [i:tʃ]	jede/jeder/jedes	
	title ['taɪtl]	Titel, Überschrift	
88	**field** [fi:ld]	Feld, Acker →	 a *field*
	plural ['plʊərl]	Plural, Mehrzahl →	The *plural* of 'child' is 'children'.
	form [fɔ:m]	Form	
	alphabetical [ˌælfə'betɪkl]	alphabetisch →	alphabet → *alphabetical*

For my folder: Phone calls

Du kannst jetzt auf Englisch telefonieren. Schreibe ein Telefongespräch, in dem du dich für eine bestimmte Uhrzeit mit jemandem verabredest, für deinen *English folder* auf.

Das sagst du	Das sagt dein Gegenüber
Hi!/Hello.	*Hi, it's …*
What are you doing?	*I'm …. And what about you?*
…	…

Word game

Spiele Bingo mit deinen Freunden/Freundinnen. Jeder malt sich eine Bingokarte mit neun Feldern. Sucht euch dann einen Bereich aus dem *vocabulary* aus, z. B. alle Wörter aus der *story* in dieser Unit. Aus diesem Bereich schreibt jeder Wörter in die Kästchen auf seiner Karte. Der Spielleiter/die Spielleiterin liest durcheinander die Wörter aus dem festgelegten Bereich vor. Jedesmal wenn ein Wort von eurer Bingokarte kommt, dürft ihr es durchstreichen. Es gewinnt, wer als erster eine Dreierreihe senkrecht, waagerecht oder diagonal durchgestrichen hat und laut „Bingo" ruft.

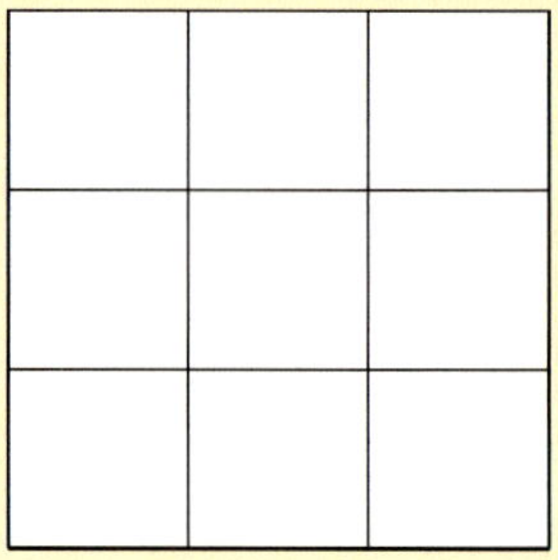

Unit 7 The school year

Lerntipp: Bastel dir ein Lernspiel.

Schreibe die englischen Wörter, die du lernen willst, auf kleine Zettel. Die deutsche Bedeutung kommt in einer anderen Farbe auf die Rückseite. Lege die Zettel mit den deutschen Wörtern nach oben vor dich hin. Jedesmal wenn du das englische Wort weißt, darfst du die Karte einsammeln. Kannst du das Wort noch nicht, legst du die Karte wieder zu den anderen.

90	**event** [ɪˈvent]	Veranstaltung, Ereignis →	A school disco is an *event*.
	between [bɪˈtwiːn]	zwischen →	May is *between* April and June.
	lantern [ˈlæntən]	Laterne	
	last [lɑːst]	letzte/letzter/letztes →	'Z' is the *last* letter in the alphabet.
	to **act** [ækt]	spielen (Theater)	
	play [pleɪ]	Theaterstück, Spiel →	a school *play* 
	at the moment [æt ðə ˈməʊmənt]	im Augenblick, momentan	
	moment [ˈməʊmənt]	Moment, Augenblick	
	to **rehearse** [rɪˈhɜːs]	proben (*ein Theaterstück*) →	We are *rehearsing* our new play.
	make-up [ˈmeɪkʌp]	Make-up, Schminke	
	to **paint** [peɪnt]	malen, anmalen →	Let's *paint* our faces.
	to **organize** [ˈɔːɡənaɪz]	organisieren	
	to **sell** [sel]	verkaufen →	*sell* ↔ buy
	ticket [ˈtɪkɪt]	Ticket, Fahrschein, Eintrittskarte →	Do you sell *tickets* here?
	sports day [ˈspɔːts deɪ]	Sportfest	
	long jump [ˈlɒŋ ˌdʒʌmp]	Weitsprung →	
	summer fair [ˈsʌmə ˌfeə]	Sommerfest	
	fair [feə]	Messe, Jahrmarkt →	A *fair* is a big event.
	charity [ˈtʃærɪti]	Wohltätigkeit, Wohltätigkeitsverein →	We collect money for *charities*.
	stall [stɔːl]	Stand, Bude →	
	sponge [spʌndʒ]	Schwamm	
	even [ˈiːvn]	selbst, sogar	a *stall* 
	to **welcome** [ˈwelkəm]	willkommen heißen	
91	activity [ækˈtɪvəti]	Aktivität	
	along [əˈlɒŋ]	entlang	
	other [ˈʌðə]	andere/anderer/anderes →	The *other* pupils are over there.
	to compare [kəmˈpeə]	vergleichen	

Language

92	to **do sports** [duː ˈspɔːts]	Sport treiben →	The pupils are *doing sports*.
	reporter [rɪˈpɔːtə]	Reporter/Reporterin	
	to **time** [taɪm]	stoppen, die Zeit nehmen	
	runner [ˈrʌnə]	Läufer/Läuferin	
	race [reɪs]	Wettlauf, Rennen	
	to **run a race** [ˌrʌn‿ə ˈreɪs]	einen Wettlauf machen →	They're *running a race*.

cricket [ˈkrɪkɪt]	Kricket	
ice-cream [aɪs ˈkri:m]	Eis, Eiscreme →	I like *ice-cream.*
to describe [dɪˈskraɪb]	beschreiben	
right now [ˌraɪt ˈnaʊ]	jetzt gleich, in diesem Augenblick →	What is he doing *right now?*
sports field [ˈspɔ:ts fi:ld]	Sportplatz →	Lisa is on the *sports field.*

Machen

*to **do** homework*	Hausaufgaben **machen**	*to **do** the long jump*	Weitsprung **machen**
*to **do** sports*	Sport **machen**	*to **do** an excercise*	eine Übung **machen**

93 to bring in [brɪŋ‿ɪn]	hereinbringen, mitbringen	
94 **must** [mʌst]	müssen →	You *must* do your homework.
scone [skɒn]	Scone *(Gebäck)*	
exchange [ɪksˈtʃeɪndʒ]	Austausch, Tausch	
visit [ˈvɪzɪt]	Besuch →	*visit* → visitor
Miss [mɪs]	Frau *(Anrede)* →	You say *'Miss'* to your teacher.
afternoon tea [ˌɑ:ftənu:n ˈti:]	Nachmittagstee	
tea [ti:]	Tee, Abendessen →	
fine [faɪn]	gut, in Ordnung, fein, schön	
fantastic [fænˈtæstɪk]	fantastisch, großartig →	Your scones are *fantastic.*
recipe [ˈresɪpi:]	Rezept →	Achtung Aussprache!
needn't [ˈni:dnt]	nicht brauchen, nicht müssen →	You *needn't* go now.
as long as [əz ˈlɒŋ‿əz]	solange →	*As long as* they are quiet, they can stay.
to **taste** [teɪst]	schmecken →	This cake *tastes* fantastic!
jam [dʒæm]	Marmelade →	You can eat *jam* for breakfast.
butter [ˈbʌtə]	Butter →	milk, cheese, *butter*

Ausdrücke mit *to be* und *to have*

*to **be** fed up*	die Nase voll haben	*to **be** in a hurry*	es eilig haben	*to **have** a good time*	sich amüsieren
*to **be** fun*	Spaß machen	*to **be** lucky*	Glück haben	*to **have** fun*	Spaß haben
*to **be** good at*	gut sein in	*to **be** pleased with*	zufrieden sein mit	*to **have** a party*	eine Party feiern
*to **be** good with*	gut mit … umgehen können	*to **be** worried*	besorgt sein	*to **have** got*	besitzen, haben

Chats with Charlie

95 **food** [fu:d]	Essen, Nahrung, Lebensmittel →	Sandwiches are my favourite *food.*
drink [drɪŋk]	Getränk →	
price [praɪs]	Preis	

Story

96	**bloke** [bləʊk]	Typ, Kerl →	A *bloke* is a man.
	actor ['æktə]	Schauspieler →	act → *actor*
	to **follow** ['fɒləʊ]	hinterhergehen, folgen, befolgen →	*Follow* your teacher.
	autograph ['ɔ:təgrɑ:f]	Autogramm →	Let's ask him for his *autograph*.
	white elephant stall [ˌwaɪt 'elɪfənt stɔ:l]	Trödelstand →	You can buy a lot of different things at a *white elephant stall*.
	elephant ['elɪfənt]	Elefant →	*Elephants* are very big animals.
	maybe ['meɪbi]	vielleicht →	Where is she? – *Maybe* at school.
	crazy ['kreɪzi]	verrückt	
	corridor ['kɒrɪdɔ:]	Gang, Flur, Korridor	
	Where's the fire? [ˌweəz ðə 'faɪə]	Wo brennt's denn? →	
	fire [faɪə]	Feuer, Brand →	water ↔ *fire*
97	**past** [pɑ:st]	vorbei, vorüber →	The girls walk *past* Nasreen.
	soap [səʊp]	Seifenoper, Seife →	You can watch a *soap* or you can wash with *soap*.
	double ['dʌbl]	Doppelgänger, das Doppelte →	He looks like me. He's my *double*.
98	meaning ['mi:nɪŋ]	Bedeutung	
	underlined [ˌʌndə'laɪnd]	unterstrichen	

For my folder: I like …

Schreibe alle Ausdrücke auf, mit denen du sagen kannst, was du über eine Sache denkst, was du magst/nicht magst und warum du es magst/nicht magst. Die Ausdrücke rechts helfen dir. Schau dir auch deine bisher gesammelten Ausdrücke in deinem *English folder* nochmal an. Kannst du sie ergänzen?

Was ich mag/nicht mag

I think … is …	*nice*
… is … because …	*boring*
I like … because it's …	*I have fun there*
I don't like … because I must …	*I'm good at …*
…	…

Word game

Benutze das *dictionary* am Ende des Buchs. Schlage die Wörter in der rechten Spalte nach. Sie ergeben eine Frage. Lese sie laut und antworte darauf.

Du kannst auch mit deinen Freunden/Freundinnen um die Wette nach Wörtern suchen. Ihr müsst mindestens zu dritt sein. Einer fragt die anderen nach einem Wort im *dictionary*, z. B.: *What comes after/before … ?*

Wer zuerst antwortet, bekommt einen Punkt und darf das nächste Wort nennen.

Welches Wort steht

1. vor *dog*
2. nach *yes*
3. nach *south*
4. nach *end?*

Numbers

Kardinalzahlen

1	**one** [wʌn]	eins
2	**two** [tu:]	zwei
3	**three** [θri:]	drei
4	**four** [fɔ:]	vier
5	**five** [faɪv]	fünf
6	**six** [sɪks]	sechs
7	**seven** ['sevn]	sieben
8	**eight** [eɪt]	acht
9	**nine** [naɪn]	neun
10	**ten** [ten]	zehn
11	**eleven** [ɪ'levn]	elf
12	**twelve** [twelv]	zwölf
13	**thirteen** [θɜ:'ti:n]	dreizehn
14	**fourteen** [fɔ:'ti:n]	vierzehn
15	**fifteen** [fɪf'ti:n]	fünfzehn
16	**sixteen** [sɪks'ti:n]	sechzehn
17	**seventeen** [sevn'ti:n]	siebzehn
18	**eighteen** [eɪ'ti:n]	achtzehn
19	**nineteen** [nain'ti:n]	neunzehn
20	**twenty** ['twenti]	zwanzig
21	**twenty-one** [ˌtwenti'wʌn]	einundzwanzig
22	**twenty-two** [ˌtwenti'tu:]	zweiundzwanzig
23	**twenty-three** [ˌtwenti'θri:]	dreiundzwanzig
…		…
30	**thirty** ['θɜ:ti]	dreißig
40	**forty** ['fɔ:ti]	vierzig
50	**fifty** ['fɪfti]	fünfzig
60	**sixty** ['sɪksti]	sechzig
70	**seventy** ['sevnti]	siebzig
80	**eighty** ['eɪti]	achtzig
90	**ninety** ['naɪnti]	neunzig
100	**one hundred** [wʌn'hʌndrəd]	hundert

Ordinalzahlen

first [fɜ:st]	erste (-r/-s)
second ['seknd]	zweite (-r/-s)
third [θɜ:d]	dritte (-r/-s)
fourth [fɔ:θ]	vierte (-r/-s)
fifth [fɪfθ]	fünfte (-r/-s)
sixth [sɪksθ]	sechste (-r/-s)
seventh ['sevnθ]	siebte (-r/-s)
eighth [eɪtθ]	achte (-r/-s)
ninth [naɪnθ]	neunte (-r/-s)
tenth [tenθ]	zehnte (-r/-s)
eleventh [ɪ'levnθ]	elfte (-r/-s)
twelfth [twelfθ]	zwölfte (-r/-s)
thirteenth [θɜ:'ti:nθ]	dreizehnte (-r/-s)
fourteenth [fɔ:'ti:nθ]	vierzehnte (-r/-s)
fifteenth [fɪf'ti:nθ]	fünfzehnte (-r/-s)
sixteenth [sɪks'ti:nθ]	sechzehnte (-r/-s)
seventeenth [sevn'ti:nθ]	siebzehnte (-r/-s)
eighteenth [eɪ'ti:nθ]	achzehnte (-r/-s)
nineteenth [naɪn'ti:nθ]	neunzehnte (-r/-s)
twentieth ['twentiɪθ]	zwanzigste (-r/-s)
twenty-first [ˌtwenti'fɜ:st]	einundzwanzigste (-r/-s)
twenty-second [ˌtwenti'seknd]	zweiundzwanzigste (-r/-s)
twenty-third [ˌtwenti'θɜ:d]	dreiundzwanzigste (-r/-s)
twenty-fourth [ˌtwenti'fɔ:θ]	vierundzwanzigste (-r/-s)
…	…
thirtieth ['θɜ:tiəθ]	dreißigste (-r/-s)
thirty-first [ˌθɜ:ti'fɜ:st]	einunddreißigste (-r/-s)
…	…

Mengen

How much …?	Wie viel … ?
How many …?	Wie viele … ?
a lot of money/books	viel Geld/viele Bücher
a packet of cheese	ein Päckchen Käse
a bag of apples	eine Tüte Äpfel
a bottle of water	eine Flasche Wasser
a box of eggs	eine Schachtel Eier
no chocolate	keine Schokolade

Dictionary

In dieser alphabetischen Liste ist das Vokabular von *Orange Line 1* enthalten. Namen werden in einer gesonderten Liste am Ende des Vokabulars aufgelistet.
Das Zeichen ° bei einem Eintrag weist darauf hin, dass das Wort zum rezeptiven Wortschatz zählt.
Die mit * gekennzeichneten Verben sind unregelmäßig.
Wendungen, die aus mehreren Wörtern bestehen, werden meist unter mehreren Stichwörtern aufgeführt.
So ist z. B. *at home* unter *at* und *home* zu finden.
Die Fundstellen verweisen auf das erstmalige Vorkommen der Wörter, z. B.
about [ə'baʊt] über **IU3,** 40 kommt zum ersten Mal vor in Band I, Unit 3, Seite 40
colour ['kʌlə] Farbe **ILUA,** 24 kommt zum ersten Mal vor in Band I, Link-up A, Seite 24.
U = Unit, LU = Link-up, FA = Fakultativer Anhang (nur Namen)

A

a, an [ə; ən] ein/eine **I U1,** 10
a bit [ə 'bɪt] ein bisschen **I U2,** 35
a lot of [ə 'lɒt‿əv] viel/viele, eine Menge **I U2,** 30
out and **about** ['aʊt‿ənd‿ə'baʊt] unterwegs **°I U4,** 54
about [ə'baʊt] über **I U3,** 40
What about ...? [wɒt‿ə'baʊt] Was ist mit ...? Wie wäre es mit ...? **I U2,** 30
to **act** [ækt] spielen *(Theater)* **I U7,** 90
action ['ækʃn] Handlung, Aktion **°I U6,** 81
activity [æk'tɪvəti] Aktivität **°I U7,** 91
actor ['æktə] Schauspieler **I U7,** 96
to **add** [æd] hinzufügen **°I U2,** 27
address [ə'dres] Adresse **I U5,** 70
adjective ['ædʒəktɪv] Adjektiv, Eigenschaftswort **°I U1,** 22
after ['ɑ:ftə] nach **I LUB,** 39
afternoon [ˌɑ:ftə'nu:n] Nachmittag **I U2,** 34
afternoon tea [ˌɑ:ftənu:n 'ti:] Nachmittagstee **I U7,** 94
in the afternoon [ˌɪn ði: ˌɑ:ftə'nu:n] nachmittags, am Nachmittag **I U3,** 47
again [ə'gen] wieder **I U3,** 48
alarm clock [ə'lɑ:m ˌklɒk] Wecker **I U5,** 75
all [ɔ:l] alle/alles; ganz **I U3,** 50
along [ə'lɒŋ] entlang **I U7,** 91
alphabet ['ælfəbet] Alphabet, Abc **I U1,** 15
alphabetical [ˌælfə'betɪkl] alphabetisch **I U6,** 88
already [ɔ:l'redi] schon **I U2,** 34
also ['ɔ:lsəʊ] auch **I U5,** 68
always ['ɔ:lweɪz] immer, ständig **I U1,** 16
and [ænd] und **I U1,** 11
animal ['ænɪml] Tier **I U6,** 82
answer ['ɑ:ntsə] Antwort **I U4,** 58
to **answer** ['ɑ:ntsə] antworten, beantworten **°I LUA,** 24
anything ['eniθɪŋ] etwas, irgendetwas **I U5,** 66
apple ['æpl] Apfel **I U1,** 14
April ['eɪprl] April **I U5,** 70
***are** [ɑ:] bist, seid, sind **I U1,** 11
Here you are! [ˌhɪə ju:‿'ɑ:] Bitte schön! **I U1,** 20
to **arrive** [ə'raɪv] ankommen **I U6,** 86
as long as [əz 'lɒŋ‿əz] solange **I U7,** 94
to **ask** [ɑ:sk] fragen **I U3,** 44
to ask for ['ɑ:sk fə] fragen nach, bitten um **I U4,** 60
at [æt] in, auf, bei, an **I U1,** 10
at home [ət 'həʊm] zu Hause **I U2,** 26
at least [ət 'li:st] wenigstens, mindestens **I U6,** 87
at the moment [æt ðə 'məʊmənt] im Augenblick, momentan **I U7,** 90
August ['ɔ:gəst] August **I U5,** 70
aunt [ɑ:nt] Tante **I U2,** 28
autograph ['ɔ:təgrɑ:f] Autogramm **I U7,** 96
autumn ['ɔ:təm] Herbst **I U6,** 79
away [ə'weɪ] weg **I U3,** 48
to run away [rʌn‿ə'weɪ] wegrennen **I U3,** 48

B

baby, babies *(pl)* ['beɪbi; 'beɪbiz] Baby, Säugling **I U6,** 82
back [bæk] zurück **I U3,** 42
bad [bæd] schlecht **I U5,** 74
bad luck [ˌbæd 'lʌk] Pech **I U4,** 63
badminton ['bædmɪntən] Badminton, Federball **I U3,** 40
bag [bæg] Tasche, Tüte **I U1,** 14
school bag ['sku:l bæg] Schultasche, Schulranzen **I U1,** 14
sleeping bag ['sli:pɪŋ ˌbæg] Schlafsack **I U6,** 84
ball [bɔ:l] Ball **I U1,** 20
balloon [bə'lu:n] Luftballon **°I U5,** 71
burger **bar** ['bɜ:gə ˌbɑ:] Fastfood-Restaurant **I U5,** 68
to **bark** [bɑ:k] bellen **I U3,** 48
basketball ['bɑ:skɪtbɔ:l] Basketball **I U3,** 40
bathroom ['bɑ:θrʊm] Bad, Badezimmer **I LUA,** 24
*to **be** [bi:] sein **I U1,** 23
He is on his way to ... [ˌhi:‿ɪz‿ɒn hɪz 'weɪ tə] Er ist auf dem Weg zu ... **I U3,** 42
I'm good at ... [aɪm 'gʊd‿ət] ich bin gut in ... **I U1,** 20
to be fed up [bi: ˌfed‿'ʌp] die Nase voll haben **I U2,** 34
to be fun [bi: 'fʌn] Spaß machen **I U3,** 43
to be good with ... [bi: 'gʊd wɪð] gut mit ... umgehen können **I U2,** 34
to be in a hurry [bi:‿ɪn‿ə 'hʌri] es eilig haben **I U2,** 30
to be pleased with [bi: 'pli:zd wɪð] zufrieden sein mit **I U6,** 87
to be right [bi: 'raɪt] Recht haben **°I U6,** 83
to be worried ['wʌrid] besorgt sein, beunruhigt sein **I U6,** 87

English – German

you're lucky [ˌjʊəˈlʌki] du hast Glück **I U1,** 16
beautiful [ˈbjuːtɪfl] schön, wunderschön **I U6,** 78
because [bɪˈkɒz] weil **I U2,** 30
bed [bed] Bett **I LUA,** 25
bedroom [ˈbedrʊm] Schlafzimmer **I LUA,** 24
before [bɪˈfɔː] vor; bevor **I LUB,** 39
behind [bɪˈhaɪnd] hinter **I U1,** 18
between [bɪˈtwiːn] zwischen **I U7,** 90
big [bɪg] groß **I U1,** 12
bike [baɪk] Fahrrad **I LUB,** 38
by bike [baɪ ˈbaɪk] mit dem Fahrrad **I U4,** 57
birthday [ˈbɜːθdeɪ] Geburtstag **I U5,** 68
biscuit [ˈbɪskɪt] Keks **I U5,** 68
a **bit** [ə ˈbɪt] ein bisschen **I U2,** 35
black [blæk] schwarz **I LUA,** 24
bloke [bləʊk] Typ, Kerl **I U7,** 96
*to **blow up** [bləʊ‿ˈʌp] aufblasen °**I U5,** 71
blue [bluː] blau **I LUA,** 24
board [bɔːd] Tafel, Wandtafel **I U1,** 18
book [bʊk] Buch **I U1,** 14
exercise book [ˈeksəsaɪz ˌbʊk] Heft, Übungsheft **I U1,** 14
boring [ˈbɔːrɪŋ] langweilig **I U1,** 20
to **borrow** [ˈbɒrəʊ] borgen, leihen **I U2,** 34
bottle [ˈbɒtl] Flasche **I U5,** 68
box, boxes *(pl)* [bɒks; ˈbɒksɪz] Kiste, Schachtel, Kasten **I U5,** 68
boy [bɔɪ] Junge **I U1,** 16
to **break-dance** [ˈbreɪk dɑːnts] Breakdance tanzen **I LUB,** 38
breakfast [ˈbrekfəst] Frühstück **I U3,** 44
bridge [brɪdʒ] Brücke **I LUC,** 52
*to **bring** [brɪŋ] bringen, mitbringen **I U3,** 43
to bring in [brɪŋ‿ˈɪn] hereinbringen, mitbringen °**I U7,** 93
broken [ˈbrəʊkn] kaputt, zerbrochen, gebrochen **I U6,** 84
brother [ˈbrʌðə] Bruder **I LUA,** 25
brown [braʊn] braun **I LUA,** 24
burger [ˈbɜːgə] Hamburger **I U5,** 68
burger bar [ˈbɜːgə ˌbɑː] Fastfood-Restaurant **I U5,** 68
bus, buses *(pl)* [bʌs; ˈbʌsɪz] Bus **I LUC,** 52
bus stop [ˈbʌs ˌstɒp] Bushaltestelle **I LUC,** 52
bush, bushes *(pl)* [bʊʃ; ˈbʊʃɪz] Busch, Strauch **I U6,** 86
busy [ˈbɪzi] beschäftigt, ausgefüllt **I U2,** 34
but [bʌt] aber **I U2,** 26
butter [ˈbʌtə] Butter **I U7,** 94
*to **buy** [baɪ] kaufen **I U5,** 66
by bike [baɪ ˈbaɪk] mit dem Fahrrad **I U4,** 57
bye [baɪ] tschüss **I U1,** 16

C

café [ˈkæfeɪ] Café **I U3,** 48
cafeteria [ˌkæfəˈtɪəriə] Cafeteria **I U1,** 20
cake [keɪk] Kuchen **I U5,** 68
calendar [ˈkæləndə] Kalender **I U5,** 71
call [kɔːl] Anruf °**I U6,** 83
to **call** [kɔːl] rufen, anrufen, nennen **I U3,** 48
camping [ˈkæmpɪŋ] Camping, Zelten **I U6,** 84
***can** [kæn] können, dürfen **I U1,** 19
cap [kæp] Kappe, Mütze **I U5,** 66
car [kɑː] Auto **I U3,** 49
card [kɑːd] Karte **I LUB,** 38
caretaker [ˈkeəteɪkə] Hausmeister/Hausmeisterin **I U1,** 12
to **carry** [ˈkæri] tragen **I U6,** 80
pencil **case** [ˈpensl ˌkeɪs] Mäppchen **I U1,** 14
cat [kæt] Katze **I U2,** 26
CD [ˌsiːˈdiː] CD **I U5,** 69
centre [ˈsentə] Zentrum, Mittelpunkt **I LUC,** 52
information centre [ɪnfəˈmeɪʃn ˌsentə] Informationszentrum **I LUC,** 52
chair [tʃeə] Stuhl **I U1,** 18
charity [ˈtʃærɪti] Wohltätigkeit, Wohltätigkeitsverein **I U7,** 90
chat [tʃæt] Geplauder, Unterhaltung **I U2,** 33
to **chat** [tʃæt] sich unterhalten **I U2,** 33
cheap [tʃiːp] billig **I U5,** 68
to **check** [tʃek] überprüfen **I U6,** 82
cheese [tʃiːz] Käse **I U5,** 68
child, children *(pl)* [tʃaɪld; ˈtʃɪldrɪn] Kind **I U2,** 26
only child [ˈəʊnli ˌtʃaɪld] Einzelkind **I U2,** 26
chocolate [ˈtʃɒklət] Schokolade **I U1,** 18
*to **choose** [tʃuːz] wählen, auswählen **I U4,** 54
church [tʃɜːtʃ] Kirche **I LUC,** 52
to **clap** [klæp] klatschen **I U1,** 15
class [klɑːs] Schulklasse, Klasse **I U1,** 16
classroom [ˈklɑːsrʊm] Klassenzimmer **I U1,** 16
clock [klɒk] Uhr **I U4,** 54
alarm clock [əˈlɑːm ˌklɒk] Wecker **I U5,** 75
o'clock [əˈklɒk] Uhr *(Zeitangabe)* **I U3,** 40
to **close** [kləʊz] schließen, zumachen **I LUC,** 53
closed [kləʊzd] zu, geschlossen °**I U2,** 32
club [klʌb] Klub, Verein, Arbeitsgemeinschaft **I LUB,** 39
cold [kəʊld] kalt **I U4,** 62
to **collect** [kəˈlekt] sammeln **I LUB,** 38
colour [ˈkʌlə] Farbe **I LUA,** 24
*to **come** [kʌm] kommen **I U2,** 33
Come on. [kʌm‿ˈɒn] Komm./Kommt. **I U2,** 35
to come in [kʌm‿ˈɪn] hereinkommen **I U3,** 48
to come over [kʌm‿ˈəʊvə] herüberkommen **I U2,** 27
comic [ˈkɒmɪk] Comic, Comicheft **I LUB,** 38
to **compare** [kəmˈpeə] vergleichen °**I U7,** 91
to **complete** [kəmˈpliːt] vervollständigen °**I U4,** 54
computer [ˌkəmˈpjuːtə] Computer **I LUA,** 25
cooking [ˈkʊkɪŋ] Kochen, Koch- **I U3,** 40
cool [kuːl] cool, prima **I U1,** 20
to **copy** [ˈkɒpi] abschreiben, kopieren °**I U1,** 14
cornflakes [ˈkɔːnfleɪks] Cornflakes **I U5,** 68
to **correct** [kəˈrekt] korrigieren, verbessern °**I LUB,** 38
corridor [ˈkɒrɪdɔː] Gang, Flur, Korridor **I U7,** 96
country, countries *(pl)* [ˈkʌntri; ˈkʌntriz] Land **I U2,** 29
in the country [ˌɪn ðə ˈkʌntri] auf dem Land **I U6,** 78
of **course** [əv ˈkɔːs] natürlich, selbstverständlich **I U1,** 19
cousin [ˈkʌzn] Cousin/Cousine **I U2,** 28
cow [kaʊ] Kuh **I U6,** 82
crazy [ˈkreɪzi] verrückt **I U7,** 96
ice-**cream** [aɪs ˈkriːm] Eis, Eiscreme **I U7,** 92

cricket [ˈkrɪkɪt] Kricket **I U7,** 92
crisp [krɪsp] Kartoffelchip **I U1,** 18
crossword (puzzle) [ˈkrɒswɜːd ˈpʌzl] Kreuzworträtsel °**I U5,** 71
cupboard [ˈkʌbəd] Küchenschrank, Schrank **I U1,** 18

D

dad [dæd] Papa, Vati **I LUA,** 25
to **dance** [dɑːnts] tanzen **I U3,** 40
dark [dɑːk] dunkel **I U2,** 34
date [deɪt] Datum **I U5,** 70
day [deɪ] Tag **I LUB,** 39
  sports day [ˈspɔːts deɪ] Sportfest **I U7,** 90
dear [dɪə] lieb **I U3,** 44
December [dɪˈsembə] Dezember **I U5,** 70
department store [dɪˈpɑːtmənt stɔː] Kaufhaus **I LUC,** 52
to **describe** [dɪˈskraɪb] beschreiben °**I U7,** 92
desk [desk] Schreibtisch **I U1,** 18
dialogue [ˈdaɪəlɒg] Gespräch °**I U3,** 42
different [ˈdɪfrnt] anders, verschieden **I U6,** 78
dining room [ˈdaɪnɪŋ rʊm] Esszimmer, Speisesaal **I LUA,** 24
disco [ˈdɪskəʊ] Disko **I U5,** 74
divorced from [dɪˈvɔːst frəm] geschieden von **I U2,** 28
DJ [ˌdiːˈdʒeɪ] DJ **I U2,** 33
*to **do** [duː] machen, tun **I U1,** 15 °**I U7,** 95
  to do sports [duː ˈspɔːts] Sport treiben **I U7,** 92
dog [dɒg] Hund **I U2,** 27
  to walk the dog [wɔːk ðə ˈdɒg] mit dem Hund spazieren gehen **I U3,** 42
dog-tired [ˌdɒg ˈtaɪəd] hundemüde **I U3,** 49
door [dɔː] Tür **I U1,** 18
double [ˈdʌbl] Doppelgänger, das Doppelte **I U7,** 97
*to go **down** [gəʊ ˈdaʊn] hinuntergehen °**I U4,** 61
  to sit down [sɪt ˈdaʊn] sich setzen, sich hinsetzen **I U1,** 19
  Go down … [ˈgəʊ daʊn] Geh … entlang. **I LUC,** 53
downstairs [daʊnˈsteəz] unten, im unteren Stock **I U2,** 27
drama [ˈdrɑːmə] Theater, Drama **I U3,** 40
*to **draw** [drɔː] zeichnen **I LUB,** 38
dream [driːm] Traum **I LUA,** 25
to **dress** [dres] sich anziehen **I U3,** 44
drink [drɪŋk] Getränk **I U7,** 95
*to **drink** [drɪŋk] trinken **I U5,** 75
*to **drive** [draɪv] fahren **I U6,** 86
driver [ˈdraɪvə] Fahrer/Fahrerin **I U4,** 54
drums [drʌmz] Schlagzeug **I U2,** 26

E

each [iːtʃ] jede/jeder/jedes °**I U6,** 87
early [ˈɜːli] früh **I U3,** 46
east [iːst] Osten **I U4,** 54
easy [ˈiːzi] einfach, leicht **I U1,** 20
*to **eat** [iːt] essen, fressen **I U3,** 44
egg [eg] Ei **I U5,** 68
elephant [ˈelɪfənt] Elefant **I U7,** 96
else [els] sonst, noch **I U5,** 66
e-mail [ˈiːmeɪl] E-Mail **I U3,** 44
to **end** [end] enden **I U5,** 76
English [ˈɪŋglɪʃ] englisch **I U1,** 11
er [ɜː] äh °**I U1,** 12
euro [ˈjʊərəʊ] Euro *(Währung)* **I U5,** 73
even [ˈiːvn] selbst, sogar **I U7,** 90
evening [ˈiːvnɪŋ] Abend **I U3,** 47
in the **evening** [ˌɪn ðiː ˈiːvnɪŋ] abends, am Abend **I U3,** 47
event [ɪˈvent] Veranstaltung, Ereignis **I U7,** 90
every [ˈevri] jede/jeder/jedes **I U3,** 40
example [ɪgˈzɑːmpl] Beispiel °**I U1,** 13
exchange [ɪksˈtʃeɪndʒ] Austausch, Tausch **I U7,** 94
excited [ɪkˈsaɪtɪd] aufgeregt **I U5,** 74
Excuse me! [ɪkˈskjuːz mi] Entschuldigung! **I U3,** 42
exercise [ˈeksəsaɪz] Übung, Aufgabe **I U1,** 19
  exercise book [ˈeksəsaɪz ˌbʊk] Heft, Übungsheft **I U1,** 14
expensive [ɪkˈspentsɪv] teuer **I U5,** 68
eye [aɪ] Auge **I U2,** 35

F

face [feɪs] Gesicht **I U3,** 48
fair [feə] Messe, Jahrmarkt **I U7,** 90
  summer fair [ˈsʌmə ˌfeə] Sommerfest **I U7,** 90
family [ˈfæmli] Familie **I LUA,** 25
  family tree [ˈfæmli triː] Familienstammbaum °**I U2,** 28
famous [ˈfeɪməs] berühmt **I U4,** 54
fantastic [fænˈtæstɪk] fantastisch, großartig **I U7,** 94
farm [fɑːm] Bauernhof, Farm **I U6,** 78
farmer [ˈfɑːmə] Bauer, Bäuerin, Landwirt/Landwirtin **I U6,** 82
favourite [ˈfeɪvrɪt] Lieblings- **I U1,** 12
February [ˈfebruri] Februar **I U5,** 70
*to **feed** [fiːd] füttern **I U6,** 80
  to be fed up [biː ˌfed‿ˈʌp] die Nase voll haben **I U2,** 34
field [fiːld] Feld, Acker **I U6,** 88
  sports field [ˈspɔːts fiːld] Sportplatz **I U7,** 92
to **fill** in [fɪl‿ˈɪn] ausfüllen, einsetzen °**I U1,** 14
*to **find** [faɪnd] finden **I U3,** 48
  to find out [faɪnd‿ˈaʊt] herausfinden **I U4,** 62
fine [faɪn] gut, in Ordnung, fein, schön **I U7,** 94
to **finish** [ˈfɪnɪʃ] beenden, erledigen, aufhören **I U2,** 34
fire [faɪə] Feuer, Brand **I U7,** 96
  Where's the fire? [ˌweəz ðə ˈfaɪə] Wo brennt's denn? **I U7,** 96
first [fɜːst] zuerst; erste/erster/erstes **I U4,** 54
fish, fish *(pl)* [fɪʃ] Fisch/Fische **I U6,** 78
fishing [ˈfɪʃɪŋ] Angeln, Fischen **I U6,** 78
flag [flæg] Flagge, Fahne **I U2,** 29
flat [flæt] Wohnung **I U2,** 26
flower [ˈflaʊə] Blume **I U6,** 78
foggy [ˈfɒgi] neblig **I U6,** 79
folder [ˈfəʊldə] Ordner, Mappe **I U4,** 60
to **follow** [ˈfɒləʊ] hinterhergehen, folgen, befolgen **I U7,** 96
food [fuːd] Essen, Nahrung, Lebensmittel **I U7,** 95
foot, feet *(pl)* [fʊt; fiːt] Fuß **I U4,** 54
  on foot [ɒn ˈfʊt] zu Fuß **I U4,** 57
football [ˈfʊtbɔːl] Fußball **I U1,** 12
for [fɔː] für **I U1,** 11
*to **forget** [fəˈget] vergessen **I U4,** 60
form [fɔːm] Form °**I U6,** 88
  long form [ˈlɒŋ fɔːm] Langform °**I U1,** 16
free [friː] frei **I U3,** 40
Friday [ˈfraɪdeɪ] Freitag **I LUB,** 39
friend [frend] Freund/Freundin **I U1,** 16
from [frɒm] aus, von **I U1,** 10
  divorced from [dɪˈvɔːst frəm] geschieden von **I U2,** 28
  Where are you from? [ˌweər‿ə jə ˈfrɒm] Woher kommst du? **I U1,** 11
in **front** of [ɪn ˈfrʌnt‿əv] vor **I U3,** 49

fun [fʌn] Spaß **I U3,** 41
Have fun! [ˌhæv ˈfʌn] Viel Spaß! **I U6,** 82
to be fun [bi: ˈfʌn] Spaß machen **I U3,** 43
to have fun [ˌhæv ˈfʌn] Spaß haben, sich amüsieren **I U6,** 82
funny [ˈfʌni] komisch, lustig **I LUA,** 25
furniture [ˈfɜ:nɪtʃə] Möbel **I LUA,** 25

G

game [geɪm] Spiel **I U2,** 26
garden [ˈgɑ:dn] Garten **I U2,** 26
German [ˈdʒɜ:mən] deutsch; Deutsche/ Deutscher **I U1,** 17
*to **get** [get] kommen, bekommen, besorgen **I U3,** 44
to get into [get‿ˈɪntə] einsteigen in **I U5,** 75
to get lost [get ˈlɒst] verloren gehen, sich verirren **I U3,** 48
to get off [get‿ˈɒf] aussteigen aus **I U4,** 59
to get out [get‿ˈaʊt] aussteigen **I U6,** 86
to get up [get‿ˈʌp] aufstehen **I U3,** 44
ghost [gəʊst] Geist, Gespenst **I U2,** 34
girl [gɜ:l] Mädchen **I U1,** 16
*to **give** [gɪv] geben, schenken **I U4,** 60
*to **go** [gəʊ] gehen **I U1,** 19
Go down … [ˈgəʊ daʊn] Geh … entlang. **I LUC,** 53
Go left. [gəʊ ˈleft] Biege nach links ab. **I LUC,** 52
Go right. [gəʊ ˈraɪt] Biege nach rechts ab. **I LUC,** 52
to go down [gəʊ ˈdaʊn] hinuntergehen °**I U4,** 61
to go up [gəʊ‿ˈʌp] hinaufgehen °**I U4,** 61
goal [gəʊl] Tor, Ziel **I U1,** 12
good [gʊd] gut **I U1,** 16
Good luck! [ˌgʊd ˈlʌk] Viel Glück! **I U4,** 63
Good Morning! [ˈgʊd ˈmɔ:nɪŋ] Guten Morgen! **I U1,** 16
I'm good at … [aɪm ˈgʊd‿ət] ich bin gut in … **I U1,** 20
to be good with … [bi: ˈgʊd wɪð] gut mit … umgehen können **I U2,** 34
to have a good time [ˌhæv‿ə gʊd ˈtaɪm] sich amüsieren **I U5,** 75
goodbye [gʊdˈbaɪ] auf Wiedersehen **I U1,** 19

*to have **got** [hæv ˈgɒt] besitzen, haben **I U2,** 30
grandad [ˈgrændæd] Opa **I LUA,** 25
grandma [ˈgrændmɑ:] Oma **I LUA,** 25
great [greɪt] großartig, toll **I U2,** 26
Greek [gri:k] griechisch; Grieche/ Griechin **I U2,** 29
green [gri:n] grün **I LUA,** 24
grid [grɪd] Gitter, Tabelle °**I U1,** 14
group [gru:p] Gruppe **I U4,** 54
gym [dʒɪm] Turnhalle **I U3,** 40
to **guess** [ges] raten, vermuten °**I U6,** 81

H

half past (two) [ˈhɑ:f pɑ:st] halb (drei) **I U3,** 40
half-sister [ˈhɑ:fˌsɪstə] Halbschwester **I U2,** 26
hall [hɔ:l] Halle, Saal, Flur **I U3,** 40
Hang on! [ˈhæŋ‿ɒn] Moment mal! Warte mal! **I U6,** 82
to **happen** [ˈhæpn] geschehen, passieren **I U6,** 86
happy [ˈhæpi] glücklich, froh **I U2,** 33
*to **have** [hæv] haben **I U5,** 68
Have fun! [ˌhæv ˈfʌn] Viel Spaß! **I U6,** 82
to have a good time [ˌhæv‿ə gʊd ˈtaɪm] sich amüsieren **I U5,** 75
to have a party [ˌhæv‿ə ˈpɑ:ti] eine Party feiern **I U5,** 68
to have fun [ˌhæv ˈfʌn] Spaß haben, sich amüsieren **I U6,** 82
to have got [hæv ˈgɒt] besitzen, haben **I U2,** 30
to have supper [hæv ˈsʌpə] zu Abend essen **I U3,** 44
he [hi:] er **I U1,** 12
*to **hear** [hɪə] hören **I U6,** 78
Hello! [heˈləʊ] Hallo! **I U1,** 10
help [help] Hilfe **I U2,** 34
to **help** [help] helfen **I U2,** 34
her [hɜ:] ihr/ihre; sie **I U2,** 26
here [hɪə] hier **I U1,** 12
Here you are! [ˈhɪə ju:‿ɑ:] Bitte schön! **I U1,** 20
hey [heɪ] he °**I U1,** 16
Hi! [haɪ] Hi! **I U1,** 10
*to **hide** [haɪd] verstecken, sich verstecken **I U6,** 86
him [hɪm] ihn, ihm **I U4,** 60
his [hɪz] sein/seine **I LUA,** 25
hobby, hobbies *(pl)* [ˈhɒbi; ˈhɒbiz] Hobby **I LUB,** 38

home [həʊm] Zuhause, Heim; nach Hause **I U1,** 11
at home [ət ˈhəʊm] zu Hause **I U2,** 26
*to take home [ˌteɪk ˈhəʊm] nach Hause bringen **I U2,** 35
homework [ˈhəʊmwɜ:k] Hausaufgabe/ Hausaufgaben **I U1,** 19
to **hope** [həʊp] hoffen **I U5,** 72
horse [hɔ:s] Pferd **I LUB,** 38
hot [hɒt] heiß **I U6,** 79
hour [ˈaʊə] Stunde **I U2,** 34
hours [ˈaʊəz] Öffnungszeiten **I U4,** 62
house [haʊs] Haus **I LUA,** 25
how [haʊ] wie **I U1,** 11
How are you? [ˌhaʊ‿ˈɑ: ju:] Wie geht es dir/Ihnen/euch? **I U6,** 83
how many [haʊ ˈmeni] wie viele **I U5,** 68
How much are … ? [ˌhaʊ ˈmʌtʃ‿ɑ:] Wie viel kosten … ? **I U5,** 66
How much is … ? [ˌhaʊ ˈmʌtʃ‿ɪz] Wie viel kostet … ? **I U5,** 66
How old are you? [haʊ‿ˈəʊld‿ɑ: ju:] Wie alt bist du? **I U1,** 11
*to be in a **hurry** [bi:‿ɪn‿ə ˈhʌri] es eilig haben **I U2,** 30
Hurry up! [ˌhʌri‿ˈʌp] Beeil dich! **I U2,** 30

I

I [aɪ] ich **I U1,** 10
ice-cream [aɪs ˈkri:m] Eis, Eiscreme **I U7,** 92
idea [aɪˈdɪə] Idee, Einfall **I LUB,** 38
idiot [ˈɪdiət] Idiot, Dummkopf **I U1,** 21
I'm [aɪm] ich bin **I U1,** 10
in [ɪn] in, auf; herein **I U1,** 10
in front of [ɪn ˈfrʌnt‿əv] vor **I U3,** 49
information [ˌɪnfəˈmeɪʃn] Information/ Informationen **I LUC,** 52
information centre [ɪnfəˈmeɪʃn ˌsentə] Informationszentrum **I LUC,** 52
inside [ɪnˈsaɪd] innen, drin, nach drinnen **I U5,** 75
into [ˈɪntə] in, in … hinein **I U3,** 44
to get into [get‿ˈɪntə] einsteigen in **I U5,** 75
invitation [ˌɪnvɪˈteɪʃn] Einladung **I U5,** 70
to **invite** [ɪnˈvaɪt] einladen **I U5,** 68
***is** [ɪz] ist **I U1,** 10
it [ɪt] es **I U1,** 12
Italian [ɪˈtælien] italienisch; Italiener/ Italienerin **I U2,** 29

J

jacket ['dʒækɪt] Jacke **I U6,** 86
jam [dʒæm] Marmelade **I U7,** 94
January ['dʒænjuri] Januar **I U5,** 70
joke [dʒəʊk] Witz **I U1,** 20
to **joke** [dʒəʊk] scherzen, Witze machen **I U6,** 82
July [dʒʊ'laɪ] Juli **I U5,** 70
long **jump** ['lɒŋ ˌdʒʌmp] Weitsprung **I U7,** 90
June [dʒu:n] Juni **I U5,** 70
just [dʒʌst] nur, gerade, einfach **I U2,** 30

K

Keep out! [ki:p‿'aʊt] Eintritt verboten! **I U2,** 26
to **kick** [kɪk] treten **I U5,** 74
kid [kɪd] Kind **I U3,** 44
kitchen ['kɪtʃɪn] Küche **I LUA,** 24
knock [nɒk] Klopfen, Schlag **I U2,** 34
*to **know** [nəʊ] wissen, kennen **I U4,** 58

L

land [lænd] Land **I LUB,** 38
language ['læŋgwɪdʒ] Sprache **I U2,** 29
lantern ['læntən] Laterne **I U7,** 90
laptop ['læptɒp] Laptop **I U2,** 34
large [lɑ:dʒ] groß, riesig **I U5,** 66
last [lɑ:st] letzte/letzter/letztes **I U7,** 90
late [leɪt] spät, zu spät, verspätet **I U1,** 16
later ['leɪtə] später **I U2,** 30
to **laugh** [lɑ:f] lachen **I U5,** 74
*to **learn** [lɜ:n] lernen **I U3,** 40
at **least** [ət 'li:st] wenigstens, mindestens **I U6,** 87
*to **leave** [li:v] lassen, verlassen, abfahren **I U3,** 43
left [left] linke/linker/linkes; links **I U4,** 55
Go **left.** [gəʊ 'left] Biege nach links ab. **I LUC,** 52
on the **left** [ɒn ðə 'left] links **I U2,** 28
lemonade [ˌlemə'neɪd] Limonade **I U5,** 68
lesson ['lesn] Unterrichtsstunde **I U1,** 15
Let's . . . . [lets] Lasst uns .... **I U1,** 10
letter ['letə] Buchstabe, Brief **I U1,** 15
to **like** [laɪk] mögen, gern haben **I U3,** 44
like [laɪk] wie **I U6,** 86
line [laɪn] Zeile, Text, Linie **I U3,** 43
list [lɪst] Liste **I U5,** 68
to **listen** ['lɪsn] zuhören, anhören **I U1,** 11
little [lɪtl] klein **I U6,** 82
to **live** [lɪv] wohnen, leben **I U3,** 45
living room ['lɪvɪŋ rʊm] Wohnzimmer **I LUA,** 24
long [lɒŋ] lang **I U3,** 44
as long as [əz 'lɒŋ‿əz] solange **I U7,** 94
long form ['lɒŋ fɔ:m] Langform °**I U1,** 16
long jump ['lɒŋ ˌdʒʌmp] Weitsprung **I U7,** 90
to **look** [lʊk] sehen, schauen, aussehen **I U1,** 12
to look at ['lʊk‿ət] ansehen **I U6,** 82
to look for ['lʊk fə] suchen **I U6,** 81
*to get **lost** [get 'lɒst] verloren gehen, sich verirren **I U3,** 48
a **lot** of [ə 'lɒt‿əv] viel/viele, eine Menge **I U2,** 30
love [lʌv] Herzliche Grüße (am Briefende), Liebe **I U6,** 78
to **love** [lʌv] lieben, gern mögen **I U3,** 44
luck [lʌk] Glück **I U4,** 63
bad luck [ˌbæd 'lʌk] Pech **I U4,** 63
Good luck! [ˌgʊd 'lʌk] Viel Glück! **I U4,** 63
lucky ['lʌki] glücklich **I U1,** 16
you're lucky [ˌjʊə'lʌki] du hast Glück **I U1,** 16
lunch [lʌntʃ] Mittagessen **I U1,** 18
lunchtime ['lʌntʃtaɪm] Mittag, Mittagszeit **I U1,** 19

M

magazine [mægə'zi:n] Zeitschrift, Magazin **I U2,** 33
*to **make** [meɪk] machen, tun **I U1,** 11
to make up [meɪk‿'ʌp] erfinden, sich ausdenken **I U4,** 62
make-up ['meɪkʌp] Make-up, Schminke **I U7,** 90
man, men *(pl)* [mæn; men] Mann **I U4,** 62
manager ['mænɪdʒə] Manager/ Managerin **I U2,** 26
many ['meni] viele **I U5,** 68
how many [haʊ 'meni] wie viele **I U5,** 68
map [mæp] Stadtplan, Landkarte **I LUC,** 52
March [mɑ:tʃ] März **I U5,** 70
mark [mɑ:k] Fleck **I U2,** 30
married to ['mærid tə] verheiratet mit **I U2,** 28
to **match** [mætʃ] zuordnen, zusammenfügen °**I U1,** 13
May [meɪ] Mai **I U5,** 70
maybe ['meɪbi] vielleicht **I U7,** 96
me [mi:] mich, mir **I LUB,** 38
*to **mean** [mi:n] bedeuten, meinen **I U4,** 55
meaning ['mi:nɪŋ] Bedeutung °**I U7,** 98
medium ['mi:diəm] mittel **I U5,** 66
*to **meet** [mi:t] treffen, sich treffen **I U3,** 45
Meow! [mi:'aʊ] Miau! °**I U2,** 35
text **message** ['tekst ˌmesɪdʒ] SMS **I U6,** 80
mice *(pl)* [maɪs] Mäuse **I U3,** 45
milk [mɪlk] Milch **I U5,** 68
to **mime** [maɪm] pantomimisch darstellen °**I U6,** 81
miming game ['maɪmɪŋ] Pantomime °**I U6,** 81
minute ['mɪnɪt] Minute **I U5,** 69
Miss [mɪs] Frau *(Anrede)* **I U7,** 94
missing ['mɪsɪŋ] fehlend °**I U4,** 64
mobile ['məʊbaɪl] Handy, Mobiltelefon **I U1,** 11
at the **moment** [æt ðə 'məʊmənt] im Augenblick, momentan **I U7,** 90
moment ['məʊmənt] Moment, Augenblick **I U7,** 90
Monday ['mʌndeɪ] Montag **I LUB,** 39
on Mondays [ɒn 'mʌndeɪz] montags **I LUB,** 39
money ['mʌni] Geld **I U5,** 67
month [mʌnθ] Monat **I U5,** 70
more [mɔ:] mehr **I U2,** 29
morning ['mɔ:nɪŋ] Morgen, Vormittag **I U1,** 16
Good Morning! ['gʊd 'mɔ:nɪŋ] Guten Morgen! **I U1,** 16
in the morning [ˌɪn ðə 'mɔ:nɪŋ] morgens, am Morgen, vormittags **I U3,** 47
most [məʊst] das meiste, die meisten **I U3,** 44
mouse [maʊs] Maus **I U1,** 10
Mr ['mɪstə] Herr *(Anrede)* **I U1,** 12
Mrs ['mɪsɪz] Frau *(Anrede)* **I U1,** 12

much [mʌtʃ] viel I **U5, 66**
How much are … ? [ˌhaʊ ˈmʌtʃ‿ɑː]
Wie viel kosten … ? I **U5, 66**
How much is … ? [ˌhaʊ ˈmʌtʃ‿ɪz]
Wie viel kostet … ? I **U5, 66**
mum [mʌm] Mama, Mutti I **LUA, 25**
museum [mjuːˈziːəm] Museum I **LUC, 52**
music [ˈmjuːzɪk] Musik I **U2, 34**
*__must__ [mʌst] müssen I **U7, 94**
my [maɪ] mein/meine I **U1, 10**
My name is …. [maɪ ˈneɪm‿ɪz] Ich heiße …. I **U1, 10**

N

name [neɪm] Name I **U1, 10**
My name is …. [maɪ ˈneɪm‿ɪz] Ich heiße …. I **U1, 10**
What's your name? [ˌwɒts jə ˈneɪm] Wie heißt du? I **U1, 11**
near [nɪə] in der Nähe von, nahe I **LUC, 53**
needn't [ˈniːdnt] nicht brauchen, nicht müssen I **U7, 94**
never [ˈnevə] nie, niemals I **U3, 44**
new [njuː] neu I **U1, 10**
newsagent [ˈnjuːsˌeɪdʒənt] Zeitschriftenhändler/Zeitschriftenhändlerin I **LUC, 52**
next [nekst] nächste/nächster/nächstes I **U5, 69**
next to [ˈnekst tə] neben I **U2, 28**
nice [naɪs] nett I **U1, 12**
night [naɪt] Nacht I **U3, 44**
night nurse [ˈnaɪt nɜːs] Nachtschwester I **U3, 47**
no [nəʊ] nein, nicht; kein/keine I **U1, 12**
noise [nɔɪz] Geräusch, Lärm I **U2, 35**
normal [ˈnɔːml] normal I **U3, 44**
north [nɔːθ] Norden I **U4, 55**
not [nɒt] nicht I **U1, 16**
November [nəʊˈvembə] November I **U5, 70**
now [naʊ] jetzt, nun I **U1, 20**
right now [ˌraɪt ˈnaʊ] gleich jetzt, in diesem Augenblick I **U7, 92**
number [ˈnʌmbə] Nummer, Zahl I **U1, 11**
phone number [ˈfəʊnˈnʌmbə] Telefonnummer I **U1, 11**
nurse [nɜːs] Krankenschwester, Krankenpfleger I **U3, 47**
night nurse [ˈnaɪt nɜːs] Nachtschwester I **U3, 47**

O

observatory [əbˈzɜːvətri] Observatorium, Sternwarte I **U5, 73**
October [ɒkˈtəʊbə] Oktober I **U5, 70**
of [ɒv; əv] von I **U2, 26**
of course [əv ˈkɔːs] natürlich, selbstverständlich I **U1, 19**
*to get **off** [get‿ˈɒf] aussteigen aus I **U4, 59**
often [ˈɒfn] oft I **U3, 44**
oh [əʊ] oh °I **U1, 12**
Oink-oink! [ɔɪŋk‿ɔɪŋk] Grunz! °I **U6, 82**
OK [əʊˈkeɪ] OK I **U1, 12**
is OK with us [ɪz‿əʊˈkeɪ wɪð‿ʌs] ist uns recht I **U6, 78**
We're OK. [ˌwɪər‿əʊˈkeɪ] Es geht uns gut. I **U6, 83**
old [əʊld] alt I **U1, 11**
How old are you? [haʊ‿ˈəʊld‿ə juː] Wie alt bist du? I **U1, 11**
on [ɒn] auf, an I **U1, 14**
on foot [ɒn ˈfʊt] zu Fuß I **U4, 57**
on Mondays [ɒn ˈmʌndeɪz] montags I **LUB, 39**
on the left [ɒn ðə ˈleft] links I **U2, 28**
on the right [ɒn ðə ˈraɪt] rechts I **U2, 28**
only child [ˈəʊnli ˌtʃaɪld] Einzelkind I **U2, 26**
only [ˈəʊnli] nur, bloß, erst I **U2, 26**
Oops! [uːps] Huch! °I **U1, 20**
to **open** [ˈəʊpən] öffnen, aufmachen I **U1, 19**
or [ɔː] oder I **U1, 11**
order [ˈɔːdə] Reihenfolge, Ordnung °I **U1, 21**
to **organize** [ˈɔːgənaɪz] organisieren I **U7, 90**
other [ˈʌðə] andere/anderer/anderes I **U7, 91**
our [ˈaʊə] unser/unsere I **U2, 26**
out [aʊt] heraus, draußen, außerhalb I **U3, 42**
Keep out! [kiːp‿ˈaʊt] Eintritt verboten! I **U2, 26**
out and about [ˈaʊt‿nd‿əˈbaʊt] unterwegs °I **U4, 54**
to get out [get‿ˈaʊt] aussteigen I **U6, 86**
to sort out [sɔːt‿ˈaʊt] klären, regeln *(ein Problem)* I **U2, 30**
to take out [teɪk‿ˈaʊt] herausnehmen I **U3, 42**
out of [ˈaʊt‿əv] aus … heraus I **U3, 49**
outside [aʊtˈsaɪd] außerhalb, draußen, nach draußen I **U2, 30**
oven [ˈʌvn] Backofen I **U3, 42**
over there [ˌəʊvə ˈðeə] da drüben I **U5, 66**
to come over [kʌm‿ˈəʊvə] herüberkommen I **U2, 34**
over [ˈəʊvə] über I **U2, 26**

P

to **pack** [pæk] packen I **U6, 80**
packet [ˈpækɪt] Päckchen, Paket I **U5, 68**
page [peɪdʒ] Seite I **U1, 19**
to **paint** [peɪnt] malen, anmalen I **U7, 90**
pair [peə] Paar °I **U1, 22**
parents [ˈpeərənts] Eltern I **U2, 26**
park [pɑːk] Park I **U3, 40**
part [pɑːt] Teil °I **U6, 87**
partner [ˈpɑːtnə] Partner/Partnerin I **U1, 15**
party [ˈpɑːti] Party, Feier I **U5, 68**
to have a party [ˌhæv‿ə ˈpɑːti] eine Party feiern I **U5, 68**
past [pɑːst] vorbei, vorüber I **U7, 97**
half **past** (two) [ˈhɑːf pɑːst] halb (drei) I **U3, 41**
pen [pen] Füller I **U1, 14**
pence *(pl)* [pents] Pence *(Währung)* I **U5, 67**
pencil [ˈpensl] Bleistift I **U1, 14**
pencil case [ˈpensl ˌkeɪs] Mäppchen I **U1, 14**
penknife, **penknives** *(pl)* [ˈpennaɪf; ˈpennaɪvz] Taschenmesser I **U6, 84**
people [ˈpiːpl] Leute, Menschen I **U2, 29**
per [pɜː] pro °I **LUA, 24**
phone [fəʊn] Telefon I **U1, 11**
phone number [ˈfəʊn ˌnʌmbə] Telefonnummer I **U1, 11**
to **phone** [fəʊn] anrufen, telefonieren I **U2, 33**
photo [ˈfəʊtəʊ] Foto °I **U4, 64**
phrase [freɪz] Redewendung, Ausdruck °I **U1, 19**
to **pick** [pɪk] pflücken, auswählen I **U6, 78**
picture [ˈpɪktʃə] Bild I **U1, 14**
pig [pɪg] Schwein I **U6, 82**
pink [pɪŋk] pink, rosa I **LUA, 24**
pizza [ˈpiːtsə] Pizza I **U5, 68**
place [pleɪs] Platz, Stelle, Ort I **U2, 26**
plan [plæn] Plan °I **LUB, 39**
play [pleɪ] Theaterstück, Spiel I **U7, 90**
to **play** [pleɪ] spielen I **U1, 14**

playground ['pleɪgraʊnd] Schulhof, Spielplatz **I U1,** 18
please [pli:z] bitte **I U1,** 19
*to be **pleased** with [bi: 'pli:zd wɪð] zufrieden sein mit **I U6,** 87
plural ['plʊərl] Plural, Mehrzahl **I U6,** 88
to **point** [pɔɪnt] zeigen °**I U1,** 18
police [pə'li:s] Polizei **I U6,** 87
Polish ['pəʊlɪʃ] polnisch **I U2,** 29
postcard ['pəʊstkɑ:d] Postkarte **I U6,** 78
poster ['pəʊstə] Poster, Plakat **I U1,** 11
pound [paʊnd] Pfund *(Währung)* **I U5,** 66
present ['preznt] Geschenk **I U5,** 69
price [praɪs] Preis **I U7,** 95
problem ['prɒbləm] Problem, Schwierigkeit **I U1,** 20
project ['prɒdʒekt] Projekt **I U2,** 34
pupil ['pju:pl] Schüler/Schülerin **I U1,** 10
purple ['pɜ:pl] lila, violett **I LUA,** 24
*to **put** [pʊt] setzen, stellen, legen **I U3,** 42
to put in [pʊt‿'ɪn] einsetzen °**I U4,** 58
to put on [pʊt‿'ɒn] anziehen, aufsetzen **I U6,** 81
to put up [pʊt‿'ʌp] aufstellen, aufbauen **I U6,** 84
puzzle ['pʌzl] Rätsel, Puzzle °**I U1,** 15
crossword (puzzle) ['krɒswɜ:d 'pʌzl] Kreuzworträtsel °**I U5,** 71

Q

quarter past ['kwɔ:tə pɑ:st] Viertel nach **I U3,** 42
quarter to ['kwɔ:tə tə] Viertel vor **I U3,** 42
question ['kwestʃn] Frage **I U2,** 31
quick [kwɪk] schnell **I U6,** 86
quiet ['kwaɪət] ruhig, still, leise **I U6,** 78
quiz [kwɪz] Quiz, Rätsel °**I U1,** 13

R

race [reɪs] Wettlauf, Rennen **I U7,** 92
to run a race [ˌrʌn‿ə 'reɪs] einen Wettlauf machen **I U7,** 92
radio ['reɪdiəʊ] Radio **I U2,** 33
radio show ['reɪdiəʊ ˌʃəʊ] Radiosendung **I U2,** 33
to **rain** [reɪn] regnen **I U4,** 62
rainy ['reɪni] regnerisch, verregnet **I U6,** 79
rap [ræp] Rap **I U1,** 15
to **rap** [ræp] rappen **I U3,** 40
*to **read** [ri:d] lesen **I LUB,** 38
really ['rɪəli] wirklich **I U2,** 34
recipe ['resɪpi:] Rezept **I U7,** 94
red [red] rot **I LUA,** 24
to **rehearse** [rɪ'hɜ:s] proben *(ein Theaterstück)* **I U7,** 90
to **remember** [rɪ'membə] sich erinnern, sich erinnern an, sich merken **I U3,** 49
reporter [rɪ'pɔ:tə] Reporter/Reporterin **I U7,** 92
revision [rɪ'vɪʒn] Wiederholung °**I U2,** 32
rhyme [raɪm] Reim °**I LUA,** 25
*to **ride** [raɪd] fahren, reiten **I LUB,** 38
right [raɪt] rechter/rechte/rechtes; rechts **I U4,** 55; richtig, korrekt **I U1,** 13
on the right [ɒn ðə 'raɪt] rechts **I U2,** 28
to be right [bi: 'raɪt] Recht haben °**I U6,** 83
Go **right**. [gəʊ 'raɪt] Biege nach rechts ab. **I LUC,** 52
right now [ˌraɪt 'naʊ] gleich jetzt, in diesem Augenblick **I U7,** 92
*to **ring** [rɪŋ] klingeln **I U5,** 75
river ['rɪvə] Fluss **I LUC,** 52
road [rəʊd] Straße, Landstraße **I LUC,** 52
roof [ru:f] Dach **I U2,** 26
room [ru:m] Zimmer, Raum, Platz **I U1,** 16
dining room ['daɪnɪŋ rʊm] Esszimmer, Speisesaal **I LUA,** 24
living room ['lɪvɪŋ rʊm] Wohnzimmer **I LUA,** 24
RSVP [ˌɑ: es vi: 'pi:] um Antwort wird gebeten °**I U5,** 70
rubber ['rʌbə] Radiergummi **I U1,** 14
rubbish ['rʌbɪʃ] Abfall, Abfälle, Müll **I U6,** 84
rule [ru:l] Regel, Vorschrift **I U3,** 43
ruler ['ru:lə] Lineal **I U1,** 14
*to **run** [rʌn] rennen, laufen **I U3,** 48
to run a race [ˌrʌn‿ə 'reɪs] einen Wettlauf machen **I U7,** 92
to run away [rʌn‿ə'weɪ] wegrennen **I U3,** 48
runner ['rʌnə] Läufer/Läuferin **I U7,** 92
Russian ['rʌʃn] russisch; Russe/Russin **I U2,** 29

S

sandwich ['sænwɪdʒ] Sandwich, belegtes Brot **I U1,** 14
Saturday ['sætədeɪ] Samstag **I U2,** 34
*to **say** [seɪ] sagen, sprechen **I U1,** 11
scared [skeəd] verängstigt **I U2,** 35
school [sku:l] Schule **I U1,** 10
school bag ['sku:l bæg] Schultasche, Schulranzen **I U1,** 14
scone [skɒn] Scone *(Gebäck)* **I U7,** 94
season ['si:zn] Jahreszeit, Saison **I U6,** 79
second ['seknd] Sekunde **I U2,** 30
*to **see** [si:] sehen **I U2,** 33
See you! ['si: jə] Bis dann! Bis … **I U5,** 70
*to **sell** [sel] verkaufen **I U7,** 90
*to **send** [send] schicken **I U6,** 80
sentence ['sentənts] Satz °**I U1,** 13
September [sep'tembə] September **I U5,** 70
she [ʃi:] sie **I U1,** 12
shed [ʃed] Schuppen **I U2,** 26
sheep, sheep *(pl)* [ʃi:p] Schaf/Schafe **I U6,** 78
shelf, shelves *(pl)* [ʃelf; ʃelvz] Regal, Regalbrett **I U2,** 30
ship [ʃɪp] Schiff **I U4,** 54
shirt [ʃɜ:t] Hemd **I U3,** 44
shoe [ʃu:] Schuh **I U1,** 12
shop [ʃɒp] Laden, Geschäft **I U2,** 26
sports shop ['spɔ:ts ʃɒp] Sportgeschäft **I U5,** 66
shopping ['ʃɒpɪŋ] Einkaufen, Einkauf **I U5,** 66
short [ʃɔ:t] kurz **I U4,** 55
to **shout** [ʃaʊt] schreien, rufen **I U1,** 15
show [ʃəʊ] Show, Sendung, Schau **I U2,** 33
radio show ['reɪdiəʊ ˌʃəʊ] Radiosendung **I U2,** 33
*to **show** [ʃəʊ] zeigen **I U4,** 65
sign [saɪn] Schild, Zeichen **I U2,** 26
*to **sing** [sɪŋ] singen **I U2,** 33
sister ['sɪstə] Schwester **I LUA,** 25
half-sister ['hɑ:fˌsɪstə] Halbschwester **I U2,** 26
*to **sit** [sɪt] sitzen **I U3,** 48
to sit down [sɪt 'daʊn] sich setzen, sich hinsetzen **I U1,** 19
to sit with ['sɪt wɪθ] sich setzen zu **I U5,** 74
to **skate** [skeɪt] Inlineskates fahren, skaten **I LUB,** 38
skateboard ['skeɪtbɔ:d] Skateboard **I U4,** 54

skates *(pl)* [skeɪts] Inlineskates **I U4,** 54
*to **sleep** [sli:p] schlafen **I U3,** 46
sleeping bag ['sli:pɪŋ ˌbæg] Schlafsack **I U6,** 84
slow [sləʊ] langsam **I U2,** 34
small [smɔ:l] klein **I U2,** 26
to **smile** [smaɪl] lächeln **I U3,** 43
snowy ['snəʊi] verschneit **I U6,** 79
so [səʊ] so, also, deshalb **I U2,** 26
soap [səʊp] Seifenoper, Seife **I U7,** 97
sofa ['səʊfə] Sofa, Couch **I LUA,** 25
sometimes ['sʌmtaɪmz] manchmal **I U3,** 44
song [sɒŋ] Lied **I U2,** 33
soon [su:n] bald **I U6,** 78
sorry ['sɒri] Tut mir Leid. Entschuldigung. **I U1,** 12
to **sort** [sɔ:t] sortieren °**I U1,** 21
to sort out [sɔ:t‿'aʊt] klären, regeln *(ein Problem)* **I U2,** 30
sound [saʊnd] Ton, Geräusch, Klang **I U6,** 85
south [saʊθ] Süden **I U4,** 55
*to **speak** [spi:k] sprechen **I U4,** 62
*to **spell** [spel] buchstabieren **I U4,** 60
*to **spend** [spend] verbringen, ausgeben **I U6,** 83
sponge [spʌndʒ] Schwamm **I U7,** 90
spooky ['spu:ki] unheimlich **I U2,** 35
sport [spɔ:t] Sport **I U1,** 12
sports day ['spɔ:ts deɪ] Sportfest **I U7,** 90
sports field ['spɔ:ts fi:ld] Sportplatz **I U7,** 92
sports shop ['spɔ:ts ʃɒp] Sportgeschäft **I U5,** 67
to do sports [du: 'spɔ:ts] Sport treiben **I U7,** 92
spring [sprɪŋ] Frühling **I U6,** 78
stall [stɔ:l] Stand, Bude **I U7,** 90
word **star** ['wɜ:d stɑ:] Wortstern °**I U1,** 22
to **start** [stɑ:t] anfangen, starten **I U3,** 44
station ['steɪʃn] Wache, Station, Bahnhof **I U6,** 87
to **stay** [steɪ] bleiben **I U4,** 60
to stay with ['steɪ wɪð] wohnen bei **I U6,** 78
stepdad ['stepdæd] Stiefvater **I U2,** 26
stop [stɒp] Halt, Haltestelle **I LUC,** 52
bus stop ['bʌs ˌstɒp] Bushaltestelle **I LUC,** 52
to **stop** [stɒp] aufhören, aufhören mit, anhalten **I U3,** 42

department **store** [dɪ'pɑ:tmənt stɔ:] Kaufhaus **I LUC,** 52
story ['stɔ:ri] Geschichte, Erzählung **I U1,** 21
strange [streɪndʒ] merkwürdig, seltsam **I U2,** 35
street [stri:t] Straße **I LUC,** 52
studio ['stju:diəʊ] Studio **I U2,** 33
stupid ['stju:pɪd] dumm, blöd **I U2,** 35
suddenly ['sʌdnli] plötzlich, auf einmal **I U2,** 35
summer ['sʌmə] Sommer **I U6,** 79
summer fair ['sʌmə ˌfeə] Sommerfest **I U7,** 90
Sunday ['sʌndeɪ] Sonntag **I LUB,** 39
sunny ['sʌni] sonnig **I U6,** 79
supermarket ['su:pəˌmɑ:kɪt] Supermarkt **I LUC,** 52
supper ['sʌpə] Abendessen **I U3,** 44
to have supper [hæv 'sʌpə] zu Abend essen **I U3,** 44
sure [ʃʊə] sicher **I U1,** 16
survey ['sɜ:veɪ] Umfrage **I U4,** 56
to **swap** [swɒp] tauschen **I LUB,** 38
sweet [swi:t] süß **I LUA,** 24
*to **swim** [swɪm] schwimmen **I LUB,** 38

T

table ['teɪbl] Tisch **I U1,** 18
*to **take** [teɪk] nehmen, mitnehmen, bringen **I U3,** 42
to take home [ˌteɪk 'həʊm] nach Hause bringen **I U2,** 35
to take out [teɪk‿'aʊt] herausnehmen **I U3,** 42
to **talk** [tɔ:k] sprechen, reden **I U1,** 10
to **taste** [teɪst] schmecken **I U7,** 94
tea [ti:] Tee, Abendessen **I U7,** 94
afternoon tea [ˌɑ:ftənu:n 'ti:] Nachmittagstee **I U7,** 94
*to **teach** [ti:tʃ] lehren **I LUB,** 38
teacher ['ti:tʃə] Lehrer/Lehrerin **I U1,** 12
*to **tell** [tel] erzählen, sagen **I U3,** 49
tent [tent] Zelt **I U6,** 84
terrible ['terəbl] schrecklich, furchtbar **I U2,** 35
to **test** [test] testen, prüfen °**I U2,** 31
text [tekst] Text °**I U2,** 27
text message ['tekst ˌmesɪdʒ] SMS **I U6,** 80
than [ðæn] als **I U4,** 55
to **thank** [θæŋk] danken **I U4,** 60

thank you ['θæŋk‿ju:] danke **I U1,** 12
that [ðæt] das, jenes **I U1,** 12
the [ðə; ði] der, die, das **I U1,** 11
their [ðeə] ihr/ihre **I U2,** 30
them [ðem] sie, ihnen **I U4,** 60
then [ðen] dann **I LUB,** 38
there [ðeə] dort, da **I U2,** 26
over there [ˌəʊvə 'ðeə] da drüben **I U5,** 66
there are [ðer‿'ɑ:] da sind, es gibt **I U2,** 32
there is [ðer‿'ɪz] da ist, es gibt **I U2,** 32
these [ði:z] diese, diese hier **I U6,** 84
they [ðeɪ] sie *(Mehrzahl)* **I U1,** 16
thing [θɪŋ] Sache, Ding **I U3,** 40
*to **think** ['θɪŋk] denken **I U3,** 49
third [θɜ:d] dritte/dritter/drittes **I U5,** 70
this [ðɪs] dies; diese/dieser/dieses **I U1,** 12
those [ðəʊz] diese dort, jene **I U6,** 84
*to **throw** [θrəʊ] werfen **I U3,** 49
Thursday ['θɜ:zdeɪ] Donnerstag **I LUB,** 39
ticket ['tɪkɪt] Ticket, Fahrschein, Eintrittskarte **I U7,** 90
tiger ['taɪgə] Tiger **I U2,** 26
time [taɪm] Zeit **I U2,** 30
to have a good time [ˌhæv‿ə gʊd 'taɪm] sich amüsieren **I U5,** 75
What's the time, please? [ˌwɒts ðə 'taɪm ˌpli:z] Wie viel Uhr ist es, bitte? **I U3,** 42
to **time** [taɪm] stoppen, die Zeit nehmen **I U7,** 92
timeline ['taɪmlaɪn] Zeitleiste °**I U4,** 63
tiny ['taɪni] winzig **I LUA,** 25
tip [tɪp] Tipp °**I U1,** 13
title ['taɪtl] Titel, Überschrift °**I U6,** 87
to [tʊ; tə] zu, nach, bis **I U1,** 19
today [tə'deɪ] heute **I U2,** 29
together [tə'geðə] zusammen, miteinander **I LUB,** 38
toilet ['tɔɪlɪt] Toilette **I U1,** 19
tomato, tomatoes *(pl)* [tə'mɑ:təʊ; tə'mɑ:təʊz] Tomate **I U5,** 68
tonight [tə'naɪt] heute Abend, heute Nacht **I U6,** 84
too [tu:] auch **I U1,** 10; zu **I U5,** 66
topic ['tɒpɪk] Thema **I U2,** 33
torch, torches *(pl)* [tɔ:tʃ; 'tɔ:tʃɪz] Taschenlampe, Fackel **I U6,** 84
town [taʊn] Stadt **I U3,** 41
train [treɪn] Zug **I U4,** 54

transport ['træntspɔ:t] Transport **I U4,** 57
tree [tri:] Baum **I U1,** 20
family tree ['fæmli tri:] Familienstammbaum °**I U2,** 28
trick [trɪk] Trick, Streich **I U3,** 40
trip [trɪp] Ausflug, Reise **I U6,** 80
trouble [trʌbl] Schwierigkeiten, Ärger **I U2,** 30
to **try** [traɪ] versuchen, probieren °**I U4,** 60
T-shirt ['ti:ʃɜ:t] T-Shirt **I U2,** 30
Tuesday ['tju:zdeɪ] Dienstag **I LUB,** 39
tunnel ['tʌnl] Tunnel, Unterführung **I U4,** 54
Turkish ['tɜ:kɪʃ] türkisch **I U2,** 29
to **turn** off [tɜ:n‿'ɒf] abschalten, ausschalten **I U5,** 75
TV [ˌti:'vi:] Fernsehen, Fernseher **I LUA,** 25

U

uncle ['ʌŋkl] Onkel **I U2,** 28
under ['ʌndə] unter **I U1,** 18
underlined [ʌndə'laɪnd] unterstrichen °**I U7,** 98
unhappy [ʌn'hæpi] unglücklich **I U2,** 33
uniform ['ju:nɪfɔ:m] Uniform **I U3,** 44
Hurry **up**! [ˌhʌri‿'ʌp] Beeil dich! **I U2,** 30
to get up [get‿'ʌp] aufstehen **I U3,** 44
to go up [gəʊ‿'ʌp] hinaufgehen °**I U4,** 61
to wake up [weɪk‿'ʌp] aufwecken, aufwachen **I U3,** 48
What's up? [ˌwɒts‿'ʌp] Was ist los? **I U1,** 16
upstairs [ʌp'steəz] oben, im oberen Stock **I U2,** 27
us [ʌs] uns **I U4,** 60
to **use** [ju:z] benutzen, verwenden **I U4,** 54

V

van [væn] Lieferwagen **I U6,** 86
very ['veri] sehr **I U1,** 20
video ['vɪdiəʊ] Video **I LUB,** 38
visit ['vɪsɪt] Besuch **I U7,** 94
to **visit** ['vɪzɪt] besuchen, besichtigen **I U4,** 54
visitor ['vɪzɪtə] Besucher/Besucherin **I U4,** 55
volleyball ['vɒlibɔ:l] Volleyball **I U3,** 40

W

to **wait** [weɪt] warten **I U5,** 69
to wait for ['weɪt fɔ:] warten auf **I U6,** 86
*to **wake** up [weɪk‿'ʌp] aufwecken, aufwachen **I U3,** 48
to **walk** [wɔ:k] gehen, laufen **I U4,** 54
to walk the dog [wɔ:k ðə 'dɒg] mit dem Hund spazieren gehen **I U3,** 42
wall [wɔ:l] Wand, Mauer **I U1,** 18
to **want**, to **want** to ['wɒnt tə] wollen, mögen **I U4,** 54
wardrobe ['wɔ:drəʊb] Kleiderschrank, Garderobe **I U2,** 30
to **wash** [wɒʃ] sich waschen, waschen **I U3,** 44
to **watch** [wɒtʃ] ansehen, beobachten **I LUB,** 38
water ['wɔ:tə] Wasser **I U5,** 68
way [weɪ] Weg **I U3,** 42
He is on his way to … [ˌhi:‿ɪz‿ɒn hɪz 'weɪ tə] Er ist auf dem Weg zu … **I U3,** 42
we [wi:] wir **I U1,** 16
*to **wear** [weə] anhaben, tragen **I U3,** 45
Wednesday ['wenzdeɪ] Mittwoch **I LUB,** 39
week [wi:k] Woche **I LUB,** 39
weekend [ˌwi:k'end] Wochenende **I U3,** 45
to **welcome** ['welkəm] willkommen heißen **I U7,** 90
You're **welcome.** [jʊə 'welkəm] Bitte sehr!, Gern geschehen! **I U1,** 19
well [wel] also, na ja, nun gut **I U2,** 29
west [west] Westen **I U4,** 54
what [wɒt] was **I U1,** 11
What about …? [wɒt‿ə'baʊt] Was ist mit …? Wie wäre es mit …? **I U2,** 30
What's the time, please? [ˌwɒts ðə 'taɪm ˌpli:z] Wie viel Uhr ist es, bitte? **I U3,** 42
What's up? [ˌwɒts‿'ʌp] Was ist los? **I U1,** 16
What's your name? [ˌwɒts jə 'neɪm] Wie heißt du? **I U1,** 11
when [wen] wenn, als; wann **I U2,** 33
where [weə] wo, wohin **I U1,** 11
Where are you from? [ˌweər‿ə jə 'frɒm] Woher kommst du? **I U1,** 11
Where's the fire? [ˌweəz ðə 'faɪə] Wo brennt's denn? **I U7,** 96
white [waɪt] weiß **I LUA,** 24
white elephant stall [ˌwaɪt 'elɪfənt stɔ:l] Trödelstand **I U7,** 96
who [hu:] wer **I U1,** 16
why [waɪ] warum **I U5,** 70
wind [wɪnd] Wind **I U2,** 35
window ['wɪndəʊ] Fenster **I U1,** 18
windy ['wɪndi] windig **I U6,** 79
winter ['wɪntə] Winter **I U6,** 79
with [wɪð] mit **I U1,** 14
to be pleased with [bi: 'pli:zd wɪð] zufrieden sein mit **I U6,** 87
without [wɪ'ðaʊt] ohne **I U4,** 54
woman, women *(pl)* ['wʊmən; 'wɪmɪn] Frau **I U4,** 62
Woof! [wʊf] Wau! °**I U2,** 27
word [wɜ:d] Wort **I U1,** 15
word star ['wɜ:d stɑ:] Wortstern °**I U1,** 22
work [wɜ:k] Arbeit **I U3,** 47
to **work** [wɜ:k] arbeiten, funktionieren **I U3,** 48
worksheet ['wɜ:kʃi:t] Arbeitsblatt **I U4,** 58
*to be **worried** ['wʌrid] besorgt sein, beunruhigt sein **I U6,** 87
to **worry** ['wʌri] sich Sorgen machen **I U6,** 82
wow [waʊ] wow °**I U1,** 12
*to **write** [raɪt] schreiben **I U3,** 43
to write down ['raɪt ˌdaʊn] aufschreiben °**I LUB,** 38
wrong [rɒŋ] falsch **I U1,** 16

Y

year [jɪə] Jahr, Jahrgangsstufe **I U1,** 10
yellow ['jeləʊ] gelb **I LUA,** 24
yes [jes] ja **I U1,** 12
you [ju:] dich, dir, Sie, Ihnen, euch **I LUB,** 38; du, ihr, Sie **I U1,** 11
Here you are! [ˌhɪə ju:‿'ɑ:] Bitte schön! **I U1,** 20
thank you ['θæŋk‿ju:] danke **I U1,** 12
*you're lucky [‿jʊə'lʌki] du hast Glück **I U1,** 16
You're welcome. [jʊə 'welkəm] Bitte sehr!, Gern geschehen! **I U1,** 19
young [jʌŋ] jung **I U3,** 45
your [jɔ:] dein/deine, euer/eure, Ihr/Ihre **I U1,** 11

Boys' names

Ben [ben] **I U2,** 27
Bob [bɒb] **I U6,** 78
Charlie ['tʃɑ:li] **I U2,** 33
David ['deɪvɪd] **I U2,** 28
Eric ['erɪk] **I FA,** 102
Jack [dʒæk] **I FA,** 102
James [dʒeɪmz] **I U2,** 28
Jim [dʒɪm] **I U5,** 73
Jo [dʒəʊ] **I FA,** 105
John [dʒɒn] **I U4,** 57
Mark [mɑ:k] **I U4,** 61
Nelson ['nelsn] **I U1,** 13
Paul [pɔ:l] **I U6,** 85
Peter ['pi:tə] **I U4,** 61
Phil [fɪl] **I U2,** 28
Richard ['rɪtʃəd] **I U2,** 27
Rob [rɒb] **I U2,** 26
Sam [sæm] **I U1,** 16
Steve [sti:v] **I U1,** 23
Ted [ted] **I U2,** 26
Terry ['teri] **I U1,** 10
Thomas ['tɒməs] **I LUA,** 25
Tim [tɪm] **I LUA,** 25
Tom [tɒm] **I U1,** 10
Tony ['təʊni] **I LUA,** 25

Girls' names

Anna ['ænə] **I U3,** 47
Elena ['elɪnə] **I U2,** 28
Emma ['emə] **I U1,** 12
Farah ['fɑ:rə] **I U2,** 26
Fiona [fi'əʊnə] **I U1,** 23
Grace [greɪs] **I U2,** 26
Jade [dʒeɪd] **I U2,** 27
Jenny ['dʒeni] **I U4,** 57
Kate [keɪt] **I U4,** 57
Kath [kæθ] **I U6,** 78
Lisa ['li:sə] **I U1,** 10
Maria [mə'ri:ə] **I U2,** 28
Mary ['meəri] **I U4,** 57
Nadine [neɪ'di:n] **I U1,** 13
Nasreen [nʌs'ri:n] **I U2,** 26
Nicola ['nɪklə] **I FA,** 100
Sally ['sæli] **I U6,** 85
Sarah ['seərə] **I U2,** 28
Sue [su:] **I U2,** 27
Susan ['su:zn] **I U2,** 28
Suzanne [su:'zæn] **I U1,** 11
Tamara [tə'mɑ:rə] **I LUA,** 25
Tess [tes] **I U6,** 85
Tilly ['tɪli] **I LUA,** 25
Tina ['ti:nə] **I LUA,** 25
Tracy ['treɪsi] **I U2,** 28

Surnames

Brook [brʊk] **I U1,** 12
Carter ['kɑ:tə] **I U1,** 12
Hunter ['hʌntə] **I U6,** 82
Jackson ['dʒæksn] **I U1,** 10
Lean [li:n] **I FA,** 104
Martin ['mɑ:tɪn] **I FA,** 106
Monte ['mɒnteɪ] **I U2,** 28
Newman ['nju:mən] **I U1,** 12
Pilch [pɪltʃ] **I U2,** 28
Rose [rəʊz] **I U4,** 60
Spencer ['spentsə] **I U2,** 28
Stavros ['stʌvrəs] **I U2,** 28
Taylor ['teɪlə] **I U1,** 10

Place names

Bath [bɑ:θ] **I U6,** 79
Bow Church ['bəʊ ˌtʃɜ:tʃ] **I FA,** 108
Bristol ['brɪstl] **I U1,** 12
Cutty Sark Gardens ['kʌti 'sɑ:k 'gɑ:dns] **I U4,** 54
England ['ɪŋglənd] England **I U2,** 29
Germany ['dʒɜ:məni] Deutschland **I U2,** 29
Greece [gri:s] Griechenland **I U2,** 29
Greenwich ['grenɪdʒ] **I U1,** 10
Hither Farm Road ['hɪðə fɑ:m ˌrəʊd] **I U2,** 26
Holburne Road ['hɒlbɜ:n ˌrəʊd] **I U2,** 26
Houses of Parliament [ˌhaʊzɪz‿əv 'pɑ:ləmənt] **I FA,** 114
Isle of Dogs [ˌaɪl əv 'dɒgz] **I U4,** 54
Istanbul [ˌɪstæn'bʊl] **I U1,** 13
Italy ['ɪtəli] Italien **I U2,** 29
King William Walk [kɪŋ 'wɪljəm ˌwɔ:k] °**I U4,** 62
London ['lʌndən] **I U1,** 10
Madrid [mə'drɪd] **I U1,** 13
Nairobi [naɪ'rəʊbi] **I U1,** 13
Neston ['nestn] **I U6,** 78
New York [ˌnju: 'jɔ:k] **I U4,** 55
Park Row ['pɑ:k rəʊ] **I U4,** 60
Poland ['pəʊlənd] Polen **I U2,** 29
Pond Road ['pɒnd rəʊd] **I U2,** 27
Royal Observatory [ˌrɔɪəl əb'zɜ:vətri] **I U4,** 55
Russia ['rʌʃə] Russland **I U2,** 29
the **Thames** [temz] **I U4,** 54
Thomas Tallis School [ˌtɒməs 'tælɪs ˌsku:l] **I U1,** 10
Turkey ['tɜ:ki] Türkei **I U2,** 29
Wendover Road ['wendəʊvə ˌrəʊd] **I U5,** 70
Wildcroft ['waɪldkrɒft] **I FA,** 100
Wiltshire ['wɪltʃə] **I U6,** 78

Other names

Alice Fitzwarren ['ælis ˌfɪts'wɒrn] **I FA,** 108
Barker ['bɑ:kə] **I U2,** 27
Barny Forge [ˌbɑ:ni 'fɔ:dʒ] **I FA,** 108
Blacky ['blæki] **I FA,** 108
Boxing Day ['bɒksɪŋ ˌdeɪ] **I FA,** 114
buzz [bʌz] **I U1,** 14
Charlie Smart [ˌtʃɑ:li 'smɑ:t] **I FA,** 108
Cutty Sark [ˌkʌti 'sɑ:k] **I U4,** 54
Dick Whittington [ˌdɪk 'wɪtɪŋtən] **I FA,** 108
Discman ['dɪskmən] Discman **I U2,** 30
DLR [ˌdi: el 'ɑ:] **I U4,** 55
Docklands Light Railway ['dɒkləndz ˌlaɪt 'reɪlweɪ] **I U4,** 55
Drayton Hall [ˌdreɪtn 'hɔ:l] **I FA,** 101
Eastenders [ˌi:st'endəz] **I U7,** 96
George Buckingham [ˌdʒɔ:dʒ 'bʌkɪŋəm] **I FA,** 108
GMT ['dʒi: em 'ti:] **I U4,** 55
Greenwich Mean Time [ˌgrenɪdʒ 'mi:n taɪm] **I U4,** 55
Guy Fawkes [ˌgaɪ 'fɔ:ks] **I FA,** 114
24-hour clock ['twenti 'fɔ: 'aʊə klɒk] **I U4,** 54
I spy with my little eye, something beginning with … [aɪ 'spaɪ wɪð maɪ 'lɪtl‿aɪ 'sʌmθɪŋ bɪ'gɪnɪŋ wɪð] Ich sehe was, was du nicht siehst, das fängt mit … an. °**I U2,** 32
James Bond [ˌdʒeɪmz 'bɒnd] **I FA,** 104
Lady Anne Fitzwarren [ˌleɪdi‿æn fɪts'wɒrn] **I FA,** 108
Mario's ['mæriəʊs] **I U5,** 68
Meridian Line [mə'rɪdiən 'laɪn] **I U4,** 54
MTV [ˌem ti: 'vi:] **I U6,** 82
Queen Elizabeth [ˌkwi:n‿ɪ'lɪzəbeθ] **I U5,** 73
Radio Active [ˌreɪdiəʊ‿'æktɪv] **I U2,** 33
Shrove Tuesday [ˌʃrəʊv 'tju:zdeɪ] **I FA,** 115
Sissy Forge [ˌsɪsi 'fɔ:dʒ] **I FA,** 108
Stouty Burke [ˌstaʊti 'bɜ:k] **I FA,** 108
Thames Festival Lantern Procession [ˌtemz 'festɪvl 'læntən prə'seʃn] **I U7,** 90
Tiger ['taɪgə] **I U2,** 26
Tom and Jerry [ˌtɒm‿ən 'dʒeri] **I U3,** 46

A

Abc alphabet
Abend evening
heute Abend tonight
am Abend in the evening
zu Abend essen to have supper
Abendessen supper, tea
abends in the evening
aber but
abfahren to leave
Abfall/Abfälle rubbish
abschalten to turn off
Acker field
Adresse address
Alphabet alphabet
alphabetisch alphabetical
als than; when
also so; well
alt old
sich **amüsieren** to have a good time, to have fun
an at
andere/anderer/anderes other
anders different
anfangen to start
Angeln fishing
anhaben to wear
anhalten to stop
anhören to listen
ankommen to arrive
anmalen to paint
anrufen to call, to phone
ansehen to watch, to look at
Antwort answer
antworten to answer
sich **anziehen** to dress
anziehen to put on
Apfel apple
April April
Arbeit work
arbeiten to work
Arbeitsblatt worksheet
Ärger trouble
auch also, too
auf on
auf einmal suddenly
auf Wiedersehen goodbye
auf dem Land in the country
aufbauen to put up
Aufgabe exercise
aufgeregt excited
aufhören to finish, to stop
aufmachen to open
aufstehen to get up
aufstellen to put up
aufwachen to wake up
aufwecken to wake up
Auge eye
Augenblick moment
im Augenblick at the moment
in diesem Augenblick right now
August August
aus from
aus … heraus out of
sich **ausdenken** to make up
Ausflug trip
ausgeben to spend
ausschalten to turn off
aussehen to look
außerhalb outside
aussteigen to get out
aussteigen aus to get off
Austausch exchange
auswählen to choose, to pick
Auto car
Autogramm autograph

B

Baby baby, babies *(pl)*
Backofen oven
Badezimmer bathroom
Badminton badminton
Bahnhof station
bald soon
Ball ball
Basketball basketball
Bauer, Bäuerin farmer
Bauernhof farm
Baum tree
beantworten to answer
bedeuten to mean
Beeil dich! Hurry up!
beenden to finish
befolgen to follow
bei at
bekommen to get
bellen to bark
benutzen to use
beobachten to watch
berühmt famous
beschäftigt busy
besichtigen to visit
besitzen to have got
besorgt sein to be worried
Besuch visit
besuchen to visit
Besucher/Besucherin visitor
Bett bed
beunruhigt sein to be worried
bevor before
Bild picture
billig cheap
bis to
Bis dann! See you!
ein **bisschen** a bit
bist are
bitte please
Bitte schön! Here you are!
bitten um to ask for
blau blue
bleiben to stay
Bleistift pencil
blöd stupid
bloß only
Blume flower
borgen to borrow
Brand fire
nicht **brauchen** needn't
braun brown
Breakdance tanzen to break-dance
Brief letter
bringen to bring, to take
belegtes Brot sandwich
Brücke bridge
Bruder brother
Buch book
Buchstabe letter
buchstabieren to spell
Bude stall
Bus bus, buses *(pl)*
Busch bush, bushes *(pl)*
Bushaltestelle bus stop
Butter butter

C

Café café
Cafeteria cafeteria
Camping camping
CD CD
Comic comic
Computer computer
cool cool
Cornflakes cornflakes
Couch sofa
Cousin/Cousine cousin

D

da there
da drüben over there
da ist there is
da sind there are

German – English

Dach roof
danke thank you
danken to thank
dann then
das the; that
Datum date
dein/deine your
denken to think
der the
deutsch German
Deutsche/Deutscher German
Dezember December
dich you
die the
Dienstag Tuesday
dies this
diese/dieser/dieses this
diese dort those
diese hier these
Ding thing
dir you
Disko disco
DJ DJ
Donnerstag Thursday
Doppelgänger double
das **Doppelte** double
dort there
Drama drama
draußen outside
drin inside
dritte/dritter/drittes third
du you
dumm stupid
Dummkopf idiot
dunkel dark
dürfen can

E

Ei egg
es **eilig** haben to be in a hurry
ein/eine one; a, an
einfach easy
Einfall idea
Einkaufen shopping
einladen to invite
Einladung invitation
einsteigen in to get into
Eintritt verboten! Keep out!
Eintrittskarte ticket
Einzahl singular
Einzelkind only child
Eis ice-cream
Elefant elephant
Eltern parents
E-Mail e-mail
enden to end
englisch English
entlang along
Geh … entlang. Go down …
Entschuldigung! Excuse me!
er he
Ereignis event
sich **erinnern** to remember
erledigen to finish
erst only
erste/erster/erstes first
erzählen to tell
Erzählung story
es it
es gibt there are
es gibt there is
essen to eat
Essen food
Esszimmer dining room
etwas anything
euch you
euer/eure your
Euro *(Währung)* euro

F

Fackel torch, torches *(pl)*
Fahne flag
fahren to drive, to ride
Fahrer/Fahrerin driver
Fahrrad bike
mit dem Fahrrad by bike
Fahrschein ticket
falsch wrong
Familie family
fantastisch fantastic
Farbe colour
Farm farm
Fastfood-Restaurant burger bar
Februar February
Federball badminton
Feier party
eine Party **feiern** to have a party
fein fine
Feld field
Fenster window
Fernsehen TV
Fernseher TV
Feuer fire
finden to find
Fisch/Fische fish, fish *(pl)*
Fischen fishing
Flagge flag
Flasche bottle
Fleck mark
Flur corridor, hall
Fluss river
folgen to follow
Frage question
fragen to ask
fragen nach to ask for
Frau (Anrede) Miss, Mrs
Frau woman, women *(pl)*
frei free
Freitag Friday
fressen to eat
Freund/Freundin friend
froh happy
früh early
Frühling spring
Frühstück breakfast
Füller pen
funktionieren to work
für for
furchtbar terrible
Fuß foot, feet *(pl)*
zu Fuß on foot
Fußball football
füttern to feed

G

Gang corridor
ganz all
Garderobe wardrobe
Garten garden
geben to give
gebrochen broken
Geburtstag birthday
gehen to go, to walk
Geist ghost
gelb yellow
Geld money
Geplauder chat
Geräusch noise, sound
gern haben to like
Gern geschehen! You're welcome.
Geschäft shop
geschehen to happen
Geschenk present
Geschichte story
geschieden von divorced from
Gesicht face
Gespenst ghost
Getränk drink
gleich jetzt right now
Glück luck
du hast Glück you're lucky
Viel Glück! Good luck!

glücklich happy, lucky
Grieche/Griechin Greek
griechisch Greek
groß big, large
großartig fantastic, great
grün green
Gruppe group
gut good, fine
Guten Morgen! Good Morning!
gut mit … umgehen können to be good with …
ich bin gut in … I'm good at …

H

haben to have, to have got
halb (drei) half past (two)
Halbschwester half-sister
Halle hall
Hallo! Hello!
Haltestelle stop
Handy mobile
Haus house
zu **Hause** at home
Hausaufgabe/Hausaufgaben homework
Hausmeister/Hausmeisterin caretaker
Heft exercise book
Heim home
heiß hot
helfen to help
Hemd shirt
heraus out
herausfinden to find out
herausnehmen to take out
Herbst autumn
herein in
hereinkommen to come in
Herr (Anrede) Mr
herüberkommen to come over
Herzliche Grüße love
heute today
heute Abend tonight
heute Nacht tonight
Hi! Hi!
hier here
Hilfe help
hinter behind
hinterhergehen to follow
Hobby hobby, hobbies *(pl)*
hoffen to hope
hören to hear
Hund dog
mit dem Hund spazieren gehen to walk the dog
hundemüde dog-tired

I

ich I
ich bin I'm
Ich heiße … . My name is … .
Idee idea
Idiot idiot
ihm him
ihn him
ihnen them
Ihnen you
ihr you
ihr/ihre her, their
Ihr/Ihre your
immer always
in at; in; into
in … hinein into
Information/Informationen information
Informationszentrum information centre
Inlineskates fahren to skate
Inlineskates skates *(pl)*
innen inside
irgendetwas anything
ist is
Italiener/Italienerin Italian
italienisch Italian

J

ja yes
Jacke jacket
Jahr year
Jahreszeit season
Jahrgangsstufe year
Jahrmarkt fair
Januar January
jede/jeder/jedes every
jene those
jenes that
jetzt now
Juli July
jung young
Junge boy
Juni June

K

Kalender calendar
kalt cold
Kappe cap
kaputt broken
Karte card
Kartoffelchip crisp
Käse cheese
Kasten box, boxes *(pl)*
Katze cat
kaufen to buy
Kaufhaus department store
kein/keine no
Keks biscuit
kennen to know
Kerl bloke
kicken to kick
Kind child, children *(pl)*, kid
Kirche church
Kiste box, boxes *(pl)*
Klang sound
klären (ein Problem) to sort out
Klasse class
Klassenzimmer classroom
klatschen to clap
Kleiderschrank wardrobe
klein little, small
klingeln to ring
Klopfen knock
Klub club
Kochen cooking
komisch funny
kommen to come, to get
Komm./Kommt. Come on.
können can
korrekt right
Korridor corridor
Krankenpfleger nurse
Krankenschwester nurse
Kricket cricket
Küche kitchen
Kuchen cake
Küchenschrank cupboard
Kuh cow
kurz short

L

lächeln to smile
lachen to laugh
Laden shop
Land country, countries *(pl)*, land
Landkarte map
Landstraße road
Landwirt/Landwirtin farmer
lang long
langsam slow
langweilig boring
Laptop laptop
Lärm noise
lassen to leave

German – English

Lasst uns .... Let's ....
Laterne lantern
laufen to run, to walk
Läufer/Läuferin runner
leben to live
Lebensmittel food
legen to put
lehren to teach
Lehrer/Lehrerin teacher
leicht easy
Tut mir **Leid.** sorry
leihen to borrow
leise quiet
lernen to learn
lesen to read
letzte/letzter/letztes last
Leute people
lieb dear
Liebe love
lieben to love
Lieblings- favourite
Lied song
Lieferwagen van
lila purple
Limonade lemonade
Lineal ruler
Linie line
linke/linker/linkes left
links on the left
Liste list
lustig funny

M

machen to do, to make
Spaß machen to be fun
Mädchen girl
Magazin magazine
Mai May
Make-up make-up
malen to paint
Mama mum
Manager/Managerin manager
manchmal sometimes
Mann man, men *(pl)*
Mäppchen pencil case
Mappe folder
Marmelade jam
März March
Mauer wall
Maus mouse, mice *(pl)*
mehr more
Mehrzahl plural
mein/meine my
das **meiste** most
die meisten most
eine **Menge** a lot of
Menschen people
sich **merken** to remember
merkwürdig strange
Messe fair
mich me
Milch milk
mindestens at least
Minute minute
mir me
mit with
mitbringen to bring
miteinander together
mitnehmen to take
Mittagessen lunch
Mittagszeit lunchtime
mittel medium
Mittelpunkt centre
Mittwoch Wednesday
Möbel furniture
Mobiltelefon mobile
mögen to like
Moment moment
Moment mal! Hang on!
momentan at the moment
Monat month
Montag Monday
montags on Mondays
Morgen morning
am Morgen in the morning
Guten Morgen! Good Morning!
morgens in the morning
Müll rubbish
Museum museum
Musik music
müssen must
nicht müssen needn't
Mutti mum
Mütze cap

N

nach after
nach draußen outside
nach drinnen inside
nach Hause home
nach Hause bringen to take home
Nachmittag afternoon
am Nachmittag in the afternoon
nachmittags in the afternoon
Nachmittagstee afternoon tea
nächste/nächster/nächstes next
Nacht night
heute Nacht tonight
Nachtschwester night nurse
nahe near
in der **Nähe** von near
Nahrung food
Name name
die **Nase** voll haben to be fed up
natürlich of course
neben next to
neblig foggy
nehmen to take
nein no
nennen to call
nett nice
neu new
nicht no, not
nie never
noch else
Norden north
normal normal
November November
Nummer number
nun now
nur only, just

O

oben upstairs
Observatorium observatory
oder or
öffnen to open
Öffnungszeiten hours
oft often
ohne without
OK OK
Oktober October
Oma grandma
Onkel uncle
Opa grandad
Ordner folder
organisieren to organize
Ort place
Osten east

P

Päckchen packet
packen to pack
Paket packet
Papa dad
Park park
Partner/Partnerin partner
Party party
eine Party feiern to have a party
Pech bad luck

Pence *(Währung)* pence *(pl)*
Pferd horse
pflücken to pick
Pfund *(Währung)* pound
pink pink
Pizza pizza
Plakat poster
Platz place, room
plötzlich suddenly
Plural plural
Polizei police
polnisch Polish
Poster poster
Postkarte postcard
Preis price
prima cool
proben *(ein Theaterstück)* to rehearse
Problem problem
Projekt project

R

Radiergummi rubber
Radio radio
Radiosendung radio show
Rap rap
rappen to rap
Raum room
rechte/rechter/rechtes right
rechts on the right
reden to talk
Regal shelf, shelves *(pl)*
Regalbrett shelf, shelves *(pl)*
Regel rule
regeln *(ein Problem)* to sort out
regnen to rain
regnerisch rainy
Reise trip
reiten to ride
rennen to run
Rennen race
Reporter/Reporterin reporter
Rezept recipe
richtig right
riesig large
rosa pink
rot red
rufen to call, to shout
ruhig quiet
Russe/Russin Russian
russisch Russian

S

Saal hall
Sache thing
sagen to say, to tell
Saison season
sammeln to collect
Samstag Saturday
Sandwich sandwich
Säugling baby, babies *(pl)*
Schachtel box, boxes *(pl)*
Schaf sheep, sheep *(pl)*
Schau show
schauen to look
Schauspieler actor
schenken to give
scherzen to joke
schicken to send
Schild sign
schlafen to sleep
Schlafsack sleeping bag
Schlafzimmer bedroom
Schlag knock
Schlagzeug drums
schlecht bad
schließen to close
schmecken to taste
Schminke make-up
schnell quick
Schokolade chocolate
schön beautiful, fine
schon already
Schrank cupboard
schrecklich terrible
schreiben to write
Schreibtisch desk
schreien to shout
Schuh shoe
Schule school
Schüler/Schülerin pupil
Schulhof playground
Schulklasse class
Schulranzen school bag
Schultasche school bag
Schuppen shed
Schwamm sponge
schwarz black
Schwein pig
Schwester sister
Schwierigkeit problem
schwimmen to swim
Scone *(Gebäck)* scone
sehen to see, to look
sehr very
Seife soap
Seifenoper soap
sein to be
sein/seine his
Seite page
Sekunde second
selbstverständlich of course
seltsam strange
Sendung show
September September
sich **setzen** to sit down
  sich setzen zu to sit with
Show show
sich treffen to meet
sicher sure
sie she; her; they *(pl)*; them *(pl)*
Sie you
singen to sing
sitzen to sit
Skateboard skateboard
skaten to skate
SMS text message
so so
Sofa sofa
sogar even
solange as long as
Sommer summer
Sommerfest summer fair
sonnig sunny
Sonntag Sunday
sonst else
sich **Sorgen** machen to worry
Spaß fun
  Spaß haben to have fun
  Spaß machen to be fun
  Viel Spaß! Have fun!
spät late
  zu spät late
später later
Speisesaal dining room
Spiel game, play
spielen to play
  spielen *(Theater)* to act
Spielplatz playground
Sport sport
  Sport treiben to do sports
Sportfest sports day
Sportgeschäft sports shop
Sportplatz sports field
Sprache language
sprechen to speak, to talk, to say
Stadt town
Stadtplan map
Stand stall
ständig always
starten to start
Station station
Stelle place

Sternwarte observatory
Stiefvater stepdad
still quiet
im oberen **Stock** upstairs
im unteren **Stock** downstairs
Straße street, road
Strauch bush, bushes *(pl)*
Streich trick
Studio studio
Stuhl chair
Stunde hour
suchen to look for
Süden south
Supermarkt supermarket
süß sweet

T

Tafel board
Tag day
Tante aunt
tanzen to dance
Breakdance tanzen to break-dance
Tasche bag
Taschenlampe torch, torches *(pl)*
Taschenmesser penknife, penknives *(pl)*
Tausch exchange
tauschen to swap
Tee tea
Telefon phone
telefonieren to phone
Telefonnummer phone number
teuer expensive
Theaterstück play
Thema topic
Ticket ticket
Tier animal
Tiger tiger
Tisch table
Toilette toilet
toll great
Tomate tomato, tomatoes *(pl)*
Ton sound
Tor goal
tragen to carry, to wear
Transport transport
Traum dream
treffen to meet
treten to kick
Trick trick
trinken to drink
Trödelstand white elephant stall
tschüss bye
T-Shirt T-shirt
tun to do, to make
Tunnel tunnel
Tür door
türkisch Turkish
Turnhalle gym
Tüte bag
Typ bloke

U

über over; about
überprüfen to check
Übung exercise
Übungsheft exercise book
Uhr clock
Uhr *(Zeitangabe)* o'clock
Wie viel Uhr ist es, bitte? What's the time, please?
Umfrage survey
und and
unglücklich unhappy
unheimlich spooky
Uniform uniform
uns us
unser/unsere our
unten downstairs
unter under
Unterführung tunnel
sich **unterhalten** to chat
Unterhaltung chat
unterrichten to teach
Unterrichtsstunde lesson

V

Vati dad
verängstigt scared
Veranstaltung event
verbringen to spend
Verein club
vergessen to forget
verheiratet mit married to
sich **verirren** to get lost
verkaufen to sell
verlassen to leave
verloren gehen to get lost
verregnet rainy
verrückt crazy
verschieden different
verschneit snowy
verspätet late
verstecken to hide
sich verstecken to hide
verwenden to use
Video video
viel much
Viel Glück! Good luck!
viel/viele a lot of
viele many
vielleicht maybe
Viertel nach quarter past
Viertel vor quarter to
violett purple
Volleyball volleyball
von from, of
vor before; in front of
vorbei past
Vormittag morning
vormittags in the morning
Vorschrift rule

W

wählen to choose
Wand wall
Wandtafel board
wann when
warten to wait
Warte mal! Hang on!
warten auf to wait for
warum why
was what
Was ist los? What's up?
Was ist mit …? What about …?
waschen to wash
sich waschen to wash
Wasser water
Wecker alarm clock
weg away
Weg way
Er ist auf dem Weg zu … He is on his way to …
wegrennen to run away
weil because
Weitsprung long jump
wenigstens at least
wenn when
wer who
werfen to throw
Westen west
Wettlauf race
einen Wettlauf machen to run a race
wie how; like
Wie alt bist du? How old are you?
Wie geht es dir/Ihnen/euch? How are you?
Wie heißt du? What's your name?
Wie wäre es mit …? What about …?

wie viele how many
Wie viel kosten …? How much are …?
Wie viel kostet …? How much is …?
Wie viel Uhr ist es, bitte? What's the time, please?
wieder again
auf **Wiedersehen** goodbye
willkommen heißen to welcome
Wind wind
windig windy
Winter winter
winzig tiny
wir we
wirklich really
wissen to know
Witz joke
Witze machen to joke
wo where
Woche week
Wochenende weekend
Woher kommst du? Where are you from?
wohin where
Wohltätigkeit charity
Wohltätigkeitsverein charity
wohnen to live
wohnen bei to stay with
Wohnung flat
Wohnzimmer living room
wollen to want, to want to
Wort word
wunderschön beautiful

Z

Zahl number
Zeichen sign
zeichnen to draw
zeigen to show
Zeile line
Zeit time
Zeitschrift magazine
Zeitschriftenhändler/Zeitschriftenhändlerin newsagent
Zelt tent
Zelten camping
Zentrum centre
zerbrochen broken
Ziel goal
Zimmer room
zu to; too
zuerst first
zufrieden sein mit to be pleased with
Zug train
Zuhause home
zuhören to listen
zumachen to close
zurück back
zusammen together
zwischen between

Place names

Deutschland Germany
England England
Griechenland Greece
Italien Italy
Polen Poland
Russland Russia
Türkei Turkey

In the classroom

Talking to your friends or teachers

Before the lesson

Good morning, Mr/Mrs/Miss … .	Guten Morgen, Herr/Frau … .
Hello, Sir/Miss.	Hallo, Herr/Frau … .
I'm sorry I'm late.	Tut mir Leid, dass ich mich verspätet habe.

Asking for help

Can you help me, please?	Kannst du/Können Sie mir helfen, bitte?
How do you do this exercise?	Wie macht man diese Übung?
Is this right? I'm not sure.	Ist das richtig? Ich bin mir nicht sicher.
Sorry, I don't know. Ask … .	Tut mir Leid, das weiß ich nicht. Frag doch … !
Why don't you ask the teacher?	Frag doch den Lehrer/die Lehrerin!
Sorry. Can you say that again, please?	Wie bitte? Können Sie das bitte wiederholen?
Can you play that again, please?	Können Sie das bitte noch einmal vorspielen?
Can we open the window, please?	Können wir das Fenster aufmachen, bitte?
Can I go to the toilet please, Sir/Miss?	Kann ich bitte auf die Toilette, Herr …/Frau … ?
Can I leave the room, please?	Kann ich bitte das Zimmer verlassen?
What's the homework?	Was haben wir als Hausaufgabe?

Asking for information

What's that in English/German?	Was heißt das auf Englisch/Deutsch?
What does that mean?	Was bedeutet das?
How do you spell …, please?	Wie schreibt man … , bitte?
What's the time, please?	Wie spät ist es, bitte?
Where's the … ? / Where are the … ?	Wo ist der/die/das … ? / Wo sind die … ?
What's today's date?	Welches Datum haben wir heute?

Working together

Can I borrow your book/ …, please?	Kann ich dein Buch/ … leihen, bitte?
Thank you. / Thanks a lot.	Danke. / Vielen Dank!
You're welcome.	Bitte. / Bitte schön!
Now it's your turn.	Jetzt bist du an der Reihe.
Let's make/draw a … .	Lasst uns ein/eine/einen … machen/zeichnen.
Let's act the story/dialogue.	Lasst uns die Geschichte/den Dialog vorspielen.

Your teacher can say

Open your books at page … .	Öffnet eure Bücher auf Seite … .
Turn to page … .	Schlagt Seite … auf.
Do Exercise … on page … for homework.	Als Hausaufgabe macht Übung … auf Seite … .
Where's your book, David?	David, wo ist dein Buch?
Sit down, please, and be quiet.	Setz dich bitte und sei ruhig.
Say that again, please.	Wiederhole es, bitte.
Try again!	Versuch es noch einmal!
That's really good!	Das ist sehr gut!
That's all for today. You can go.	Das wäre es für heute. Ihr dürft gehen.

Lösungen Check-out

Unit 1 Seite 23

1 A new school

Hi Fiona! **It**'s lunchtime here. **I**'m in the playground with Terry. Who's Terry? **He**'s my new friend and **he**'s cool. **We**'re in Year Seven now. Terry's friends are Lisa and Sam. **They**'re from his old school. **They**'re in Year Seven, too. Mrs Carter is nice. **She**'s the German teacher. **I**'m good at German, but **I**'m not good at sport. **It** isn't boring here. Greenwich is OK and my new friends are nice. But **you**'re my friend, too.

2 School questions and answers

2. **Is** Mr Newman a teacher? – **No, he isn't.**
3. Hi, Terry and Lisa! **Are** you from Greenwich? – **Yes, we are.**
4. Oh, I'm sorry. **Am** I late? – **Yes, you are.**
5. **Are** the girls in the classroom? – **No, they aren't.**
6. **Is** your school bag new? – **No, it isn't.**
7. **Is** Mrs Carter a teacher? – **Yes, she is.**
8. Hello, Mrs Carter. **Are** we in the right room? – **No, you aren't.**

3 Who or where?

Who?	Where?
girl	classroom
partner	playground
boy	cafeteria
teacher	cupboard
friend	home
caretaker	bag
	school

4 A new pupil

1. **What's** your name?
2. **Where** are you from?
3. **Who's** Mrs Carter?
4. **Where** are the boys?
5. **Where's** your football?
6. **What** are 'lucky' and 'cool'?

Unit 2 Seite 37

1 Terry's shed

a)
2. That's Lisa's dog.
3. That's Tom's cupboard.
4. That's Emma's school bag.
5. That's Sam's grandma.
6. That's Nasreen's T-shirt.

b)
1. Terry has got a shed.
2. Lisa has got a dog.
3. Tom has got a cupboard.
4. Emma has got a school bag.
5. Sam has got a grandma.
6. Nasreen has got a T-shirt.

2 Two families

The Jacksons have got a cat. They haven't got a dog. They have got a shed. They have got a garden. They have got a house. They haven't got a flat.

The Taylors haven't got a cat. They have got a dog. They haven't got a shed. They have got a garden. They have got a house. They haven't got a flat.

3 Funny questions

Example: Has my dad got drums in the car?
1. Have our cousins got a shed in the playground?
2. Have we got a sofa in the bathroom?
3. Has my grandma got a computer in the garden?
4. Has our school got a garden on the roof?
5. Have I got a cupboard in my school bag?
6. Has Barker got a window in his bed?

Unit 3 Seite 51

1 Playground rules

2. Don't play football.
3. Don't skate.
4. Don't ride bikes.
5. Don't eat sandwiches.

2 They don't eat chocolate.

1. They don't eat chocolate.
2. They don't sleep on the roof.
3. They don't live in a flat.
4. They don't love cats.
5. They don't like TV.
6. They don't help in the house.

3 Tiger's Saturday

1. She **doesn't like** her bed in the house. She **likes** the shed. There are mice under it.
2. On Saturday Tiger **gets up** at 6:00 in the morning. Terry **doesn't get up** before 10:00.
3. She **likes** mice. She doesn't **like** her breakfast.
4. She **doesn't go** into the garden. She **goes** into Terry's bedroom.
5. She **doesn't sit** on the bed. She **sits** on his face.
6. Terry **doesn't say**, "Nice cat!" He **says**, "You stupid cat!"

Unit 4 Seite 65

1 Questions about Greenwich

1. Yes, it does.
2. Yes, he does.
3. No, it doesn't.
4. No, it doesn't.
5. Yes, it does.
6. No, she doesn't.

2 In Greenwich Park

1. Do you speak Italian or Greek?
2. Do you live in Greenwich?
3. Do you know a lot of nice places here?
4. Does the DLR go to the Royal Observatory?
5. Do a lot of visitors go there on foot?
6. Do buses stop next to the Observatory?
7. Does it open at 9:00 in the morning?
8. Do a lot of people visit the 24-hour clock?

3 Find the questions.

1. Where do young people skate?
2. When does the Cutty Sark Museum open?
3. What do the pupils choose?
4. How do they get to Greenwich?
5. Where does Sam read a sign?
6. When does Mr Rose come into the café?

4 What do the people answer?

1. Please put them in the cupboard.
2. Leave it on your desk.
3. Lisa knows her.
4. You can find him in the playground.
5. We can show you.

Unit 5 Seite 77

1 What do you want for your birthday?

1. Lisa wants a football because she wants to play football for England.
2. Ben wants a car because he wants to go to the disco with Nasreen. Ben wants euros because he wants to visit his friend in Germany.
3. Jade wants skates because she wants to skate in the park with her friends. Jade wants a mouse because she wants to put it in her bedroom.

2 Much or many?

a) Mrs Taylor: OK, Lisa. Let's write a list. How **much** milk have we got?
Lisa: We haven't got **much** milk but we've got a lot of eggs. We haven't got **much** cheese and there aren't **many** tomatoes.
Mrs Taylor: How **many** tomatoes are there?
Lisa: Two and they're very old.
Mrs Taylor: OK. Write them on the list, please. Let's look in the cupboard now. Oh! We've got a lot of chocolate, but we haven't got **many** cornflakes.
Lisa: What about apples? There aren't **many** apples here.
Mrs Taylor: OK. And we haven't got **much** water.
Lisa: There aren't **many** crisps here. Can we –?
Mrs Taylor: No, we can't. You children all eat too **many** crisps.

b) milk, cheese, tomatoes, cornflakes, apples, water

3 In the shop

a) Good morning! I want **three bottles of** milk, **four packets of** cheese, **a bottle of** water, **two bags of** tomatoes, **two packets of** crisps, and **two boxes of** cornflakes, please.
b) Two packets of crisps

Unit 6 Seite 89

1 What are they doing?

1. In picture one Terry is feeding the pigs. In picture two he isn't feeding the pigs. He's phoning on his mobile.
2. In picture one Sam is carrying bottles. In picture two he isn't carrying bottles. He's reading a comic.
3. In picture one Mr Hunter is working in the field. In picture two he isn't working in the field. He's talking to Bob.
4. In picture one Kath is picking flowers. In picture two she isn't picking flowers. She's playing with the dog.
5. In picture one the dog is sleeping. In picture two it isn't sleeping. It's playing with a ball.

2 What aren't they doing?

2. They aren't doing homework.
3. They aren't reading books.
4. They aren't playing football.
5. They aren't going to school.

3 Some days are different.

1. Are Ted and Bob working in the garden? – No, they aren't. They're fishing.
2. Is Sam watching MTV? – No, he isn't. He's carrying apples.
3. Are Kath and Grace talking on the phone. – No, they aren't. They're visiting Bath.
4. Is Terry playing the drums? – No, he isn't. He's feeding the pigs.

Unit 7 Seite 99

1 What must and what needn't they do?

1. I must find the caretaker.
2. We needn't buy all of them.
3. She must be in a hurry!
4. You needn't put it in a box.
5. You needn't shout!
6. You must meet my teacher.

2 Saturday at the school fair

1. On Saturdays Mr Rose often **goes** to town. Today he **is going** to Thomas Tallis.
2. On Saturdays Terry often **makes** the breakfast. Today he **is making** pizzas.
3. On Saturdays Mrs Carter often **buys** food for the family. Today she **is buying** books.
4. On Saturdays Lisa often **throws** a ball for Barker. Today she **is throwing** sponges.

3 Tom's sports day

2. Tom is swimming. He isn't washing.
3. Tom is timing the runners. He isn't waking up Sam.
4. Tom is running a race. He isn't running away from the cat.
5. Tom is playing cricket. He isn't drawing a picture.

Bildquellen: Umschlag: Ernst Klett Verlag (Hacker), Stuttgart; S.8: Corbis (Greenwich Aerial Photo), Düsseldorf; S.9: ullstein bild (Minehan), Berlin; Collections Picture Gallery (Nigel Haggerty), London; Corbis (Patrick Ward); Corbis (John Van Hasselt); Corbis (Ed Bock); Alamy Images (Greenhill), Oxfordshire; S.10: Ernst Klett Verlag (Hacker); S.11: Ernst Klett Verlag (Fletcher); Ernst Klett Verlag (Fletcher); Fotosearch RF (Banana Stock), Waukesha, WI; Mauritius, Mittenwald; S.13: Bananastock RF, Watlington/Oxon; Corbis (RF); Bananastock RF; S.19: Ernst Klett Verlag (Fletcher); S.26: Ernst Klett Verlag (Richard McBride); Ernst Klett Verlag (Fletcher); Ernst Klett Verlag (Fletcher); Ernst Klett Verlag (Susann Edele); S.27: Ernst Klett Verlag (Fletcher); Ernst Klett Verlag (Fletcher); Mauritius (age); S.28: Bananastock (RF); S.29: Alamy Images (Paula Solloway/ Photofusion), Oxfordshire; S.31: mecom (Bilderbox/Erwin Wodicka), Hamburg; S.33: mecom (ddp/ Gerhard Blank), Hamburg; Fotosearch RF (Brand X Pictures), Waukesha, WI; S.40: Corbis (Peter Poby); 2–5 Ernst Klett Verlag (Fletcher); Mauritius (Steiner); Ernst Klett Verlag (Fletcher); S. 41: aus: Grzimeks Tierleben Bd. 11; Getty Images (taxi/Justin Pumfrey), München; S.43: Ernst Klett Verlag (Fletcher); S.44: Ernst Klett Verlag (Fletcher); S.45: Getty Images (PhotoDisc); S.46: Fotosearch (Photodisc RF); Getty Images (Photogr. Coice/ M+S Westmorland); S.47: Getty Images (Image Bank/Alan Thornton); S.49: Mauritius (age); S.54: Alamy Images (Janine Wiedel Photolibrary); Alamy Images (RF/FCL); S.55: National Maritime Museum, London; Mauritius (O'Brien); National Maritime Museum, London; Corbis (Colin Garratt; Milepost 92 ½); Ernst Klett Verlag (Dekelver); Corbis (Firefly Productions); MEV, Augsburg; Sipa Press (Trippett), Paris; S.56: Fotofinder (G. Schiefer), Berlin; S.59: Ernst Klett Verlag (Fletcher); Mauritius (Fergusson); Ernst Klett Verlag (Fletcher); S.61: Ernst Klett Verlag (Hacker); Imagine (RF/Brand X Pictures), Houston TX; S.63: Mauritius (age); S.64: Robert Harding Picture Library Ltd. (RF), London; Alamy Images (SHOUT); Mauritius (age/Lluis Real); Mauritius (age/Fotostock); Mauritius (Vidler); Corbis (RF); S.65: Ernst Klett Verlag (Stefanie Schmid); S.66: Ernst Klett Verlag (Hacker); S.67: Mit freundlicher Genehmigung der Bank of England, London; Mauritius (age); Corbis (Rob Lewine); S.69: Ernst Klett Verlag (Hacker); Mauritius (age); S.70: Ernst Klett Verlag (Fletcher); S.72: 1–4 Ernst Klett Verlag (Fletcher); Getty Images (taxi/Benelux Press); S.77: Ernst Klett Verlag (Fletcher); S.78: Mauritius (age); Corbis (Michael Boys); MEV; S.79: Corbis (Richard Klune); Corbis (RF); S.81: Getty Images (Image Bank); S.83: Bananenstock RF; S.85: Mauritius (age); S.90: Fotosearch RF (Photodisc); Ernst Klett Verlag (Hacker); Picture-Alliance (dpa/Oliver Weiken), Frankfurt; Das Fotoarchiv (Markus Dlouhy), Essen; Mauritius (Pöhlmann); Topham Picturepoint, Edenbridge Kent; Corbis (Rob Lewine); S.91: Das Fotoarchiv (Rupert Oberhäuser), Essen; Mauritius (age/Picture Partners); S.93: Mauritius (age); S.94: Alamy Images (Jack Sullivan); Fotosearch RF (Digital Vision); S.112: MEV; MEV; S.113: Reinhard-Tierfoto, Heiligkreuzsteinach; MEV; Mauritius (Reinhard); Ingram Publishing, Tattenhall Chester; MEV; MEV; J. Salmon Ltd., Kent; S.114: Mary Evans Picture Library (Bruce Castle Museum), London; Alamy Images (Guy Somerset); S.115: Picture-Alliance (dpa/John Stillwell); Picture-Alliance (dpa/William Conran); S.118: Corbis (Yann Arthus Bertrand); Corbis (Tim Hawkins/Eye Ubiquitous); Corbis (Anthony Cooper/Ecoscene)

Bye!

Flags (after Unit 2)

Match the flags with the countries. Use the Internet for help.

EUROPE

Country	Adjective	Country	Adjective	Country	Adjective
1 Albania	Albanian	13 Greece	Greek	25 Poland	Polish
2 Austria	Austrian	14 Hungary	Hungarian	26 Portugal	Portuguese
3 Belgium	Belgian	15 Iceland	Icelandic	27 Romania	Romanian
4 Bosnia-Herzegovina	Bosnian	16 Ireland	Irish	28 Russia	Russian
5 Bulgaria	Bulgarian	17 Italy	Italian	29 Serbia and Montenegro	Serbian Montenegrin
6 Croatia	Croatian	18 Latvia	Latvian	30 Slovakia	Slovak
7 Czech Republic	Czech	19 Lithuania	Lithuanian	31 Spain	Spanish
8 Denmark	Danish	20 Luxembourg	Luxembourgish	32 Sweden	Swedish
9 Estonia	Estonian	21 Macedonia	Macedonian	33 Switzerland	Swiss
10 Finland	Finnish	22 Moldavia	Moldavian	34 Turkey	Turkish
11 France	French	23 The Netherlands	Dutch	35 Ukraine	Ukrainian
12 Germany	German	24 Norway	Norwegian		